HOW TO DESIGN AND BUILD

THE COOLEST WEBSITE IN CYBERSPACE

Nick Nettleton

4

CONTENTS

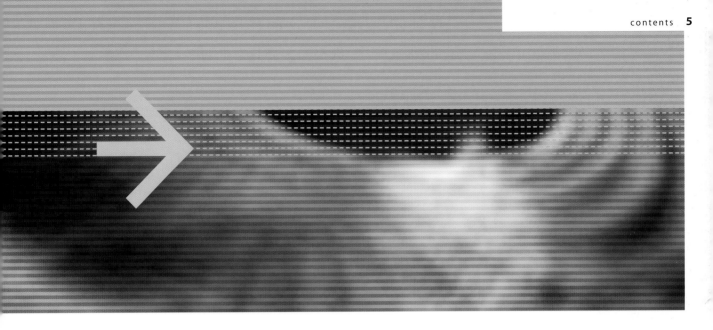

INTRODUCTION

How do you design and build the coolest website? That's a big question... you'd need to know all the basic stuff first, such as how the Web works, what HTML is, and how to get a website online.

Then you'd need to know all about the major website design applications, not to mention the graphics packages, complete with step-by-step run-throughs.

Of course, you'd need to find out about good design as well... that's really important. How to plan a site, for example, and create a design that matches your brief, with fonts, colors, and graphics to go.

Then there's all the fun stuff: all those animations, rollovers, and buttons. And what about sound and video? How do you do that?

Even if you did find out all these things, how do you build a community? Get feedback from your visitors? Or publicize your work?

Where can you find a book like that?

You've just picked it up!

Enjoy your read...

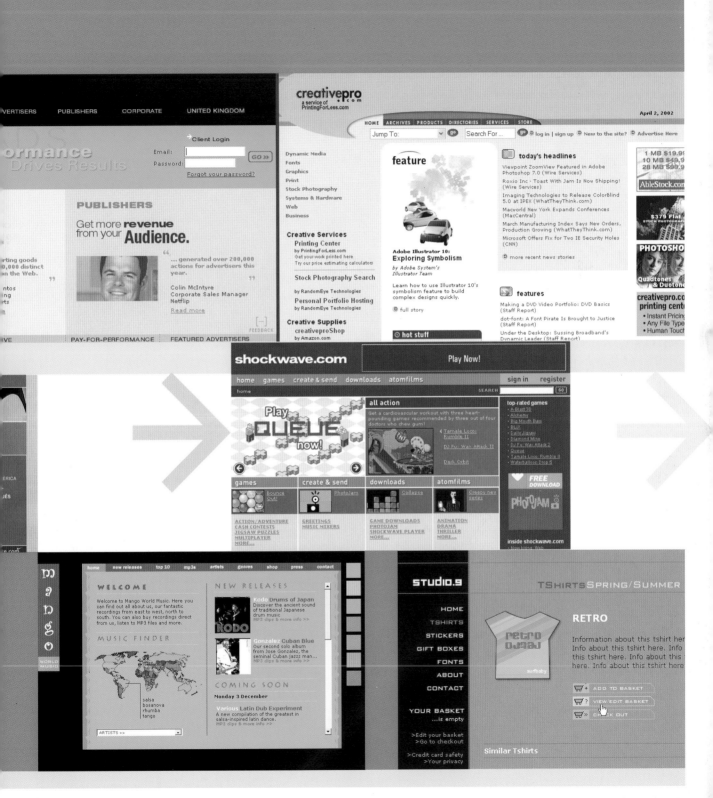

A WEBSITE IS THE VISUAL (AND SOMETIMES AURAL) REPRESENTATION OF WHAT WOULD, OTHERWISE, BE A DRAB COLLECTION OF TEXT FILES AND THE DIRECTORIES THAT CONTAIN THEM. HTML DOCUMENTS CONTAIN THE ESSENTIAL INSTRUCTIONS FOR PUBLISHING YOUR PAGE IN CYBERSPACE, AND THESE DOCUMENTS ARE ALMOST ALWAYS ACCOMPANIED BY SUPPORT FILES SUCH AS ILLUSTRATIONS, BUTTONS, AND ANIMATIONS.

GETTING STARTED

WHAT IS THE WEB?

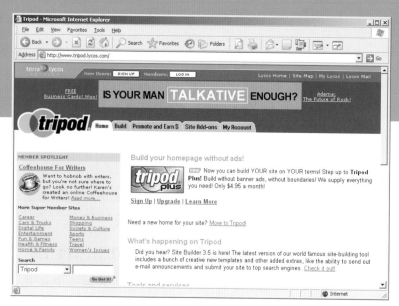

Taking part in the Web community can mean taking part in one of the many discussion groups, like at ezboard (far right) *www.ezboard.com*, creating your own fan site at Tripod (top) *www.tripod.com*, or designing a fully fledged business or hobbyist site.

The Internet is surely the great revolution of our era. Just as the middle decades of the last century came to be called the Space Age, so the first decades of this one will be remembered as the Cyberspace Age. For the first time, anyone with just a computer, a few ideas, and the right know-how can publish a magazine, distribute a movie, or sell their music. You don't need a deal with a mega-bucks company to get your ideas out there. You don't even need to spend much money of your own; many of the greatest and most innovative websites are built on a budget of coffee and hotdogs.

The most exciting thing about the Internet is not surfing the Web and reading hourly news bulletins; it's getting involved in the online community, and building your own little corner of cyberspace. It's also the possibility of exchanging information with people similar to yourself, but thousands of miles away on the other side of the world. Without the Internet, you might never have spoken to each other in a thousand lifetimes. The size and variety of the online community is so great, it's impossible not to come into contact with someone who shares the same interests and passions as yourself—and by creating a website, you can plant a flag saying, "This is me...this is what I do."

The World Wide Web, WWW, or just plain Web, is the collective name for all the websites, which link to each another and which you can browse using Internet Explorer, Netscape Navigator, Opera, or any of the other available browsers. The Internet, in contrast, is the name of the interconnected network (hence "Internet") or infrastructure that holds and transports the World Wide Web. It can also support other "webs," such as private groups of sites, or file-sharing facilities like FTP sites, and so on.

HOW THE WEB WORKS

A website is a collection of files, usually in a single folder, on a computer that is permanently connected to the Internet and specifically set up with software to deliver them to people's Web browsers. This computer is called a Web server. When you type in a Web address, your own server—the computer you dial up via your modem—searches a vast, central database to find the name of the computer that holds the files for this site.

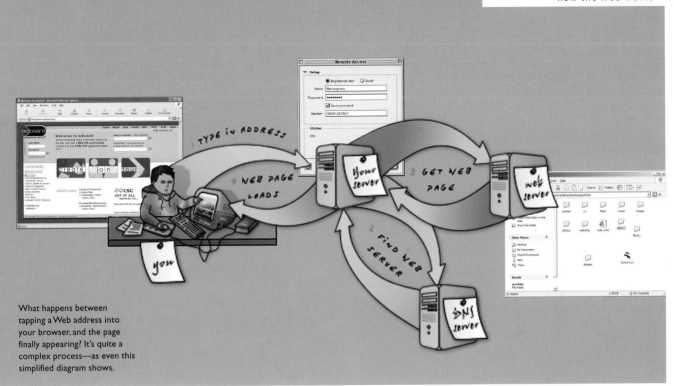

What happens between tapping a Web address into your browser, and the page finally appearing? It's quite a complex process—as even this simplified diagram shows.

It then contacts the Web server to put in a request for the relevant file. In the case of normal webpages, this is an HTML file—one HTML file for each webpage—which gets channeled down the Internet to you.

An HTML file only contains text, information about positioning and formatting, and interactive commands. It doesn't, for example, contain images or sounds. Instead, these are stored as separate files using an image or sound file format. As the HTML file downloads into your browser, your browser finds references to these other files and their whereabouts on the Internet. Again, it contacts the server with requests for these files, and the process continues. Finally, you have all the files downloaded into a temporary folder on your computer—in the case of Windows, it's usually in C:\WINDOWS\Temporary Internet Files—and your browser can display the complete webpage, with all the relevant images and sounds in the right place.

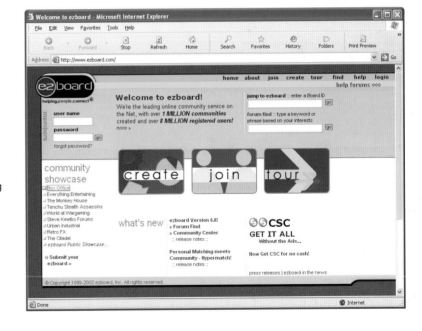

WHAT IS HTML?

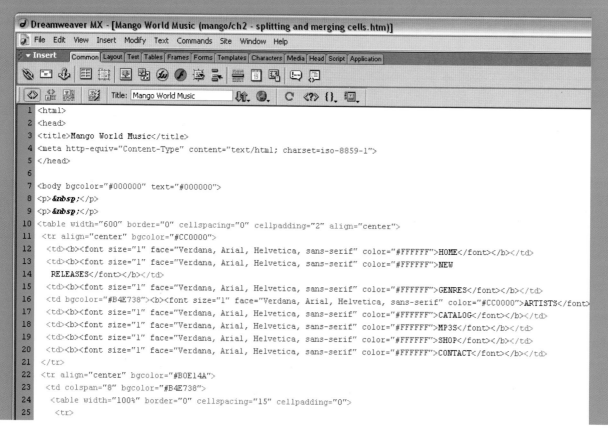

```
1  <html>
2  <head>
3  <title>Mango World Music</title>
4  <meta http-equiv="Content-Type" content="text/html; charset=iso-8859-1">
5  </head>
6
7  <body bgcolor="#000000" text="#000000">
8  <p> </p>
9  <p> </p>
10 <table width="600" border="0" cellspacing="0" cellpadding="2" align="center">
11  <tr align="center" bgcolor="#CC0000">
12   <td><b><font size="1" face="Verdana, Arial, Helvetica, sans-serif" color="#FFFFFF">HOME</font></b></td>
13   <td><b><font size="1" face="Verdana, Arial, Helvetica, sans-serif" color="#FFFFFF">NEW
14    RELEASES</font></b></td>
15   <td><b><font size="1" face="Verdana, Arial, Helvetica, sans-serif" color="#FFFFFF">GENRES</font></b></td>
16   <td bgcolor="#B4E738"><b><font size="1" face="Verdana, Arial, Helvetica, sans-serif" color="#CC0000">ARTISTS</font>
17   <td><b><font size="1" face="Verdana, Arial, Helvetica, sans-serif" color="#FFFFFF">CATALOG</font></b></td>
18   <td><b><font size="1" face="Verdana, Arial, Helvetica, sans-serif" color="#FFFFFF">MP3S</font></b></td>
19   <td><b><font size="1" face="Verdana, Arial, Helvetica, sans-serif" color="#FFFFFF">SHOP</font></b></td>
20   <td><b><font size="1" face="Verdana, Arial, Helvetica, sans-serif" color="#FFFFFF">CONTACT</font></b></td>
21  </tr>
22  <tr align="center" bgcolor="#B0E14A">
23   <td colspan="8" bgcolor="#B4E738">
24    <table width="100%" border="0" cellspacing="15" cellpadding="0">
25     <tr>
```

HTML, the language that underpins the Web. It looks a bit scary, but you only need to know what it is, *not* how to write it!

WHAT IS HTML?

HTML stands for HyperText Markup Language. It is the lynchpin of the Web, and has evolved far beyond it's original intentions. In principal, HTML is simple: it's about putting marks (known as "tags") into text to say how it should appear. For instance <I> to start italics, and </I> to finish italics. Or <B>…</B> for bold, <H1>…</H1> for heading 1, the top-level style of heading. Finally you save your text with the suffix .htm (instead of .txt), and you've got a webpage!

HyperText is also the technology that makes links, the raison d'etre of the Internet, possible. You click on a link, and that sends a request to the Web server to load a new webpage. That page could be part of the same website, or be on another website on a server located anywhere in the world. Again, it's a simple bit of markup, the <A> tag, but this time you need to include some information about the name and location of the new file you want to load when people click on the link. For this, you type <A href="web address of the file in here">Link text</A>.

This is very simple, but as your webpages become more complex, hand-coding HTML becomes dull and laborious. Fortunately, you won't need to do this, because there are many software tools out there that do it all for you. We'll take a look at some of the best ones over the page.

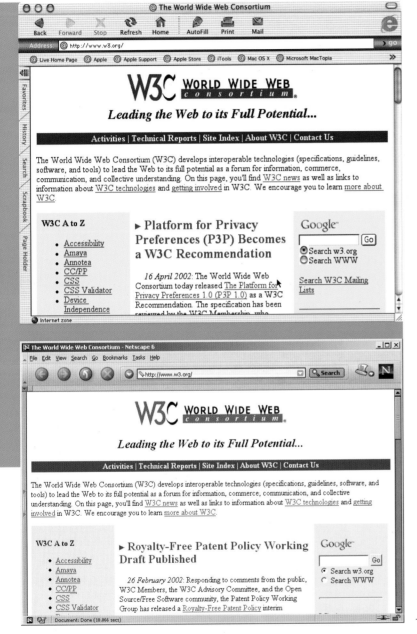

WEB BROWSERS

The browser is to a Web designer as the stage is to an actor. This is your medium. But you have no way of knowing what browser, or browsers, visitors to your website might be using. Unfortunately, Web browsers don't all work in the same way, so you can't guarantee that a webpage that looks good in one will look the same in another. The differences aren't usually fatal, but they're bad enough to frustrate Web designers, who have to be sure their websites work for all viewers, and look exactly the way they are supposed to. Things are further complicated by the fact that there are two main computing platforms that your visitors might be using: Windows PC and Apple Macintosh (known as the Mac). Not all websites work in all browsers across both. But a site that has been well thought-out and fully tested should not present any problems.

The situation is improving as the World Wide Web Consortium, or W3C (*www.w3.org*), works to introduce tough, shared standards. But it's important for you to make sure you have the major Web browsers installed on your computer—which means the latest versions of Internet Explorer and Netscape Navigator at least. Many technology pundits believe that Opera, a fast, secure browser that is growing in popularity, could be a major contender within a few years. Use them to check your webpages constantly as you work on them. If you don't do this, then you'll only need to learn the lesson once: there's nothing more frustrating than putting in two or three days' work to get a webpage looking great in Internet Explorer, only to open it in Netscape and find a travesty of broken design. You should also check your work on both a Mac and a PC. The popular browsers are slightly different on either platform, so borrow a friend's computer, or maybe head to your local Internet café if the computers there are a different platform to yours.

Microsoft Internet Explorer (top) is the most popular browser on the Web by far, with Netscape Navigator (above) second. You should have both of these installed on your computer, and use them to test your webpages as you work on them. The pictured site is *www.w3.org*, hosted by the World Wide Web Consortium, an organization that is working to improve browser standards. Opera, another browser, is fast, secure, and gaining in popularity.

< IE, Netscape + Opera

CREATING WEB PAGES

WHAT DO YOU NEED TO CREATE A WEBPAGE?

In principle, a computer, a text editor such as Windows Notepad or MacOS SimpleText, and a Web browser to check it on are all you need. HTML is a text-based file format, and you can see the code for any webpage just by dragging the file into an ordinary text editor. Alternatively, if you are viewing the page in your browser, choose View>*Source* (Internet Explorer) or View>*Page Source* (Netscape).

It's a good idea to try this so you can get an idea what HTML is about and looks like; but in practice, hand-coding HTML is neither practical nor necessary. Today's software market is literally bulging with "What You See Is What You Get" (WYSIWYG) tools, which enable you to design and prepare the elements of your webpages onscreen while the app does the coding in the background. Some of these applications really shine in terms of their ease of use and variety of features—we look at Dreamweaver, GoLive, and others on page 16. It's well worth spending some money to get the one that works for you. Remember, this is going to be the hub of your Web design work, and you can always get a "save-disabled" demo or fully working 30-day trial before you buy.

GRAPHICS

If you want to put an image onto your webpage, you need to create it in a graphics package—Web authoring software doesn't include drawing or photo enhancing tools. Photoshop, Photoshop Elements (its cheaper, beginner-level sibling), Fireworks, Paint Shop Pro and Corel Photo-Paint are the most popular options, and we'll take a closer look at these in chapter 3—where we'll start creating graphics for our webpages!

OTHER SOFTWARE

There are many other apps you can use in Web design —such as Macromedia Flash for animation, and RealProducer for preparing sound and video. We'll look at the options as we come to these topics in the book. Meanwhile, it might be worth getting hold of a good font previewer and organizer, such as BitStream's Font Navigator (*www.bitstream.com*), or Moon Software's Font Xplorer (*www.moonsoftware.com*). If you have Windows XP, however, you won't need one.

You need a variety of different applications to create a complete website...

MAC OR PC?

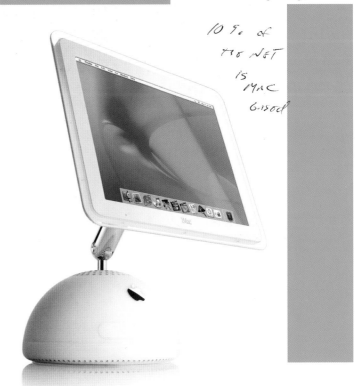

10 % of the net is mac based

RIGHT: The iMac (top) is another innovative piece of hardware from Apple, and uses the new Unix-based operating system, OS X. But high-specification Windows PCs (bottom) are now commonplace and have the greatest market share.

Beginners often wonder whether they should go for a Mac or a PC-based set-up. The Mac has the tradition of being the more creative-led, design-oriented platform, but over the last few years the differences have become far fewer.

PCs have by far the greater user base—roughly 10% of Internet surfers are on a Mac—which means that if you want to see your webpages exactly the way most of your visitors do, you need to work on a PC. There are also many more applications, resources, plugins, extensions, free fonts, and so on available to Windows users, and these are both fun and helpful in the Web design process.

If you go for a Mac, you may find it harder to share files with the Internet community—but in compensation, there are many more Mac users in the traditional design community, especially those who come from a print background. Just make sure you check your Web design work on a PC before you publish it—things don't always look the same!

WEB AUTHORING SOFTWARE

YOUR WEB AUTHORING APP IS THE HUB OF YOUR WEB DESIGN WORK.
YOU NEED TO FEEL BOTH COMFORTABLE AND CAPABLE OF USING IT.
HERE WE LOOK AT FOUR OF THE BEST. THEY ALL HAVE SIMILAR
FEATURES AND CAPABILITIES, COMBINING WEB AUTHORING WITH DRAG-
AND-DROP DYNAMIC BEHAVIORS AND SITE MANAGEMENT TOOLS.

DREAMWEAVER

Over the years Macromedia's Dreamweaver has become the industry standard application for Web designers, and it was one of the first to introduce high-powered features with an attractive, user-friendly interface. In remains one of the most intuitive Web-authoring apps on the market, and its wide user-base means there are literally thousands of free extensions you can download, which add new features to your software. *www.macromedia.com*

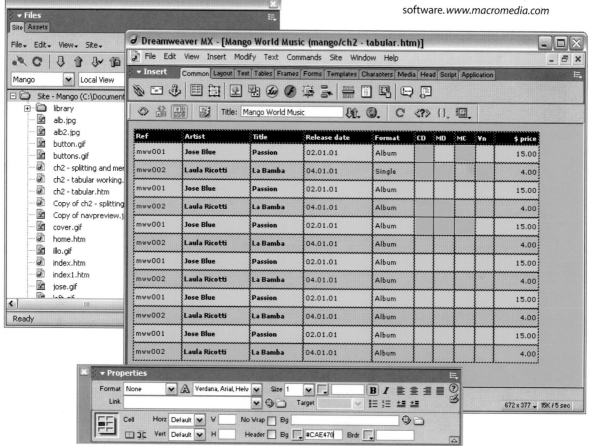

SOFTWARE ROUNDUP

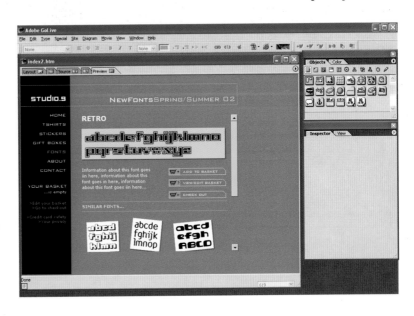

GOLIVE

Adobe, as the maker of Photoshop, is still the biggest player in the design market, and this makes its Web authoring software, GoLive, popular with traditional designers. It works well for beginners, with its numerous Wizards and shortcuts for working with files created in other Adobe packages. For the expert, it includes powerful features for dynamic, or database-driven site work, and also for group working. *www.adobe.com*

HOMESITE

Macromedia HomeSite (formerly Allaire HomeSite), is often (wrongly) perceived as the "beginner's Dreamweaver", but the program is not a WYSIWYG product and relies on the user coding the HTML by hand (which is also possible in Dreamweaver). Many successful, professional Web designers use it as their software of choice. It is, however, relatively inexpensive and is worth considering if you want to explore HTML in more depth. *www.macromedia.com*

OTHER OPTIONS

There is no shortage of Web authoring packages for you to buy—Microsoft FrontPage is another popular one. But if you are on a tight budget, Netscape Navigator, which you can get free from *www.netscape.com*, comes with the simple, easy-to-use Composer (pictured); while Microsoft Windows itself includes a number of basic tools for creating webpages, depending on your installation. Word allows you to save a Word document as a webpage, but not all its features are available in this context.

However, you may swiftly tire of the limited functionality of the free products or of the webpage building elements of larger software suites.

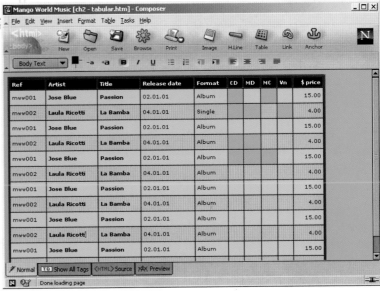

GETTING YOUR SITE ON THE WEB

ONCE YOU'VE CREATED YOUR WEBSITE, YOU NEED TO GET IT ONTO THE WEB. AND FOR THIS, YOU NEED THREE THINGS: A WEB ADDRESS, SOME WEBSPACE, AND AN FTP PROGRAM.

A Web address, otherwise known as a URL or Uniform Resource Locator, is simply a unique reference to a particular file on the Internet. Every file in your site has a Web address—but when people speak of "my Web address," they mean their home page. A Web address is made of two parts. The first is a domain name, such as *www.mysite.com* or *news.bbc.co.uk*, which usually refers to a particular folder on a Web server. When you buy a Web address, the company you buy it from will usually—but not always—allocate you a folder on one of their servers, together with a certain number of megabytes of storage space for your files. This is your Web space.

The second part is the path to the file you want to open—so *www.mysite.com/news.htm* will open the file called *news.htm*. In exactly the same way, *www.mysite.com/news/ latest.htm* will open the file *latest.htm*, which is in a subfolder called *news*. If the file isn't there, you will get the error message "404— File Not Found."

If you just type the address of a site, *www.mysite.com*, or a folder, *www.mysite.com/news*, most Web servers will automatically send you the file called *index.htm*, which is why you should usually give your home page this name. It is a hangover from the days when Internet home pages used to be a simple index of content on a site.

Once you have a Web address and some webspace, you need a way of uploading your website to this space on the Web server, or host computer. For this you use FTP, or File Transfer Protocol, which is a way of exchanging files with other computers. Using FTP, you can browse the files and folders on the Web server just as easily as you can using Windows Explorer or Mac Finder on your own. These are the same files which, if you were to look at them in the usual way via HTTP (HyperText Transfer Protocol) on your Web browser, would open directly in the browser window. Follow the steps over the page that cover choosing and using FTP software.

HOW TO // REGISTER A WEB ADDRESS

1 The best way to register a Web address is directly online. It's usually easiest to do this with the same company that you are already using as your ISP for connecting to the Internet (if they offer this service). Often you'll find your address comes as part of a package including webspace. You can also register an address via sites like *www.mediatemple.net* (pictured), *www.whois.net,* and *www.verisign.com.*

2 Type your preferred address in the search box, and you will find out if it is available. Most addresses using common words and phrases are already taken, so you may have to try a few times, and be imaginative. If your address is taken, some sites will offer similar alternatives that are still available. For example, you might find that the *.com* version of your preferred name is taken, but that a different suffix (eg *.net*) is available.

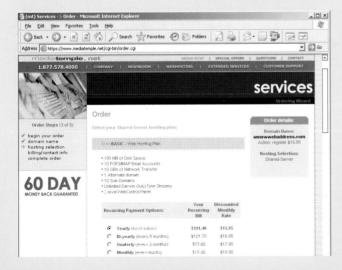

3 Once you've found an address you like, click the button to order it. Fill in the forms to complete your order—you will need to provide quite a lot of information, so you can be properly identified as the owner later on. Be careful only to give confidential information if the page is on a secure server—it should have the prefix https:// in the address bar. You should receive email confirmation of your purchase. Congratulations! You own your own Web address!

← SECURE

FTP SOFTWARE

FTP Client

If you go for a Web authoring app like Dreamweaver, GoLive, HomeSite, or FrontPage, you'll find that you have FTP software built in, as part of your site management features. This is known as an FTP client, where a client is the opposite of a server. If your Web app doesn't include FTP tools, you need to use separate software—Windows Explorer or Internet Explorer often does the job, but if not, try CuteFTP (*www.cuteftp.com*), WS_FTP Pro (*www.wsftp.com*). If you are on a Mac, try Fetch (www.fetchsoftworks.com). Even if you have built-in FTP software, you may find these useful for their speed and dedicated features.

FTP uses addresses, which work in exactly the same way as a Web address, but begin with ftp:// instead of http://. Generally, they also have the prefix "ftp." Instead of "www." So the FTP address for http://www.mysite.com is often ftp://ftp.mysite.com.

Your FTP should require you to log in with a username and password, so other people can't go changing the files in your site. But not all FTP sites do—some are "public" FTPs where anyone can go to download, and sometimes upload, files for sharing.

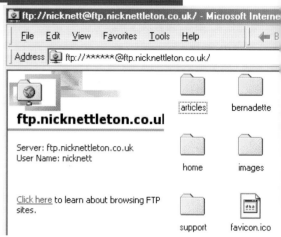

WINDOWS OR INTERNET EXPLORER

1 Most FTP software works in the same way, with exception of Windows or Internet Explorer, which is the easier. Here you just type your FTP address in the address bar, and if you need to log-in, a dialog will pop up asking for your usename and password. Now you can simply browse files and folders on the remote computer in the same way as you do on your own computer.

STANDALONE FTP SOFTWARE

1 Dedicated FTP clients like CuteFTP ,WS_FTP, and Fetch (for the Mac) work in much the same way. Usually, you will have a Site Manager, Connection Wizard, or similar, which you use to enter the settings for your FTP site.

2 Then hit *OK* and connect to your ftp site. On the left, you can see files and folder on your own computer, and on the right are the files and folders in your website. Just drag and drop to transfer files between them…

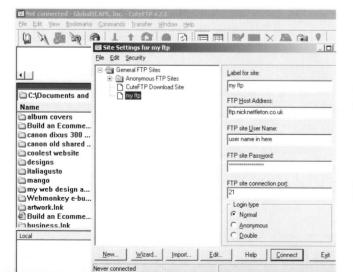

BUILT-IN FTP SOFTWARE

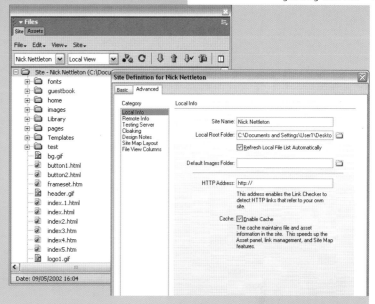

1 Web authoring apps with built-in FTP clients ask you to give FTP information as part of setting up your website in its site management tools. In Dreamweaver, for instance, you choose Window>*Site Files* to open the Site Management window, and then Site>*New Site* to define a site.

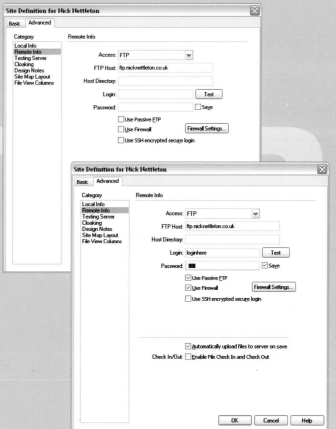

2 In the Remote section, choose FTP from the menu, and then type your FTP domain name in the FTP Host field. You don't need to put ftp:// in front, but if it has an ftp. prefix, you do need this. If your FTP site is in a subfolder of a larger site, for instance *ftp.myhost.com/mysite*—then put the name of this folder in the Host Directory field. Directories are effectively the same as folders.

3 The log-in and password dialogs speak for themselves. The Firewall and Passive FTP preferences depend on whether you are accessing your FTP site from behind a firewall (security zone).

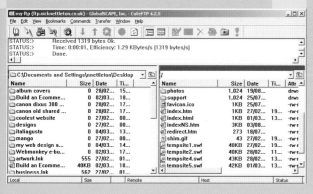

WHETHER YOU WANT TO BUILD A FANSITE, BECOME PART OF A GLOBAL COMMUNITY OF
PEOPLE WITH SHARED INTERESTS, SET UP A VIRTUAL SHOP WINDOW TO PUBLICIZE YOUR
WORK, OR DESIGN A FULLY FUNCTIONAL ECOMMERCE PRESENCE, THE BASIC PRINCIPLES
OF GOOD DESIGN ARE THE SAME

2

CREATING
WEBPAGES

PLANNING YOUR SITE

Before you get stuck into the software, grab a pad, some coffee and a couple of pencils...

Mango World Music

1. Tell people about the company

2. Latest releases, what's coming, other news

3. Sound clips for people to listen to

4. Directory of all recordings and artists

5. Info & pictures for the press

6. Later on add online purchase

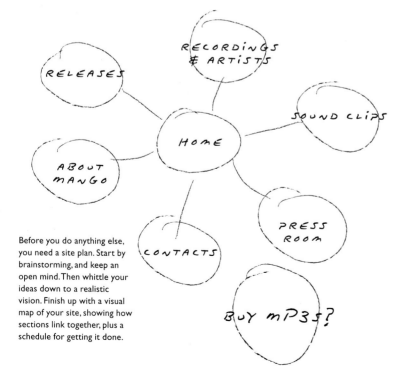

Before you do anything else, you need a site plan. Start by brainstorming, and keep an open mind. Then whittle your ideas down to a realistic vision. Finish up with a visual map of your site, showing how sections link together, plus a schedule for getting it done.

Preparation is about identifying your goals and obstacles, and making decisions about form and function. On the face of it, this sounds dull, particularly if you're eager to dive straight in with fonts and buttons and all things bright and shiny. But don't rush, because this is where the fun really is, and where most of your best ideas will be seeded. While creative work is taxing on your inner resources, and implementing is often just a rote process, preparation is about brainstorming, compiling a wish list, and working out how much of it you can really achieve.

Most designers opt to ditch their computer at this point in favor of a pencil, a sketch pad, and a strong coffee—and if you're working with someone else on your site, you should do this separately first and *then* as a team. The idea is draw up a grand "mind map" of all the things you want and hope for, then to try to rationalize it into a single, clear concept, with each element numbered according to which is the most important. It's good to set yourself a deadline for completing the site, and prioritize your wish list, otherwise you may never see a finished piece of work.

So what do you need to think about?

Schedule:
Site plan: 20 July
First design proof: 15 August
Final design proof: 30 August
Go live: 15 September

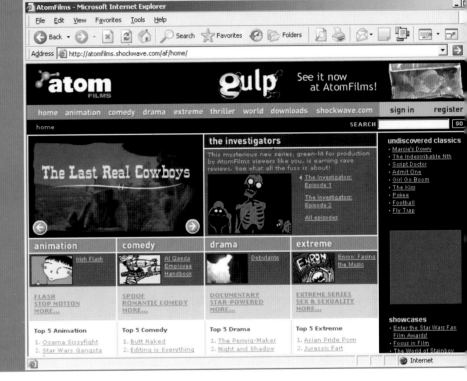

After reading the first sentence on any page, visitors should know what your site is about. A successful site has clear, well defined subject matter, which is reflected in every word and every graphic it uses. Filmmakers' site AtomFilms (*www.atomfilms.com*) is a superb example of this.

CONTENT, CONTENT...

The first and the most important question is what is your website about? This may seem a bit too obvious, but it's the stumbling block at which 90% of beginners' websites fall: they have no clear topic beyond "Here's me and a few things I like", or "Here's my top 10 links: Yahoo!, Alta Vista, Google". This has little significance to anyone beyond a few close friends. Another fault is that they cover too many diverse, unconnected topics to shine in any one area.

If you've got a business, your starting point is predefined: to show off your products or services. If you've got an overriding passion in life, go for that. If not, find something that interests you generally, and do a little research. If your aim is to make money, this should govern your choice of subject matter.

Whichever route you take, the objective is to create a single, clear theme, and focus on it. Your website has to know what it's about—otherwise your visitors won't!

We have chosen four specific site concepts for you to follow through this book, so you can see how an individual idea can evolve from drawing board to Web to business opportunity. One is a world music site, Mango World Music; another is about Italian food, called ItaliaGusto. The third promotes a designer's T-shirt designs, while the last is a photographer's personal portfolio. All four are very different, not only in subject matter, but also in their target audience and objectives. You can take a first look at them over the next few pages. We've jumped ahead a few steps with the designs, so you can get a good idea of what we're talking about before trying it out yourself.

PLANNING YOUR SITE 2

OUR USER...

*GENDER -
PROBABLY MORE
FEMALES*

AGE - 25 - 40?

*INTERESTS: ITALIAN
FOOD OF COURSE,
EATING, DRINKING,
COOKING
TRAVEL, OTHER
TYPES OF FOOD,*

*COMING TO OUR SITE FOR:
RECIPES
TIPS & TRICKS
JUST A GOOD READ
TO TALK TO OTHER
PEOPLE...*

*LANGUAGE STYLE:
CHATTY, EASY GOING,
LOTS OF INFORMATION,
BUT NOTHING TOO TECHNICAL
OR HARD*

*THINKS THEY'D LIKE?
PRINT OUT RECIPES
SEND THEM TO FRIENDS
CHAT WITH OTHER PEOPLE INTO
ITALIAN FOOD*

Why not write down a profile of your ideal user? Think carefully about who you want to attract to your site, and what kind of things appeal to these people. This identity should make its mark in the colors you choose and the words you use. This is called branding; it's an expression of confidence in what you do.

YOUR VISITORS

After you've chosen a topic, you need to think about who you want to attract to your site, and why you want them to come. Is it to promote something about yourself or your business? Is it to provide information that you want to share? Or is it pure entertainment? Do you want your visitors to spend money, or simply enjoy themselves? What sort of thing is going to meet that objective for you?

At this point, you should start to plan the type of content you want on your site—news, product information, images, resource archives, profiles, and so on—in line with what your visitors will be looking for.

And you should also start to get an idea of the look you want: are you going for a serious design, or a basic shell for presenting information? What sort of colors and styles make your visitors tick—strong and bright, or subtle and muted?

By this time, you've probably got 10 or 20 pages of thoughts and ideas sketched out —far more than is realistic—and you need to start slimming these down. You also need to think how you want to present and organize your information—or, to put it another way, how will your visitors find the information they're interested in? And, just as importantly, how long are they prepared to wait for a page to download?

SPEED VS. GRAPHICS

Unfortunately, there is a straight trade-off between the complexity of graphics (as opposed to text) in a webpage, and the time it takes to download. Surveys suggest that users will wait seconds, not minutes, for a webpage to load, before they give up and go somewhere else; and the proportion that loses patience increases rapidly after about 15 or 20 seconds. But this is going to depend entirely on what you're offering: no one expects an image gallery to load double-quick, because everybody knows that images take time to download. News, in contrast, should be swift, accessible, and easy to read.

The only way to get a true picture of how fast a webpage will download is to put it on the Web and try for yourself at different times of day (the speed depends how many other people are on the Web). But as a guideline, 3K a second is average on a 56K modem —or about 30K in 10 seconds. A 100K page, images included, is therefore going to take half a minute to download, and for most sites that is too long!

THE COMPANY SITE: MANGO WORLD MUSIC

The first of our sites is a medium-scale showcase for a fictional recording label, Mango World Music. The company wants to take its music to a new audience, using cutting-edge technologies, and the brief has four points: to reflect and promote the identity of the company; to include a catalog of recordings, which you can buy online, with a directory of artists signed to the label; to offer sound clips for people to download and listen to; and to showcase forthcoming releases on the home page. The site also has to be easy to update.

This is a very clear brief, as briefs go, and it's typical of what small companies are looking for in a website. The label's existing identity material—logo, brochures, and so on —will suggest a look for the site, and we've got no problems working out what the content and structure are going to be.

So we can quickly draw up a map of main features and sections of the website, but we'll plan to add the ecommerce section later on. In the brainstorming session, the obvious question is how people will want to go about browsing the titles they're interested in: the easiest way is by type of music (African, Cuban, Andean…), or by the name of the artist. But they may simply want to browse the latest recordings. So, let's offer all these routes, and make a fun interactive map, where people click on an area of the world to find out about music from that region.

WEBSITES BY GENRE

How long is your visitor prepared to wait for a page to appear? Err on the side of caution. Most users will click off and go to someone else's site if yours isn't downloading fast enough.

PLANNING YOUR SITE 3

THE "MAGAZINE" SITE: ITALIAGUSTO

While Mango World Music majors in intimacy and character, our second site offers something altogether different: information. This is a dedicated magazine-style site, aiming to attract people with an interest in Italian food —both cooks and food-lovers.

The core proposal is to offer hoards of information on different topics, with articles, archives, and more. This is a good approach if you want to attract a high level of traffic, but it's probably the hardest type of site to design, and it's intensive to update. You can bolster this with some some community "sharing" features, such as a discussion board and a chatroom, where users generate the content.

The home page offers literally hundreds of links and options, and this means the design has to be strong, clear, and gentle on the eyes, to make sure it all works. The information needs to be rigorously organized, otherwise you'll end up with a confusing hodgepodge. Here the design helps your viewer understand what's what, and how different bits of information relate to each other.

The other key issues with this site will be speed and usability. Information sites are primarily about giving people answers, and for the most part, they want them quickly. The Web is complex enough without added fluff. So, we pair down the graphics to a bare minimum, choose clear, well-labelled sections for the site, and add in a search tool for good measure.

TSHIRTS 9

Intro text intro text intro text intro
intro text intro text intro text intro t

RE

THE SMALL COMMERCE
SITE: STUDIO.9

Our third concept offers another approach again. Here, the
objective is purely to show off and, ultimately, sell products.
The presentation is simple and straightforward, yet attractive.
It's important with this kind of site not to distract your users
in any way from exactly what you want them to do. Offer just
enough information to tell them what they're getting and why
they're getting it, and leave it there.

Unless you've got a lot of money to spend, you'll need
to find business partners to fulfil the commerce aspects of
the site—and we'll take a look at that later in the book. In
the meantime, focus on creating an effective shop window.

Buying online can be confusing for new users, with
shopping baskets, forms, virtual checkouts, and more—not
to mention the fears many people still have about giving
their credit card details online. So be sure to provide clear
instructions about how it all works. Label your links well,
and think all the time about how you can reassure your
customers. Offer a security statement and privacy policy if
you can—you should be able to get these through your
business partners. Thoughtful details like this will go a long
way towards helping your customers trust you.

Above all, go for a clear and easy-to-browse layout
when you're designing ecommerce pages. If you find you
need to supply a lot of information about individual
products, do this on a separate page, which users can
choose to read if they wish. And don't forget to include
another "Buy it" button on that page. It's always a good idea
to show a few similar products there as well—you might
generate more sales!

STUDIO.9

HOME
TSHIRTS
STICKERS
GIFT BOXES
FONTS
ABOUT
CONTACT

YOUR BASKET
...is empty

>Edit your basket
>Go to checkout

>Credit card safety
>Your privacy

TSHIRTS SPRING/SUMMER 02

Intro text intro text intro text intro text intro text intro text intro text
intro text intro text intro text intro text intro text intro text...

pop*
>Enlarge
>Add to basket

ugly kid
>Enlarge
>Add to basket

red stripes
>Enlarge
>Add to basket

retro
>Enlarge
>Add to basket

fly
>Enlarge
>Add to basket

fruity
>Enlarge
>Add to basket

Similar Tshirts

fly
>Enlarge
>Add to basket

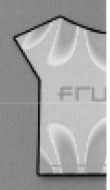

fruity
>Enlarge
>Add to

PLANNING YOUR SITE 4

Andy Butterby Portfolio

HOME | WEBSITES | PHOTOGRAPHY | CV | CONTACT

Photography
Taking landscape photos is my passion.
Click the images on the left to see the
whole image.

Many of these I do for myself and
friends, by I also do the odd commission
or exhibition here and there. If you're
interested, do please get in touch.

I use a combination of natural and digital
techniques to create and enhance the
images, although they all begin with an
amazing view or interesting feature.

Using a computer, I can enhance the
light, colour and other appearances in the
image, to bring out its unique character
or details.

THE PORTFOLIO SITE:
ANDY BUTTERBY

Our fourth and final site is a portfolio—something you might
want to create for yourself after you've designed a couple of
other sites. This one showcases photographs.

As with the ecommerce site, the design is deceptively simple,
but for different reasons. The point of a portfolio is to show off
your work at its best, and like an art gallery or the fashion pages of
a magazine, the best way to do it is to keep it clean and simple. You
don't want too many diversions from the core message, and
clutter should be avoided at all costs.

You will also need to design an interface that allows different,
contrasting images to work together well, and which looks
attractive but is also unobtrusive enough to remain in the
background. Content-wise, we've kept to the basics: a couple of
sections for different types of work, plus a C.V. and some contact
details. The gallery sections can include some descriptions of what
the work is about and how it is made.

This site might look simple enough, but we're going to include
some extra features to show off the work. The home page has a
little interactive animated browser of some favorite pieces, with
"Previous" and "Next" links at the bottom. The gallery pages,
meanwhile, use thumbnails which, when you click on them, open a
popup window showing the full image.

In short, this site is clean, easy and effective: just what a portfolio
should be. And like any portfolio, the design should show off the work
and nothing else: that's what you want your visitors to look at.

STRUCTURE
The final step in planning your site is to work out the
structure itself: what sections are you going to use to
divide up the content? And what features will you add
to help visitors find their way around?

A popular format for product-oriented sites
breaks down into home, news, products, support,
company info, and contact details. Many magazine-
style sites use a similar structure: home, news, reviews,
interviews, community, shop, commercial info, and
again, contact details.

Alternatively, you might want to organize your
site by topic, location, or time period. For example, a
history site might be organized under Prehistoric,
Ancient, Middle Ages, and Modern. For our Mango
World Music concept site, we're going to use different
types of music—Salsa, Indian and so on—as a
secondary navigation route.

Andy Butterby Portf

HOME | WEBSITES | PHOTOGRAPHY | CV | C

Welcome. On the left is a selection
favourite recent work - use the Nex
Back buttons to browse. Or click the
above for specific information.

Websites
I have desigbed a few websites, so
big, some small. Take a look and fi
more. More >>

Photography
Landscape photos are my passion.
a little gallery fo some of my favou
work. More >>

CV
My straight-up CV - education,
employment, interests and so on.
More >>

◄ BACK   Atlanta, Georga - 2002   NEXT ►

SETTING UP A SITE

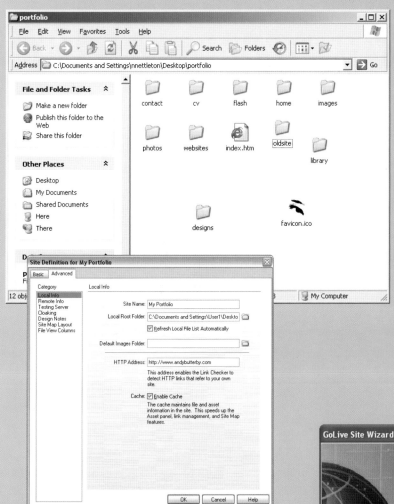

1 You should keep all the webpage, graphics and related files for your site in a single, dedicated folder to avoid problems with links later on. Traditionally, designers then create a folder within this for each section of the site, such as news and archives. This means you can give people an attractive address like *www.mysite.com/news* if you want them to go straight there.

2 Using Dreamweaver, you can open the *Window>Site Files* window and then choose *Site>New Site* to use the software's site management tools, and make overall site settings. The first two sections, Local and Remote info, are the important ones.

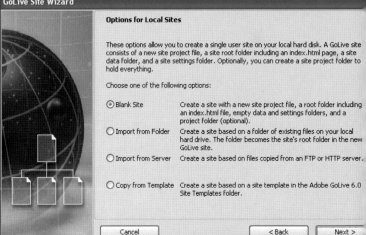

3 In Adobe GoLive, you can just choose *New Site* from the opening wizard, and follow the easy steps here. You'll find the settings dialog under *Site>Settings*. To set up your FTP, choose *Edit Server* from the FTP menu, and in the dialog click the little "page" icon to add a new server.

YOUR FIRST WEBPAGE

Once you've thoroughly planned out your website, decided what you're going to put on it and how, it's time to start sketching out design ideas and creating sample webpages.

Don't be afraid to experiment with lots of different ideas. For every design you decide to use, you will probably create two that end up on the cutting room floor. But never throw anything away...

Creating a complete and polished design takes time, inspiration, and practice. You will probably ditch more ideas than you keep. This is normal, so don't get frustrated if you're not getting the results you want. Just follow this book through and keep trying.

It's a good idea to use the same basic design concept for all the pages in your site. This not only saves time, it helps your viewer understand they are still in the same website. So your objective here is not to create a single, finished page, but a general template. You can then copy and adapt this for your different sections, just by changing the main content area: logo, navigation, fonts, and so on all stay the same. Good design is all about simplicity, not being flashy.

1 Kick off by creating a new page, and call it index.htm. This is the name your final home page should have, and although it's not necessarily always the best bet to design your home page first, let's use it for now for your working template...

STEP BY STEP

2 It's easy to forget this, but your first job is to give your page a title. This will appear in the title bar of your viewers' browser and on search engines, and "Untitled" or "index.htm" looks scrappy. Sometimes you'll see the option for this directly in your apps interface; in other software it's in a *Head* section of the toolbox, and still others have it under *Page* or *Document* properties.

4 You should have a toolbar or *Properties Inspector* with basic formatting options, including font face and size, as well as bold and italic. You should always specify a font face for your text, otherwise your viewer's browser will apply its own default face, which can vary from Arial to Times and other options. This may also cause text flow problems. Generally, it's a good idea to avoid serif faces like Times New Roman, because these are harder to read on screen.

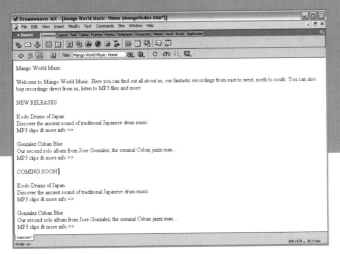

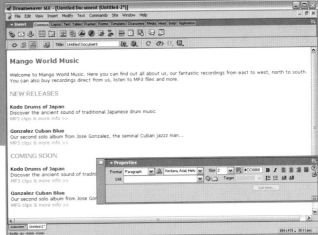

3 Adding text to your webpage is as easy as using a wordprocessor: you just type it in. In fact, it's a good idea to write your text in your normal wordprocessor first, where you can easily spell check it and so on. Then copy and paste it into your webpage. In some Webapps, you'll find that to get a single, rather than double, line space, you need to hit *Shift+Return*.

5 You can change the background color of your webpage and the default colors for text, usually using the *Page* or *Document* properties menu option. But be careful: you should make sure these are easy to read. Bright red on bright green or on dark blue isn't going to work. You can also change the color of specific bits of text, by selecting your formatting toolbar, which you should make good use of for headings and subheadings. This helps to break up your page into easy-to-read chunks.

USING TABLES

So far, so good, but your webpage doesn't have much...well, design. It's just another text document with a splash of color. So, how do you go about putting together an attractive design scheme to match your bright ideas?

The cornerstone of webpage layout is the table. Like a table in your wordprocessor or spreadsheet program, tables in Web design have rows and columns, which are made up of grids of cells. Tables might seem a clumsy and unattractive technique, but their history is almost as long as the Web's itself. They derive from the earliest days of HTML, when the medium was used for sharing mainly academic information. Tables were introduced to the mark-up language so people could display data —for instance the results of a scientific study—in an accessible, tabular format.

But by hiding the gridlines, combining and splitting cells, and controlling the widths and heights of rows and columns, designers found they could control the appearance of webpages, and to date this remains the most reliable technique. More recent versions of HTML have introduced layers, intended as a more intuitive way of controlling layout, but the technology is still new, difficult to work with, and the results are unpredictable. Steer clear for now!

In addition to controling the width and height of your table cells, you can give them individual background colors. In this way you could have blue columns down the left side of your webpage, or a black bar as a background to a white subheading in your main text. You can even use a graphic or photo as a background, instead of a color.

More and more complex webpages rely mainly on a designer's increasingly ingenious use of these simple techniques.

This working shot of the portfolio site in progress shows how you can use tables to create a layout. The gridlines mark out the individual table cells.

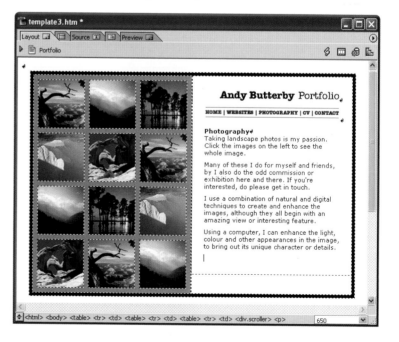

TABLE BASICS

1 To add a table to your webpage, put your cursor in your chosen place on the page, then click the *Table* button in your main toolbar or toolbox. Some software gives you a dialog where you can set the number of rows and columns, as well as the width and other properties of your table. In other apps, you need to select the table or different portions of it, and use your *Inspector*. You'll often find additional instructions in your right-click menu.

3 The *Align Property* controls set where the table appears, and whether it floats to the left or right, with content wrapping around it.

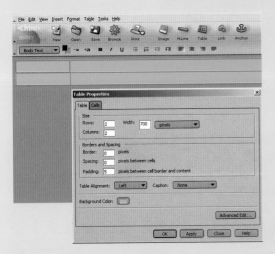

2 The key properties of a table are number of rows and columns; width and height (which you can set as a percentage, or as a precise number of pixels); border size; cell padding and cell spacing (which are in pixels); and background color or image. If you have a background image, this will override the color—but be aware that in Netscape 4.x the image won't look the same as in other browsers. It repeats again from the top-left in each cell.

4 The main settings for a table cell include *Row Span*, which represents a number of cells merged horizontally; and *Column Span*, which represents cells merged vertically. You can set the height and width of individual cells, and also give a cell its own background color or image.

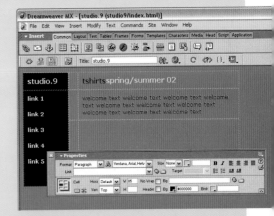

5 The *Horizontal* and *Vertical Alignment Properties* control how text and other content in your table cell appears, while the *No Wrap* setting stops content from wrapping onto a new line where it normally would.

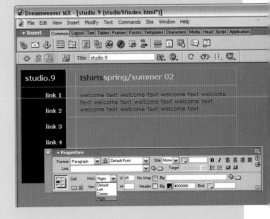

USING TABLES

2

A TABULAR DESIGN

There is no end to what you can do with tables, but one of the easiest designs to achieve is a simple, tabular layout. Such designs remain popular on many sites because they are compact and easy to understand when you've got a lot information to get through. This would be ideal for a complete catalog of Mango World Music releases, for example.

1 Start by creating a new table with 10 columns and 3 rows. The black borders are a key feature here, but the border settings for tables don't give you this level of control. Instead, try setting cell spacing to 1, and put your table inside another 1x1 table that has a black background. This is called nesting. Don't forget to set the borders to 0.

2 Give the whole top row a black background color, and make the text white. The whole table uses Verdana as the font.

3 Choose two complementary background colours for alternating rows—this makes the table easier to read—and a background color for the whole page. Then add text in the two rows. Set cell spacing for the inner table to 2 or 3, to create some space around the text.

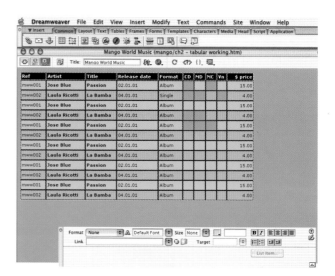

4 Next, duplicate the two rows as many times as you need for all the information, and update the text. We've set the Artist and Title columns bold, since these are the most important; and we've left the widths and heights of the cells to size automatically.

5 Finally, change the background colors of the CD, MD, etc., cells to indicate which formats the title is available in. You can now copy and paste this layout into a general page template.

SPLITTING & MERGING CELLS

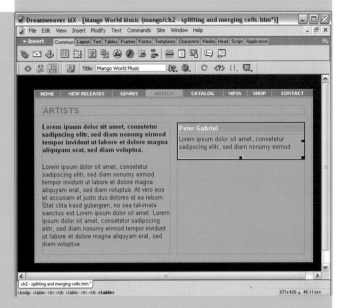

1 To create a more free-form layout or page template, you need to get to grips with splitting and merging cells. For this design, start by creating a table with 8 columns and 2 rows, setting cell padding to 2. Put your main section headings in the cells in the top row, with a medium red background color. Don't forget to set the font, size, and color.

2 Next, merge all the cells in the bottom row into one, and give this a muted green background.

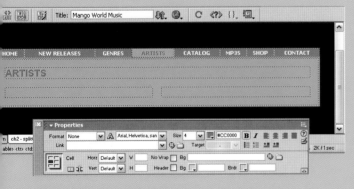

3 In this bottom row, nest a new 100%-wide table with 2 rows and 2 columns, with cell spacing set to 15. This will create a spacious gutter around the edges of the page, and between the columns. In this table, merge the top row into one cell, and put your heading in there.

4 Now you have a basic two-column layout, with navigation and a heading going right across it. In the first column, you can add some general, introductory text and information for the section.

5 In the second column, we're going to add the main information: a list of artists. First, nest a new table in the second column, this time with 1 column and 2 rows, 100%-wide with cell padding at 2. Give the top row a background color a little darker than the main background, and put your subhead—or artist's name— in there. Put some information about the artist in the second row.

6 You may need to set the *Vertical Align* of both columns of the layout to Top, to get the alignment right.

7 Finally, duplicate the last table as many times as you need for your list of artists. This design will make a good template for several pages in a site.

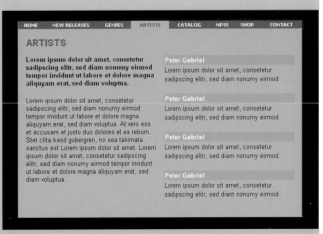

CREATING A LAYOUT

WE ARE STILL A LONG WAY AWAY FROM A COMPLETE DESIGN. IT'S ALSO MUCH HARDER TO DEVISE AN ATTRACTIVE SHAPE AND STRUCTURE OF YOUR OWN, WHEN ALL YOU'VE GOT TO GO ON IS A BLANK PAGE...

WHERE TO BEGIN?

If you have started your site by devising a grand plan, as we suggested in chapter one, then you'll find the problem is already halfway solved. Use this as your starting point, complete with all those details about the type of content you want, the features you plan to offer, and the look you're after. On this basis, you can draw up a list of everything you need on a particular page, then tick points off as you sketch out ideas, and head toward a complete design. And, of course, much of this will be the same for every page in your site: the logo, the navigation, the footer, and so on.

We'll take a step-by-step look at working out a layout for your webpages in this way over the page. But first there's another issue you need to deal with: the size of your page.

This might sound elementary, but it's actually one of the many thorny, cross-platform problems that threaten to chip away at Web designers' hard work. When you look at most websites online, any webpage appears at the same size, no matter how large or small your monitor. So, if your design completely fills the display of a large monitor, users with smaller screens won't be able to see the whole page without scrolling sideways as well as down. So how big, or small, should your page be?

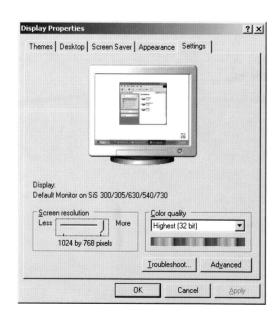

1 Unlike TV, webpages don't scale to fit the window (without a lot of hard work; we'll look at this later). Hence your designs can look great on a 17" display, but take a look on a 14" and you may only see two-thirds of your webpage. The key factor isn't the size of the monitor, but the resolution. On a PC, you can find out your resolution by selecting Display in your Control Panel, and then the Settings tab. On a Mac, select Monitors and Sounds in the Control Panel. The most common resolutions are 1024x768 and 800x600.

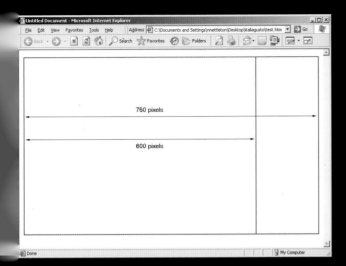

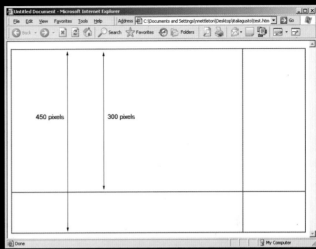

2 The important thing is to make sure your webpage fits width-wise into the smaller resolutions —scrolling down is less of an issue than scrolling across. This means that if you want your website to work for 800x600 displays, it should be 760 pixels wide at most. The leaves room for a scrollbar and other possible interface elements. If you want to appeal to 640x480 viewers, you'll need to stick to just 600 pixels width.

3 You may want your website to display entirely in one window space, with no scrolling at all. In this case, your working height is 420 pixels for 800x600 screens, and a tiny 300 pixels for 640x480.

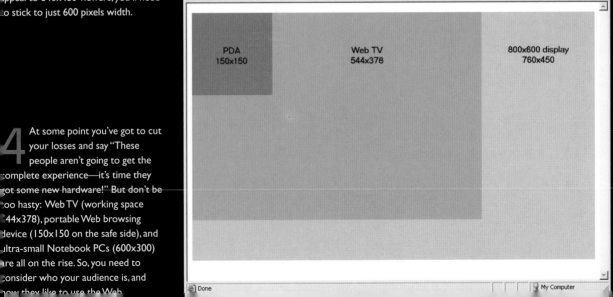

4 At some point you've got to cut your losses and say "These people aren't going to get the complete experience—it's time they got some new hardware!" But don't be too hasty: Web TV (working space 544x378), portable Web browsing device (150x150 on the safe side), and ultra-small Notebook PCs (600x300) are all on the rise. So, you need to consider who your audience is, and how they like to use the Web.

CREATING A LAYOUT 2

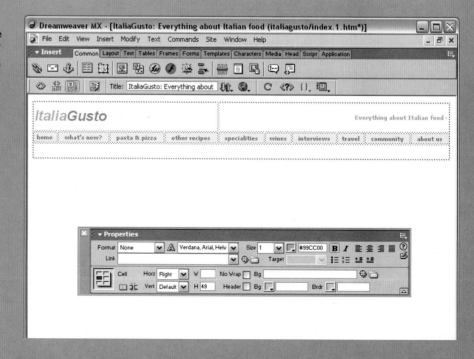

ItaliaGusto - Recipe Page

HEADER: LOGO
 STRAP LINE
 MAIN NAVIGATION

TITLE: NAME OF DISH
BIG PIC DISH
HOW LONG TO COOK?
INGREDIENTS
STEPS
LINKS TO OTHER RECIPES IT GOES WELL WITH
LINKS: CHAT ABOUT THIS RECIPE
 ADD A COMMENT
 PRINT IT
 EMAIL IT TO A FRIEND

FOOTER: BACK, TOP, RELATED, COPYRIGHT...

1 Once you've settled on a page width, you're ready to start devising a page layout. Start with a page that will be most typical of your site, rather than the home page; in the case of ItaliaGusto, we're going for a simple recipe page, which we can easily adapt for interviews, news, and so on later. Then make a list of everything you want to go on it.

2 Create a new HTML page, and add in a table that is the full width of your chosen page size. Within this, you can start devising a layout. Here we're using a 10-column, 3-row table with cell spacing of 1, cell padding of 3, and several merged columns.

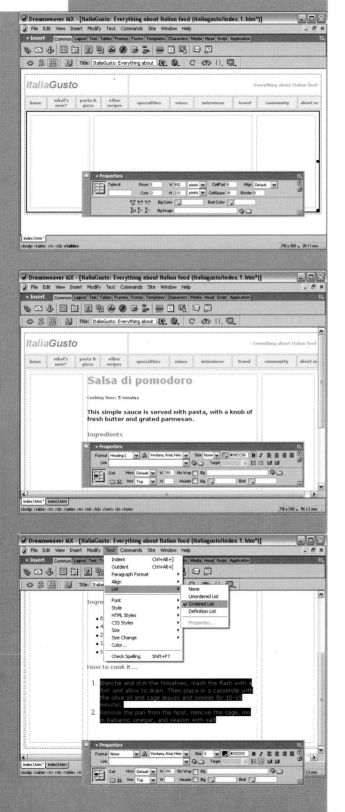

3 Let's try a 3-column layout for the main content. A wide central column will hold the recipe, and you can use the columns to the left and right to show various links, bits of extra information, advertisements, and so on. In the bottom row, add a 100%-wide table with 3 columns and plenty of spacing and padding. Roughly set the column widths.

4 Next, add some sample content in the central column, using different heading settings and colors to organize the content on the page. You should find your text formatting options include heading levels, written as *H1, H2,* etc. Make good use of these—it's much quicker than using font size settings, and later we'll learn how you can control the appearance of all headings in one go.

5 HTML text also includes options for ordered (or numbered) lists, and unordered lists, which are bulleted. We've used these for the ingredients and instructions.

CREATING A LAYOUT **3**

CREATING LINKS

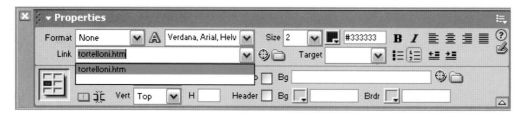

1 It's always good to include links to related pages on your site, if you can—especially if you're aiming for lots of traffic or sales. To create a link in a webpage, you simply select the text, then find your Link or URL tool.

2 You should have a *Browse* button or icon here. Click this to browse for the HTML file you want to open when people click on the link. For the time being, make sure the link type is set to *Relative*, or *Relative To Document*.

3 Using your *Page* or *Document* properties, you can control the color of unvisited, visited, and active links. Make sure the colors you choose work well with your site, and help links to stand out. We'll look at links in more detail in chapter 4.

FINISHING OFF

1 We need a footer for the page, so start by adding a Horizontal Rule (often just called HR), under the main content table, but within the cell that holds it. Insert a new row below this.

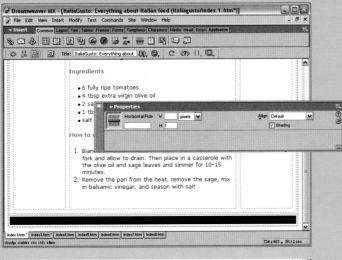

2 We split this row into two columns, adding a copyright statement on the left, and some footer links on the right.

3 To create the "Top" link, you need to add an *Anchor*, or *Target* as it is called in Netscape, at the top of the page. Give it the name "top." Then in the Link box for your Top link, simply put "#top."

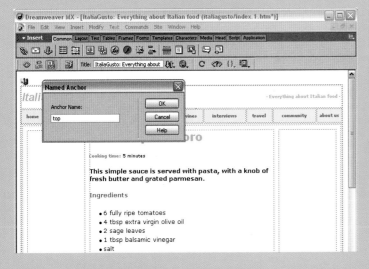

4 Using the same techniques as for the tabular layout (pages 36-7), create a box on the left to show an index of different recipes in this section of the site.

5 You can then quickly duplicate and adapt this to show different groups of information and links down the side of the page.

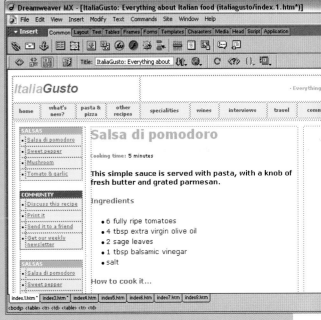

FONTS AND COLORS

IN THE PREVIOUS SECTION, YOU SAW HOW YOU HAVE TO THINK CAREFULLY ABOUT YOUR PAGE SIZE, TO MAKE SURE YOUR SITE WORKS FOR USERS WITH SMALLER SCREENS. THERE ARE SIMILAR PROBLEMS IN WEB DESIGN TO DO WITH FONTS AND COLORS, THE FIRST BEING THE MOST SERIOUS.

PHOTOCLUB
PHOTOCLUB
PHŌTŌ♀LÛ÷
PHOTOCLUB
PHOTOCLUB
PhotoClub
PhotoClub
PHOTOCLUB

Arial
Verdana
Helvetica
Times New Roman
Courier New

1 You've probably experimented already with using different fonts in your webpages: fun and funky, or just fresh and classic. This is a key step in devising an identity for your designs, and tailoring your webpages to appeal to the right people.

3 This is because, like an ordinary text file, a webpage doesn't include the font file itself, or details of the shapes of the letters.

It just has a reference to the name of the font. There are two solutions to this. The first is to use only standard fonts in your webpages. These include Verdana, Arial, Helvetica, Times New Roman, Courier, and Monaco.

2 But, if you use a typeface that your visitor doesn't have installed on their computer, it just won't work. Instead, they will see the same text in a "standard" font—but you can't be sure which one, because that depends on their browser settings. Arial, Times New Roman, or Helvetica are the most likely candidates...

4 Using these won't help you jazz up your pages much. Instead, you can create text that uses special fonts as an image file, and then embed this in the Web. We'll look at creating and using image files in the next chapter. Because image files tend to be slower to download, though, most designers opt for a combination of the two techniques: standard fonts for the body text, and graphical text for headings and navigation.

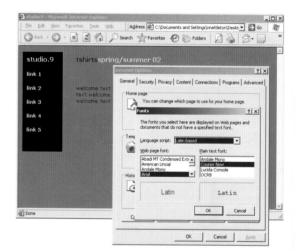

COLORS

1 Choosing the right color scheme for your site is an important part of identifying its style and target market. You've got to select colors that work together, and that will also appeal to your audience. This can be as simple or as complex a color scheme as you like, but if you want to use a lot of colors, it's generally a good idea to use different tones rather than hues.

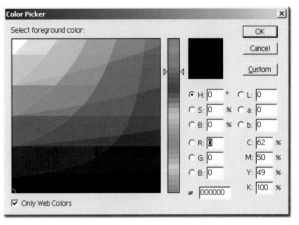

2 There is a similar, but less serious, problem to the font issue when using colors on the Web. Many older monitors can only display 256 colors, rather than the 16.7 million of newer displays. Even people with newer displays don't make the most of their settings: you can see these for yourself in your Display Properties' Settings tab. On the Mac, they're in the *Monitors Control Panel* (OS 9) or the *Display* pane in *System Preferences* (OS X).

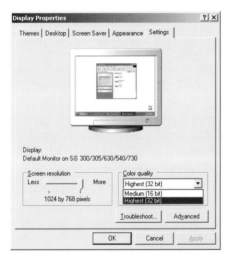

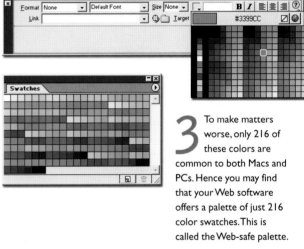

3 To make matters worse, only 216 of these colors are common to both Macs and PCs. Hence you may find that your Web software offers a palette of just 216 color swatches. This is called the Web-safe palette.

4 But you can use other colors, and many designers do. If a computer can't display a color you've specified, it will usually show the nearest possible match— but you can't always be sure. In particular, this can lead to color distortion or mismatching edges between image files and your webpage layout.

Since the dull, text-based early attempts at web publishing, images—graphics, photos, photo montages, and a whole host of other visual stimuli—have come to represent the new generation of websites. Pictures and graphics, when combined with links and interactivity, truly bring life and color to the Web

WORKING WITH IMAGES

IMAGES
HOW AND WHY?

THE KEY TO DESIGNING A GREAT WEBSITE IS GETTING YOUR MESSAGE ACROSS AS QUICKLY, EASILY, AND APPROPRIATELY AS YOU CAN, USING WHATEVER TOOLS AND TECHNOLOGIES YOU HAVE AT YOUR DISPOSAL. ONE OF THE MOST POWERFUL TECHNIQUES IS USING IMAGES. AS THE OLD ADAGE GOES, A PICTURE IS WORTH A THOUSAND WORDS...

Here we've circled all the parts of the Mango design Web plan that relate to using graphics: pretty much all of it, except the basic layout and positioning, the background colors, and the body text. The focus of graphics should be on the "page furniture"—those details that identify your site and make it unique.

...Of course, other pictures are designed to represent a simple idea or action online, rather than a "brand" (a complex set of associations and aspirations). But even a picture that says just one thing—an envelope icon next to an email link for example—will enhance your design. Visitors can take in a page full of images and know what they mean at a glance.

There are other reasons why you need to use visual content on your webpages. First, don't assume that all your visitors speak English, or find it easy to read. Images can overcome the language barrier. And second, they also add visual interest and stimulus.

As we discussed as the end of the last chapter, if you want to use nonstandard fonts in your webpages, you'll need to treat them as graphics. The same applies if you want to make use of other design features that you can't achieve with tables—a drop shadow, a diagonal line, or a rounded button effect, for example.

In fact, you'll find you'll almost always need graphics (rather than pure text) for logos, navigation, buttons, section headings, and other "page furniture", as designers call it. These are the bits and pieces that go around and enhance your main page content on every page, and stay the same throughout the site.

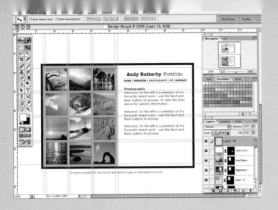

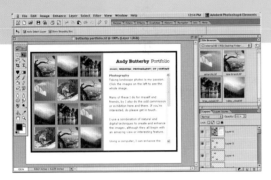

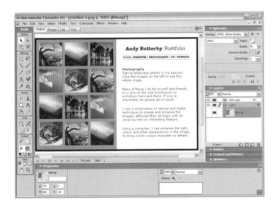

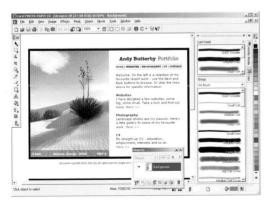

BEFORE YOU START CREATING GRAPHICS AND IMAGES, YOU NEED TO MAKE SURE YOU'VE GOT SOME GOOD SOFTWARE FOR THE JOB, WITH DEDICATED WEB FEATURES. HERE'S OUR PICK OF THE BUNCH...

ADOBE PHOTOSHOP

Probably the best image editing software in the world, Photoshop has also become the industry standard for Web and print design. On the plus side, it has immensely powerful tools for graphics and preparing photos; you can get literally thousands of plugins and effects, and it comes bundled with the dedicated Web app, ImageReady. On the minus side, with such a comprehensive feature set, Photoshop can be hard to use, and it's expensive too. www.adobe.com

PHOTOSHOP ELEMENTS

For the beginner, Adobe's Photoshop Elements may be a better bet: it's simply a cut-down version of the main app, and much less expensive with it. You'll find you have all the most important tools, and it's certainly recommended over Paint Shop Pro. But in the long term, you'll be looking for more. www.adobe.com

MACROMEDIA FIREWORKS

Fireworks is a dedicated Web-only design and animation package, and is the best in this niche field. As well as bitmap images, it works with vector graphics, which means you can easily go back and change them, resize them, and so on, and it has powerful built-in tools for creating navigations, rollovers, menus, and other "behaviors." Fireworks has only basic features for manipulating photos, and it's not appropriate for print work, but if you don't need that functionality, it's much cheaper than Photoshop and probably a better bet. www.macromedia.com

CORELDRAW AND PHOTO-PAINT

Corel's all-in graphics suite is perhaps the most comprehensive package on the market, bundling in an app for every conceivable aspect of design, except HTML authoring. Both DRAW (a vector app, like Fireworks) and Photo-Paint (a bitmap app, like Photoshop) have strong Web-oriented features, and are popular in the US. The only danger is overwhelming the user with the sheer number of features on offer. But in the long term, that can hardly be a bad thing! www.corel.com

FONTS, HEADINGS & TEXT EFFECTS

MANY OF THE GRAPHICS YOU CREATE FOR YOUR WEBPAGES WILL BE TEXT-BASED— PARTICULARLY WHEN YOU'RE USING NONSTANDARDS FONTS, PERHAPS WITH SOME SPECIAL STYLING, FOR A HEADING OR BUTTON. REMEMBER THAT IF YOU WANT TO USE ANYTHING OTHER THAN ARIAL, VERDANA, OR TIMES NEW ROMAN, YOU NEED TO CONSIDER CREATING THE TEXT AS A GRAPHIC.

Type is the easiest place to begin with graphics: choose an attractive font, type in your text, and you've already got something that looks great. You barely need do more. As a designer, it's important to have a packed and varied arsenal of typefaces, from the straightforward to the fun and funky. And it's useful to have a font manager to browse them with, like Bitstream's FontNavigator (*www.bitstream.com*).

TEXT EFFECTS

The sheer variety of things you can do with type is immense, from applying the on-board filters and effects in your graphics app, to mixing in other images, to simple contrasts of color, character, and positioning. The best way to kick off is open up your software and start experimenting.

Using your type tool, you can add text, either in a separate dialog or directly onto the page. The *Fill* color is the main color for your text, while most software also offers a *Stroke* color for the outline. You can experiment with using an image or texture for the fill (in Photoshop you'll find these under the *Effects* button at the bottom of your Layers palette). And try using the *Free Transform*, *Distortion,* or *Envelope* tools to warp your text into unexpected shapes.

CHOOSING FONTS

There are thousands of fonts available on the Web for download, both free and for a fee—the latter usually being of better quality. Try sites like *www.myfonts.com, www.fontalicious.com,* and *www.fontparadise.com* for starters. But how do you choose a font?

1 Your first criterion, especially on the Web, is readability: how small do you want your text to go, and is the font readable at that size? If you want a font to work at small sizes, you need to go for something clear and simple—although this doesn't have to mean boring. Bank Gothic works well for our Studio.9 site.

2 Capitals are often a good solution for very small text, while you can also get bitmap fonts, *pictured*, specially designed to be readable and look good at small point sizes.

nokia mobile

verdana 10pt

04b_03b

04b_03b

04b_03b

04b_03b

3 Small type is important because, as you'll realize, you don't have an awful lot of space on a webpage, especially if you want to cut down on scrolling. Once you've got 100 words or so, plus a couple of images, logos, links, navigation, and all the trimmings, you're starting to run out of space, as here at *www.pixelsurgeon.com*.

4 On the other hand, you might decide that scrolling is no problem, and you've got plenty of space to play with: time to bring out the big fonts. Once you up the size of your text, you can get a lot more playful with your typefaces. Here you need to be really thinking about the topic of your web page and what sort of typeface is going to complement that. How traditional or way-out are you going to go? For ItaliaGusto, we go for the casual, fun, but less readable FatboySlim typeface.

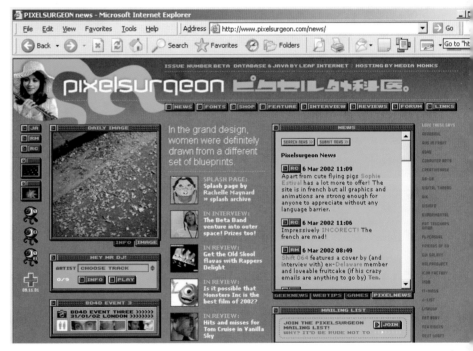

FATBOY SLIM

5 For Mango, meanwhile, we can use the funkier Curlz MT for larger type, and for Studio.9's logo we go for the ultra-cool but barely readable Luggage Round.

Mango
Curlz MT

studio.9
luggage round

EASY TEXT EFFECTS

1 You can use type "as is," with just a color from your scheme to mark it out. With more unusual fonts this is often the best way. But there's also a lot you can do to add your own mark to headings and other features. Your software should come with a variety of on-board effects, like the ubiquitous drop shadow…

2 In Photoshop (pictured) you'll find these under the *Effects* icon at the bottom of your *Layers* palette. In Fireworks you have a dedicated *Effects* palette, while in other apps you have a special *Effects* or *Filters* menu.

3 But you don't want your shadow to look just the same as everyone else's. Experiment with very soft, distant shadows, or a very tight, nearby shadow. Try combining it with an outline color for your text, too.

4 Creating an inner shadow can be an attractive alternative, for a cut-out look.

5 You can also apply different types of bevels, adjust the settings to get a smooth or chiseled effect. This works well with an outer shadow.

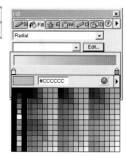

6 You can work creatively with the way the text is filled. Your software will have a gradient fill option, which you can use for simple transitions…

7 …or a complete metallic effect.

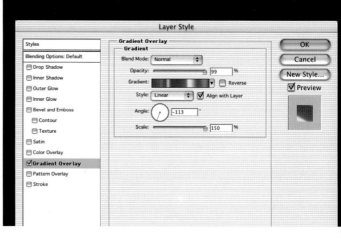

STEP BY STEP

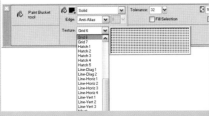

8 Another approach is to use textures to fill the type, which you can quickly adapt to create a variety of different looks. This works quite differently depending on your software. In Fireworks, use the *Texture* menu in your *Fill* palette.

9 In Photoshop, on the other hand, you need to use the *Pattern Overlay* effect from the *Effects* menu at the bottom of your *Layers* palette. Try different *Blending Modes* and scaling with the pattern to get an effect that works.

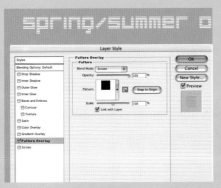

10 You can also use another image to fill your text. In Fireworks, just align the image with your text in the page, then choose Edit>*Cut* and Edit> *Paste Inside*.

11 In Photoshop, paste your image into the page first, then select your Text tool, and choose the dotted *T* icon in the *Options* bar before you type.

12 Then open your *Layers* palette, select the image layer, and click the *Mask* button at the bottom—this looks like a little dotted circle.

OPTIMIZING IMAGES

BEFORE YOU CAN ADD IMAGES TO YOUR WEBPAGES, YOU NEED TO TAKE CARE OF TWO THINGS: THE FILE FORMAT AND THE FILE SIZE.

As a rule, webpages only support two out of the numerous image formats you can use: GIF and JPEG. You need to save a copy of your image in one of these to get it onto your webpage.

But if you save the image "as is" with no preparation, you'll find that the file size is huge—maybe 100K or more. You want your images to download as quickly as possible when someone comes onto your site, so you need to get the file size down. This is called compressing, or optimizing graphics. Your graphics software should already include tools for doing this, and using these you can often reduce the size of your graphics files by 80% or more. That means much swifter downloads, and much happier visitors to your site.

Optimizing images is a fine art, and one that usually represents a trade-off between image quality and file size. So how do you choose the right format for your design? GIF compression is good for graphics, or cartoon-style images with large areas of flat color, while JPEG compression is good for photos and images with continuous (or gradually changing) tones. GIF optimization works by reducing the number of colors stored in the file format, which is no big deal if your graphic only needs 8 or 16 colors anyway. JPEG optimization, on the other hand, directly reduces the level of detail, sharpness, and overall quality in an image, although even barely visible reductions here can cut your file size by half or even more.

We'll take a look at how to use your optimization tools for each format over the page…

REUSING GRAPHICS

THERE IS ANOTHER TECHNIQUE YOU CAN USE
TO SPEED UP IMAGE DOWNLOADS...

When you open a webpage over the Internet, your computer downloads all the files into a temporary folder on your computer. It then holds onto these files in a "cache", often for months, depending on the your personal browser settings. The idea is to speed up your Internet experience, because if you go back to that page the next day, your computer doesn't need to download everything again—it only needs to check it has got the latest versions. The same applies if you click through to another webpage, but one which includes some of the same files: these can be retrieved quickly from the cache, rather than downloaded.

So it makes sense, as a Web designer, to reuse the same graphics files across your site wherever you can. You should be aiming to use the same or similar page furniture and design idioms anyway, as a matter of consistency and identity. This particularly applies to elements like the logo, your navigation graphics and common buttons.

A lot of the graphics you'll use on a website will be the same (they'll appear on every page). Reusing the same files on each webpage massively speeds up your website, as well as saving you time in preparing the files.

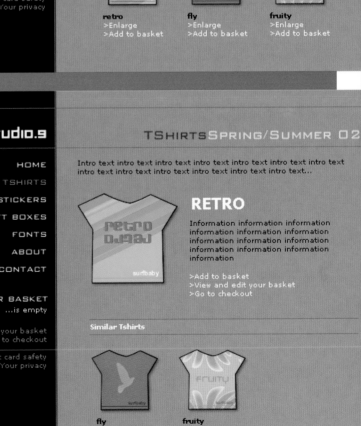

YOUR SOFTWARE'S OPTIMIZATION TOOLS

HOW YOUR OPTIMIZATION TOOLS WORK DEPENDS ON YOUR SOFTWARE, BUT THE FEATURES THEY OFFER ARE BROADLY THE SAME.

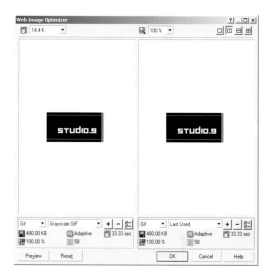

1 In Photoshop, choose *Save for Web* from the *File* menu. This opens your image in a new optimization dialog window, where you can choose your settings and preview the results. You can have a 2-up or 4-up view to compare the results of different settings, while figures at the bottom of each show the resulting file size and estimated download time. Try to get this as short as possible.

3 Corel PhotoPaint's Optimization tools are perhaps the most baffling. You need to start by choosing the File>Publish to the Web>*Web Image Optimizer* command, which opens a dialog similar to the other apps. All the important settings are in here, but the trouble is the number of buttons you need to click to achieve anything. If you get stuck, focus on the key settings and forget the rest.

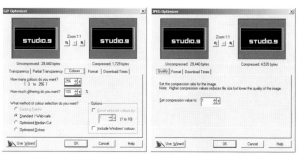

2 In Fireworks, you can do all this direct in the main workspace, by flicking through the *Preview* tabs at the top of the document window. To adjust the export settings, open the *Optimize* palette from your Window menu. Again, the view offers dynamic feedback about the file size and expected download time. Choose File>*Export* to complete the job.

4 Paint Shop Pro offers separate dialogs for GIF and JPEG optimization, which makes it hard to compare outcomes of the different formats side by side, but the settings are easy enough to deal with. You'll find them in the File>*Export* menu, and when you're using the *GIF Optimizer*, head straight for the *Colors* tab, because that's where all the action is.

HOW TO//JPEG OPTIMIZATION

OPTIMIZING JPEGS IS THE EASIER OF THE TWO FORMATS. IT'S IDEAL
FOR PHOTOS AND IMAGES WITH A CONTINUOUS TONE APPEARANCE.

1 Your core tool is the *Compression* or *Quality* slider: the more compression, the lower the quality of your final image. This works by reducing the detail in the file, and at extreme levels creates nasty "blocky" effects. These are called artifacts.

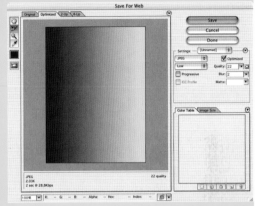

2 You can also reduce your JPEG file size with smoothing or blurring, which reduces the sharpness of your image. The result is more attractive, but has much less effect on file size, and will quickly ruin a crisp photo. Usually, it's best to go for a combination of the two techniques, balanced carefully according to the content of your image and the download speed you are aiming for.

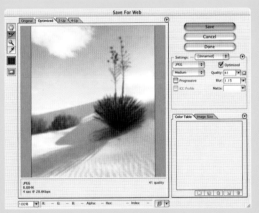

4 Another option is a simple gradient: you can't create these directly in HTML, so if you want a gradient or shadow effect on your webpage, you need to create it as a graphic. Here you can turn the blurring right up, and apply a lot of compression without great loss.

5 You may have a Progressive setting. A progressive JPEG appears gradually as it downloads, while a normal, nonprogressive JPEG needs to download completely before it can appear on the page.

3 You can apply massive compression to some types of graphic without losing much quality. A very soft, transparent photo for use in the background can be compressed to the max.

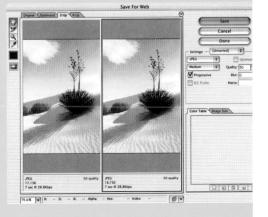

HOW TO//GIF OPTIMIZATION

1 Generally, GIF compression is best for graphics with a limited, discrete palette of colors, without continuous tones. Text, graphics, cartoon illustrations, and similar designs are all suitable...

2 The core feature of GIF optimization is reducing the number of colors stored in the file. The maximum number of colors you can have in a GIF is 256, which generally makes it a poor choice for photos, unless you choose to go extreme and make a feature of it, which can be attractive.

3 This image is more normally suited to GIF compression. The idea is you can reduce the file size in steps, by dividing the number of colors by two—choosing to use 128, 64, 32, 16, 8, 4, or just 2 colors in your graphic.

5 Dithering is a process which combines tiny dots of two or more colors to create the illusion of another color, like mixing paint. You can use this technique in GIF optimization, but be aware that it often dramatically increases your file size.

6 You can also use transparency in GIF files—say if your graphic is to go on a textured background. But you can only have total transparency or none at all there is no semi-transparency in the GIF format, which means your software needs to work out what color any semi-transparent pixels in your design (e.g. at the edges of text) should have. Use the *Matte* setting to help your software work this out.

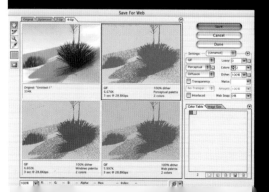

4 Your software may offer different palette options, like *Adaptive, Selective,* and *Perceptual.* These control how the app chooses which colors to keep and which to drop. Choose the one with the result you like best.

HOW TO//ALIASING AND ANTIALIASING

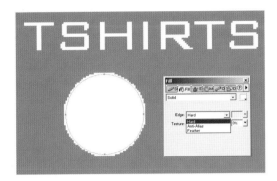

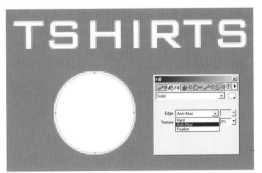

1 There is a problem associated with GIF transparency, to do with aliasing and antialiasing. Aliasing is when you draw a curve or type a character onscreen and it appears to have a jagged edge. This is because your display is made up of square pixels, and although these are very small, they are not small enough to create a good illusion of a curve. Look closely at text in your wordprocessor or an icon on your desktop, and you'll see.

2 Antialiasing is a process that makes curves display more satisfactorily. The edges are slightly blurred to give a better illusion. This is achieved by giving pixels around the edges a color that falls somewhere between the color of the curve and its background. Most software does this automatically.

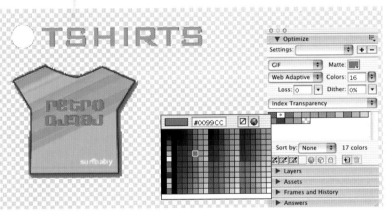

3 If the background is transparent, this usually means taking the color of the curve and making it semitransparent. But because the GIF format doesn't support semi-transparency, use the *Matte* setting to indicate an assumed background color, so it can calculate what color these pixels should be.

4 This works well until you put your transparent, anti-aliased GIF on a background color that is very different from the *Matte* you specified. Here you can see that edge pixels are completely the wrong color. The solution is either to always put them on the same background color, or, if you can't be sure of this—as in the case of desktop icons—turn anti-aliasing off in your software.

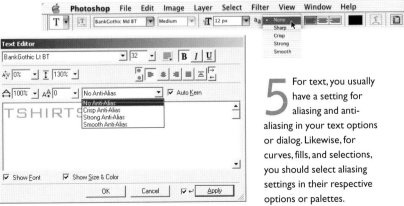

5 For text, you usually have a setting for aliasing and anti-aliasing in your text options or dialog. Likewise, for curves, fills, and selections, you should select aliasing settings in their respective options or palettes.

ADDING GRAPHICS TO A WEBPAGE

VISUALLY, HTML IS PRETTY LIMITED: IT'S GOOD FOR INFORMATION AND LAYOUT, BUT NOT FOR DESIGN. IT'S GRAPHICS THAT REALLY GIVE A WEBPAGE ITS "LOOK", OR UNIQUE IDENTITY AND APPEARANCE. SO YOU'LL PROBABLY FIND YOU WANT SEVERAL GRAPHICS IN EACH OF YOUR WEBPAGES—ALTHOUGH REMEMBER TO REUSE FILES WHEREVER POSSIBLE.

You want these to look as good as they can, and to sit seamlessly within the design. The idea is for your general user not to be able to tell the difference between a graphic and nongraphic part of your page, because they blend together naturally.

This can be a little hard to achieve at first, but you will get better at it with practice. A good trick is to take a screengrab of your webpage without graphics (*Print Screen* on a PC, or *Shift+Apple+3* on a Mac) and paste this into your graphics app. Then, design your webpage graphics over this, on a new layer, and when you're finished, copy and paste the separate bits into their own document, ready to be optimized and saved. Always keep a copy of the original, editable file, though, because it's not a good idea to do more work later on the compressed version—repeated compression does terrible things to an image.

When you've exported all your graphics, you need to put them in your website folder. It's a good idea to keep them within their own subfolder called "images." Then you're ready to use your Web authoring tools to insert them into your webpages…

HOME

PHOTOGRAPHY

WEBSITES

CV

CONTACT

Andy Butterby Portfolio

1 Here are the standard template graphics, and some sample content images, for our fictional portfolio site. The template graphics are very simple: this means they will load fast, and we can place more emphasis on the photos.

STEP BY STEP

2 By contrast, the Mango site has a stronger design emphasis on the furniture, and we've gone to town on these. We've also prepared a couple of sample album covers, just to make designing the page template easier. Once the template is ready, you can prepare all your content images and start creating individual webpages.

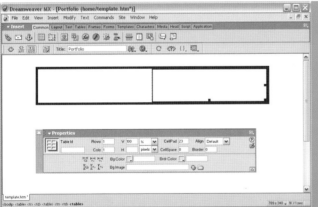

3 We create the main template for the portfolio site using a centered, 1x1 table with a black background and 6 pixels of cell padding to create the border. Inside this is another, two-column table with a white background. The rightmost column contains another 1x1 table with 20 pixels padding, to hold the content.

4 Adding an image to your webpage is easy: just click the *Image* icon in your toolbox (insert bar) or main toolbar, and browse to the file in your website folder using the dialog that appears. HTML offers a number of settings for your images, the most important being *Width, Height, Border,* and *Align.*

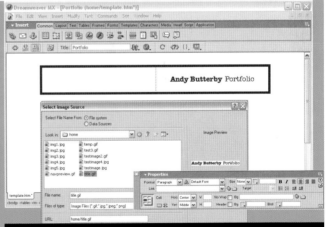

5 The *Width* and *Height* settings speak for themselves: these give the width and height at which you want the image to appear. You should almost always set these to the actual dimensions of the graphic itself, because resizing an image via HTML, or "in browser," gets bad results—as you can see. If your image is the wrong size, check what size you want it to be, then go back and edit the original image file in your graphics software.

ADDING GRAPHICS 2

6 The border setting controls the size of border you want to give your image—most appropriate for photos and illustrations. This will appear in the font color you give to the text around the image, or the link color if you give your image a link. Be aware that this adds to the width of your image, and you may feel more in control if you include the border in the file itself instead, using your graphics app.

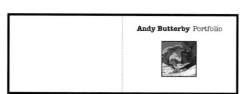

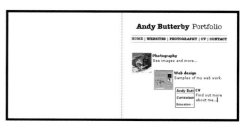

7 The *Align* setting controls where you want the image to appear. Often you will just leave this at default setting, but if you want the graphic to appear within the flow of text, you can set alignment to either left or right. The text then wraps around.

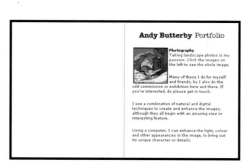

9 None of these settings are really useful if you want a several rows of images with text beside them—for a list of links, for example. Even with the *Align* property set to left, you'll get a messy result, as you can see.

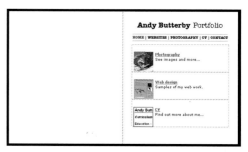

8 Two other useful settings are *vspace* and *hspace*. *Vspace* adds a certain number of pixels spacing above and below an image, while *hspace* adds spacing to the left and right. Use these to space the links properly. However, you can't use this to control the space just at the top, or just to the left, for example.

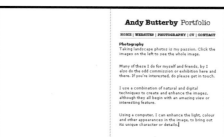

10 The best way to exactly control the positioning of images and text in a tight layout is to put them in their own table cells. The same tables rules apply for images as for text—see the previous chapter if you get stuck.

11 To take our portfolio site's design template near to completion, all we need to do is add a large image to fit the left-hand column. But what about the Mango World Music site?

12 First off, we need to export all the graphics, including a couple of sample album covers for good measure. Create a new document with a black background, and set all the page margins to 0. Then hit return once or twice, and add a 760px-wide table with 2 columns, the left column being about 110 pixels wide.

13 The left column holds the logo, while the right column is for the content. Adjusting sizes slightly, you should be able to paste in the starter template we made in the last chapter.

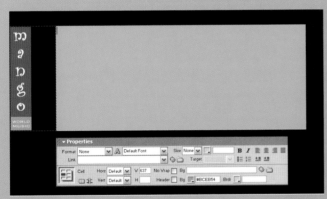

14 Clear out the links at the top and replace them with your graphical navigation; then split the title row into two columns and add a graphical title into each.

15 Dotted lines created using a *Texture* or *Pattern* overlay feature here. You only need to export this once, as a very thin graphic, then reuse the file with *vspace* to give it room on the page.

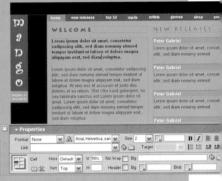

16 Finally, you can juggle some links down the right-hand side and include images if you like. We'll take a closer look at preparing images over the next few pages, and later on how to create textures and lines .

PHOTOS AND ILLUSTRATIONS

PHOTOS ARE A QUICK AND POWERFUL MEANS TO ENHANCE YOUR
WEBPAGES. THEY CAN GIVE YOUR VIEWER THE GIST OF A STORY—
MAYBE EVEN THE WHOLE STORY—AT A GLANCE.

Photos are different from simpler graphics in that they are about something, rather than simply there to look pretty or enhance the character of your design (although they should do this too). Illustrations, such as our sample T-shirt site, fall into a similar category; if your site is about software, you may go for screengrabs of the apps instead; or if it's about finance, then charts and diagrams would be good.

You can use photos and images like this in your webpages in several ways, although the most obvious is to support a story, article, or promotional text. Sometimes an image will suggest itself, as in the case of Mango World Music, where we can use a picture of an album cover or an artist. Other times, you might have to do a bit of thinking, and come up with a visual idea that enhances the text.

In different contexts, like our T-shirt and portfolio sites, it's the image that counts; the text is secondary. In this case, you want to put the picture at the top, make it big or use other design techniques to draw your viewer to it. In some cases, you may feel there is no need for any text: all that matters is the picture. But the important thing is to choose an attractive and relevant photo, and make it look as good as you can. Nothing can bring down a beautiful design like bad photos.

1 You prepare photos for the Web using your graphics app, in much the same way as you prepare other graphics files. It's important to kick off by establishing what size you want the image to be: getting this in an attractive proportion to your layout is an important part of making the most of the image. It's common for designers to divide a page up into even columns, with gutters, and use this as a basis for sizes.

HOW TO//PREPARE PHOTOS FOR THE WEB

2 If your design demands a fixed width and height, you need to crop your photo to exactly the right proportions. The easiest way to do this is use your Marquee tool (the dotted rectangle), and in the *Options* toolbar or palette, set it to *Fixed Ratio*. For the width and height, add the dimension of your final image. Then choose your software's *Crop* menu command, which is often found in the *Edit* menu.

3 Next, you need to resize the image, which will be another menu option in your software—usually in the *Edit, Image,* or *Modify* menus. It's important when you're resizing an image not to squash or stretch its width or height—this usually looks terrible. If you keep the *Constrain Proportions* option selected, your software will automatically ensure height and width are calculated correctly.

4 Try to avoid enlarging an image by more than 25%, if at all. Your software just doesn't have enough information in the pixels to work out what the extra detail should be, even though it's easy enough for you and I with our more sophisticated brains to visualize it. The result will just be blurry, as you can see.

5 Finally, save a copy of the image, then save a Web-optimized version, using your usual compression tools. You'll generally get a better result compressing photos in JPEG format.

ENHANCING IMAGES

1 There's a lot more you can do with your photos than just crop, resize, and compress them. By digitally enhancing photos, you can drastically improve their appearance, and even completely change them for some extreme effects. It's a good idea to do most processing after you crop, but before you resize the image.

2 Adding contrast is the quickest way to improve your photos, and even slight changes can have an immense effect. You'll often find this setting in the *Image, Filter,* or *Xtras* menu of your software, alongside other commands for changing the tone and color balance of your photo. If there's an *Auto Contrast* tool, try this for size, or go it alone. As a rule of thumb, the smaller your final image will be, the more contrast you want, but don't overdo it.

3 *Levels*, or *Auto Levels*, and *Hue/Saturation* are other useful controls, which deal with the balance of colour as well as light in your images. These can be hard to master, so use the *Auto* features if you have them, or experiment with settings on different images to get the hang of how they work. Go gently—it's easier to ruin an image than improve it.

4 One effect you should consider using after you've resized your image is sharpening. You should find this feature in your *Filter, Effects,* or *Image Enhancing* menu, and there will be several options. Most home photos could do with a degree of sharpening, and if you resize any image downward a lot, it will usually benefit. Experiment and see what works best for each picture. Don't overuse it.

1

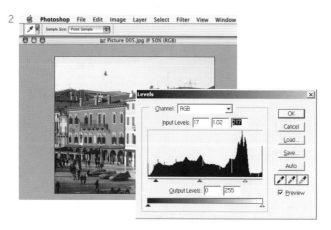

2

4

HOW TO//CREATE A THUMBNAILS PAGE

1 Thumbnails are important in Web design, and not just in galleries. These small images are particularly good with links to larger images or to other webpages. They do for links what photos do for stories—helping your viewer to understand more by reading less.

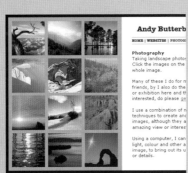

2 Try to give all your thumbnails the same dimensions. At the very least, make them the same width for a vertical layout and same height for a horizontal layout. You can also aim for other elements of continuity: showing objects at the same scale, or using the same balance of light.

3 Thumbnails can be as small as you want—even 20x20 pixels can work. You don't have to show the whole of the bigger picture in your thumb: try zooming in on a particular part of it, like a teaser.

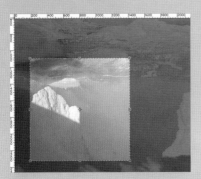

4 Once you've exported your thumbnails, the quickest way to create an attractive layout is using a single table with cell padding or spacing to control the gutters between the images. For the portfolio site, we've used a 3x4 table with cell spacing set to 10.

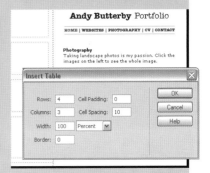

5 Then just add in the images and link them up…

6 In the case of Mango, the margins created around the outer limits of the table by cell padding and spacing mess up the layout, so instead use an empty, 10-pixel wide column to create space between thumbnail and the text, and an empty row to space the individual entries.

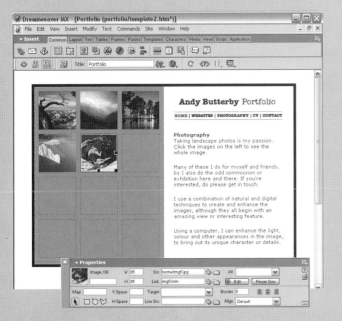

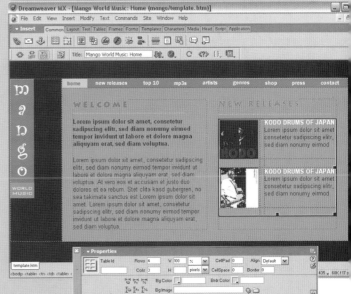

FRAMING AND EFFECTS

Modern graphics software offers an ever-increasing range of tools for enhancing and altering your images in different ways. Many of these are one-click, easy effects, which is appealing; but they can also be a little cheesy. Experiment with such effects as much as you can, but do exercise your better judgement about whether one result or another really does improve the overall design of your webpage, and whether it works in the context of your subject matter and audience.

Gimmicky, just-for-the-sake-of-it effects will do your site no favors. Simple is often best, and it's the details that make the difference. So try to choose just one or two combinations of effects for your whole site, and stick with them.

Often, as with most design, you'll decide that simple *is* best, and here we take a look at three easy but effective ways to alter your images…

HOW TO//TINTING

2 There are several techniques, with different results. One is to create a background layer filled with the tint colour you want, then put your image on a layer above it, and set its blending mode to *Luminosity*. This takes the light and darkness of the image, and applies it to the colour on the layer below.

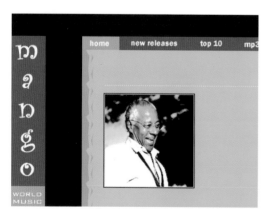

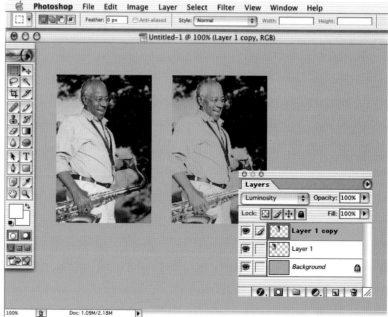

1 One way to do something a bit different with your images is tinting. You need to choose the tint carefully—the color should be one that comes from your website's existing scheme, and not look too garish. This can be particularly effective if your tint is the same as the background color.

HOW TO//TINTING

NORMAL   SCREEN   OVERLAY   HARD LIGHT   COLOR BURN

3 Another technique involves using the *Saturation* setting in your *Hue/Saturation* dialog to make the image black and white, then placing it over a colored layer as before, and experimenting with the other blending modes.

4 Here we combine this with a heading graphic to enhance the appearance of an artist's biog on the Mango site. This is an attractive and creative way to bring together text and images, but you need to take care when superimposing text to make sure it's still legible. You can slightly darken or lighten the image behind the words if you need to.

6 Because of the reduced color palette in the photo, this image exports much better as a GIF file—and we can reduce the colors here even more without losing much quality.

5 To create this effect in the webpage, we only need to export these two images. The rest we'll do using HTML, and the dotted line is a graphic we already have from the home page.

FRAMING

1 Framing or bordering an image is a quick means to enhance, or just bring attention to it. Many designers add keylines (one-pixel black borders) to images as a matter of course—especially in magazines and newspapers. You can do the same.

2 But don't feel restricted to one pixel, or to black. Try 2 pixels in white, for a stronger border on a mid- to dark-toned background. Or use another color from your site color scheme. Fashion magazines and photographers often go for big, chunky borders—a technique we've used to outline the entire design for the portfolio site.

5 Try combining framing with other effects—but don't go overboard. Posterizing is a fun, Pop Art-style process that reduces the number of colors in an image, like GIF compression. This works especially well with strong colors and tinting, and you can combine it with a fat, tinted border colour to great effect.

MANGO

3 You can create a soft edge, or vignette, by using the *Feather* setting of your *Marquee* tool. Set this to about five, then select the area of your image you want to keep, invert the selection (*Control+Shift+I* in many applications), and hit *Delete*. Finally, add a background color in a layer beneath the image.

4 You can also go for more inventive border effects, either your own creation or using dedicated software for the job. Two good options are Extensis PhotoFrame (www.extensis.com) and Photo/Graphic Edges (www.autofx.com), which both work as plugins.

CREATING A SCRATCHY FRAME

THE FINAL EFFECT WE WANT TO CREATE, FOR SPECIAL PAGES ON THE MANGO WORLD MUSIC SITE, BRINGS TOGETHER ALL THESE TECHNIQUES, WITH A SPECIAL SCRATCHY BORDER EFFECT. WE'RE DOING IT IN PHOTOSHOP, BUT YOU SHOULD BE ABLE TO GET SIMILAR RESULTS IN OTHER GRAPHICS SOFTWARE.

1 Paste your image into a large canvas space, then select a medium, scruffy brush, and scribble onto a new layer an area about the size of the image.

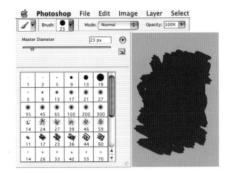

2 Control+click on the layer in your Layers palette to select its outline, then hide this layer and select the one with your image on instead. Click the Mask icon at the bottom of your Layers palette— it's the little dotted circle.

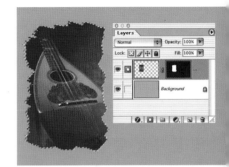

3 Control+click on the black-and-white layer Mask icon to bring back the selection, then use the Fill/Adjustment layer icon at the bottom of your Layers palette to create a new solid white layer. Drag this below your image layer, and set the latter's blending mode to Luminosity.

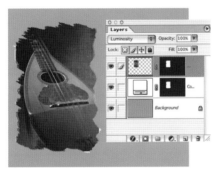

4 Use Image> Adjust>Posterize to posterize the image layer with just two levels, then link this to the white layer and merge them together.

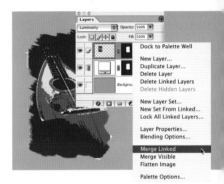

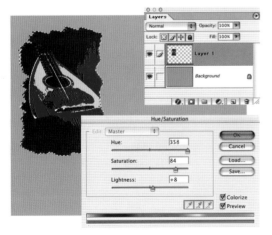

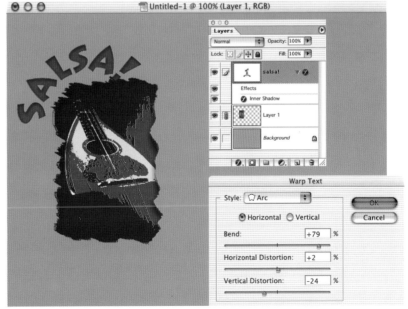

5 Use Image>Adjust> Hue/Saturation with the Colorize setting on to color up the result, then add an inner shadow to it when you're done.

6 To finish off, add some text and apply a Warp to it…

BUTTONS ETC.

Buttons are one of the features that makes the Web go around: click here to go over there. Without them, it'd be a very different place, and much less popular. But what makes a button a button? Or more to the point, what makes a button look like something you can click on? If your buttons don't stand out, then your viewers won't realize they can click on them, and you'll get a lot less traffic or business.

There are traditional and well established techniques for making graphics look clickable. A bullet point effect, a slight 3D bevel, a drop shadow, and grip-like shading are four of the most popular; and with modern software all are quick and easy to do. Don't be afraid of using these just because everybody else does: they are part of the established language of Web design, one which everybody immediately understands. But on the other hand, don't be afraid of experimenting. You can take these basic concepts, evolve them, and mix and match to create new appearances. Or try something altogether different.

What's important is this: as with fonts, as with colors, as with everything in your website design, choose a style for buttons that fits in with your overall look, makes sense in the context of your subject matter, and will appeal to your audience. Choose just one or two styles for buttons, and then stick with them.

Typically, you'll need to use buttons or button-like effects in several different ways. First, in your navigation. Second, for take-action links at the end of a piece of information—"Cast your vote" or "Submit form" for instance. And third, you may need a button-like appearance for short lists of links to other pages.

Tell me more

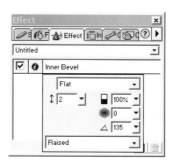

1 The basic button: a simple 3D beveled effect. You should find one-click effects like this in one of your application's menus or palettes, along with a variety of different settings. In Photoshop, you'll find it under the *Effects* icon at the bottom of your *Layers* palette; in Fireworks, you have a dedicated effects palette. For a traditional, Windows interface-style button, go for a very tight, sharp bevel—just one or two pixels—and a high opacity or low transparency settings.

Tell me more

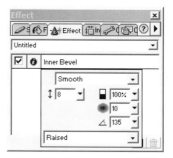

2 For a softer effect, go for a smooth bevel and increase its depth and spread. You could now add an inverted bevel to the text on the button, to make it appear inset or engraved…

3 Another classic button effect: the drop shadow. Again, you should have a one-click command for this, so you don't have to create the shadow by hand. You can go from a very tight, sharp shadow to a soft distant one—the differences in appearance are immense. Choose a style of shadow and stick to it throughout your site.

4 Grip shading may take a little more effort, but has a powerful appearance, and is less ubiquitous. There are several approaches: a line of simple text colons is a quick route to achieve the effect. Try creating the text in a darker color than the background, then duplicate this and nudge it one pixel up and across. Give the copy a lighter color, and you get a simple, clean 3D grip effect.

5 For the ItaliaGusto site, we can use angled lines at the corners of heading tabs to emphasize their appearance.

COMMUNITY

6 Other simple techniques for making buttons look "buttonlike" include outlining some text, adding different-style bullets, and using arrows or pointers to suggest motion.

CONTACT US

● CONTACT US

CONTACT US >>

ICON GRAPHICS

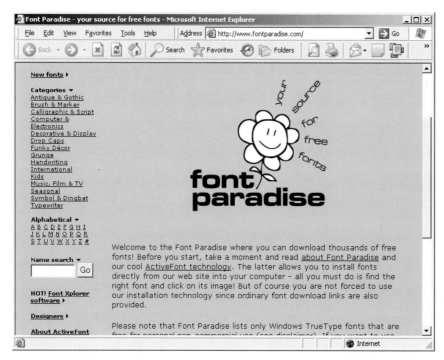

1 Adding small graphical drawings to your webpages is a sure-fire way to impress. But don't worry: you don't need to start learning how to draw with a computer. There are stacks of websites where you can download free icons, or dingbat fonts which you can quickly adapt. Try sites like *www.arttoday.com* and *www.fontparadise.com* for starters.

Icons are an impressive and attractive way to enhance buttons, links, and general graphics. An icon is a small, graphical picture or symbol representing what the link is about, or what will happen when you click on it. Using icons with buttons helps your viewers to understand quickly what they mean without having to read the text—especially where you are using well-established symbols, like a postal envelope, a shopping cart, or simply an arrow. As your website grows, you will have more and more information to present to your viewers; but the less they have to read, and the more you can get across visually, the better.

Don't worry if your drawing skills aren't up to scratch. There are many sites on the Internet offering free downloadable icons covering subjects both popular and unusual. You should always credit and link to your sources when you use free resources like this,

but if you prefer to have a little more control over the appearance of your graphics—and especially if your website design has a strong visual identity there is another option: dingbats.

A dingbat is a font, like any other font, but instead of letters it contains black-and-white line drawings, which you can use at any size. There are literally thousands of dingbats, from the universal Wingdings on PC, or Zapf Dingbats on the Mac, to the specialist, the amusing, and the simply bizarre. Whatever you need, there is probably a dingbat font for it, and you can download them from many ordinary font sites.

Because a dingbat behaves like any other font, it's easy to adapt and evolve its appearance with colors and effects to make it match the overall style of your site.

HOW TO//CREATE ICON GRAPHICS

2 These are especially great with buttons and icons, but you can use them with other page furniture and headings too. Here we've adapted a couple of dingbat characters from the Bon Appetit collection for an ItaliaGusto recipe page, along with a typeface called Dad's Recipe.

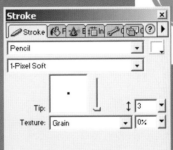

5 Because the spaces within the characters are transparent, apply a thick outline, or stroke, so you can easily distinguish the different shapes.

6 Finally, add the text, export the image, and add it to your webpage. It's simple.

3 Begin by typing each of the characters separately, on their own layer or in their own text box, using a color from the site scheme…

4 …then carefully arrange them with a triangular composition, giving each character a slightly different tone.

7 Here we've used a stronger, darker, and fatter outline for a different appearance.

NOW WE'VE LOOKED AT SOME OF THE INDIVIDUAL ELEMENTS THAT MAKE WEBSITES MORE ATTRACTIVE. YOU'RE PROBABLY THINKING THAT THERE MUST BE MORE TO DESIGN THAN CREATING EXCITING GRAPHICS AND PLAYING AROUND WITH FONTS. YOU'D BE RIGHT...

4

BUILDING YOUR WEBSITE

DESIGNING A TEMPLATE

Creating individual graphics and adding them to your webpages is all very well, but as your ideas get more sophisticated, you'll quickly realize that this isn't the easiest way to come up with a consistent, seamless design.

1 Start off with a blank canvas, as in chapter two, and brainstorm as many ideas as you can come up with. Don't delete anything, don't reject any idea at this stage, but try to find groups of colors, fonts, button styles, and so on that work together.

It's a hassle getting all the colors and sizes for your graphics just right, so that when you bring them into your webpages everything matches up as you intended. And you can never tell quite how it's going to look until you've created and added all the graphics, then viewed the whole thing in a couple of Web browsers, which is maybe a day or so's work. If you then decide you don't like what you've done, you've had it: it's back to square one.

Many designers prefer to work in a way that allows them to get a good idea of the overall appearance of a webpage before they even open their Web authoring software. First you design the whole page within your graphics software—whether it is Photoshop, Fireworks, or another package—then recreate this as closely as possible using HTML, cutting out and exporting the graphics as you go.

At first, this will take you longer; and you need to consider carefully as you work whether the ideas you are pursuing in your graphics app are really achievable in HTML. You need to keep it simple and focus on what's possible. As you get more practice, you will find that this is a quick and effective way of creating appealing designs that really work alongside the features, text, and content you plan to use. So how do you go about creating a site in this way?

DESIGNING A WHOLE PAGE

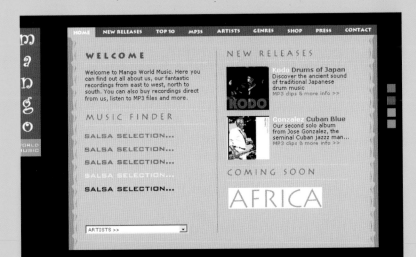

2 Now save a copy of your "sketch pad," and start to slim down the ideas to your favorites. Experiment with developing these in different ways. At some point, you will feel that one concept is stronger than the rest: copy your work for this into a new, 1,000x1,000-pixel document, adapt these ideas, and map out a layout for your webpages. The reason for working on a larger canvas is this helps you see how the page will look to viewers with larger screens.

3 Finally, settle on an exact color palette, a couple of fonts, and a couple of graphical styles for buttons. We've got the idea for Mango to use a different color for each section—you can see these down the side. Then polish up your layout to include the information you need on a page. Don't forget the size constraints of your webpage—particularly the width!

4 Developing the idea further, you can create a sample layout for a different type of page on the site—maybe the hub page for a particular section, or an end page, which contains a single article or product.

FROM DESIGN TO WEBPAGE

HAVING CREATED YOUR DESIGN IN A GRAPHICS APP, YOU NEED TO TURN THIS INTO A CONVENTIONAL, FAST-LOADING WEBPAGE. THERE ARE TWO TECHNIQUES FOR THIS, AND YOU WILL PROBABLY END UP USING A COMBINATION OF THE TWO. THE FIRST IS TO CREATE A TEMPLATE IN YOUR WEB AUTHORING APP FOLLOWING YOUR GRAPHICS DOCUMENT AS CLOSELY AS POSSIBLE. THE OTHER IS CALLED SLICING.

1 Using the first technique, begin by dragging guides in your graphics app to mark out how you propose to break up your design. These show the key table and cell boundaries, as well as which bits you expect to create as image files or in HTML.

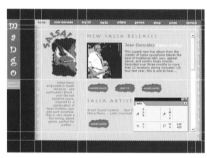

2 With this as a basis, you can begin to create the layout tables within your Web authoring app. Use your software's *Ruler* or *Marquee* and the *Info* palette to take measurements from your graphic that translate into table and columns widths in HTML.

3 To recreate the Mango design in HTML, we begin with a 3x1 table, and give the right-most column the appropriate background color.

4 Then we copy and paste the logo into a new document, and export it into the website folder. This goes in the left column of the layout, while we add another table in the right-hand column to reflect the position of the navigation bar, the main content, and the margins left, right, above, and below it.

5 We add a third table to divide the main content area into two columns, with a gutter between.

6 Finally, add in the graphics and main content, using an extra table to align the album cover properly to the left of the text; and then you can place the navigation and other page furniture. The borders and scrollbar need special techniques, which we'll look at later…

HOW TO//SLICING

1 An alternative to creating tables for your layout by hand is a technique called slicing, and most good graphics apps should have the tools for you to do it. Photoshop users may need to open the document in ImageReady, where there is a range of slicing tools and a palette. Photoshop 7, though, includes a slice tool.

2 Fireworks also has Slice tools, which you use in combination with the *Object* palette, and the Web layer in your *Layers* palette.

3 The idea is that you use the *Slice* tool to draw a rectangle marking out the edges of an individual graphics file, which will usually correspond to the edges of table cells.

4 The software then automatically calculates the tables you need to create the layout, and creates the HTML file for you when you export the graphics.

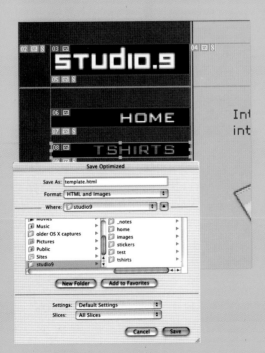

5 Ordinarily, everything is exported as sliced-up graphics. But for areas of your design that don't contain graphics—they might be empty, or contain only text—you can minimize file sizes by turning a slice into a *Text Slice*, and set the background color for its table cell.

6 You can add a link to ordinary slices, which will be exported as part of the HTML.

7 One problem with slicing is that it isn't suitable for layouts that need to be malleable or stretchy, because of the style of HTML that is created. We don't yet know the length of text in the main content area on different pages, so a slicing technique won't work well for this. We can only really use it for the navigation bar down the left.

ADVANCED TABLE TECHNIQUES

As your skills develop, you will want to achieve more and more sophisticated layouts for your webpages, using columns, lines, boxes, and different edge effects. But as we saw on the previous page, you really need to create these by hand in your Web authoring app: you can't rely on slicing to deal with anything that needs to be flexible. Nevertheless, just about anything is possible, if you're prepared to put the time into it; and one or two unusual or impressive layout effects can do a lot for a simple page design. Here are some useful techniques:

VERTICALLY CENTERING A PAGE

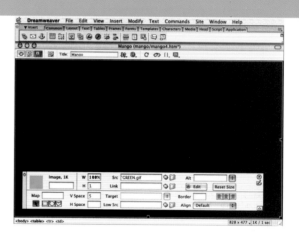

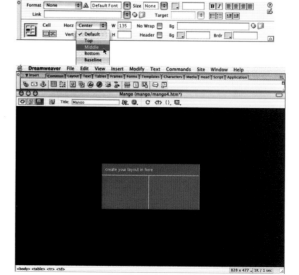

2 Start by adding a 1x1 table to your webpage, and set both its height and width to 100%.

3 Select the table cell, and set *Vertical Align* to *Middle*. You can also set the *Horizontal Align* to *Center* if you like, although for Mango we've gone for left alignment.

1 You may be wondering how we do this for the Mango site. It's actually really quick to achieve, and much better than just putting a couple of returns at the top of your page to "sort of" create the layout.

4 Then paste your main page layout in here. The position of the page now moves depending on the height of your browser window.

HORIZONTAL AND VERTICAL LINES

1 It's effective in a webpage to have lines that divide content horizontally and vertically between columns. The *Horizontal Rule* works fairly well, but you can't reliably control its appearance.

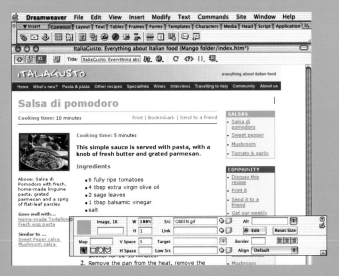

2 There are three other techniques for horizontal lines. One is to create a 1x1 pixel graphic in the color you want. Then just add this to your webpage, stretching it width-wise to the size you want.

3 Another is to create an empty table row between the two content sections, and change its background color. You will normally find, however, that the row is too high. This is because most Web authoring software automatically puts a blank space character (written   in HTML) in empty cells, to make sure they display correctly in older browsers.

4 The solution is to replace this space character with a single, transparent 1x1-pixel GIF image. Job done. Web designers' use these little images a lot for different techniques; they are often called spacers or shims. You only need one file for your whole site.

ADVANCED TABLE TECHNIQUES 2

HORIZONTAL AND VERTICAL LINES//2

5 If you want a line with a special appearance, like a dotted line, you'll need a different technique. This relies on the repeating behavior of background images in table cells. First we create a dotted line in the graphics app, but crop it to the size of just one of its dots and one space. Then we export this. The file size is tiny!

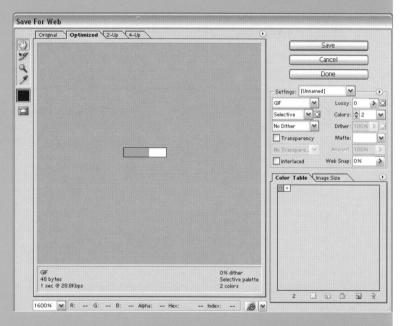

7 Instead, you set the mini dotted line graphic as its background image. Background images automatically repeat across and down to fill the space—this is called tiling. It's very useful for creating textured or patterned effects that load quickly, because the graphic only has to be downloaded once.

8 Vertical lines work in exactly the same way—you just use a column instead of a row to create it.

6 Next we create a table row with a 1-pixel spacer where the line is to go, but leave its background color alone.

EDGE EFFECTS

1 We use exactly the same technique to create the patterned borders for the Mango site, and the edge shading for ItaliaGusto. For the first, you just need to make sure your pattern tile matches seamlessly when it repeats…

2 …and that you get the width of the column right.

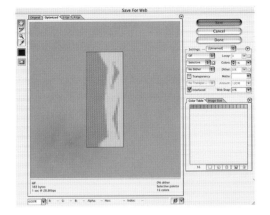

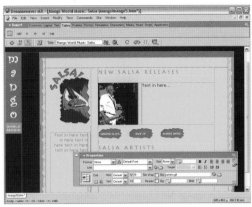

3 For the shading in ItaliaGusto, create small vertical and horizontal shading tiles, and a nontiling graphic for the bottom-right corner.

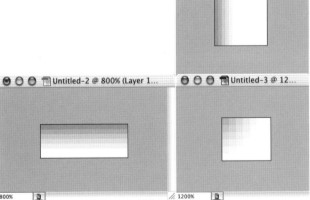

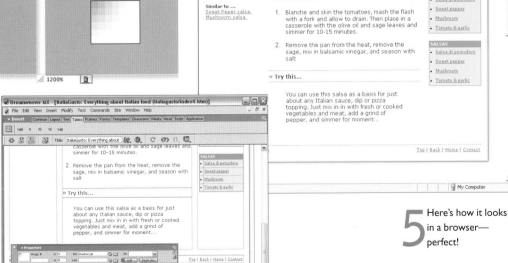

4 Set up the shading tiles as a background graphic in a new row at the bottom of the design, and in a new column to the far right. Then add in the small corner graphic, where the shading has a slightly different character.

5 Here's how it looks in a browser—perfect!

NAVIGATION

THE NAVIGATION IS AT THE HUB OF YOUR SITE. LIKE A MINI HOME PAGE THAT SHOULD APPEAR ON EVERY PAGE OF YOUR SITE, IT GIVES YOUR VIEWERS BOTH A QUICK OVERVIEW OF WHAT YOUR WEBSITE HAS TO OFFER, AND ONE-CLICK ACCESS TO ALL THE MAIN SECTIONS. THIS SAVES VISITORS USING THEIR BROWSER'S BACK BUTTON.

A well-designed navigation is one that's clear, fast, and easy to use. Its visuals and text should give a good indication of where the link is going, and what you can find there. "Cryptic" is out; "to the point" is in! What you decide to put on it depends on how you choose to organize your website, and what you think its most important elements are. But it should closely follow the site plans you mapped out in chapter one.

WHERE SHOULD YOU PUT YOUR NAVIGATION?

1 At the top, down the left, or both together, such as *www.mtv.com* (pictured), are the most popular options, simply because that gives you plenty of page space left over for presenting the main content. You don't have to follow traditions like this—but think carefully if you wander off the beaten track, because there are good reasons for it being so well trodden.

2 It can be effective to put your navigation at the bottom of the page, like a car dashboard. The galleries at *www.lucasarts.com* use this style. But don't forget, this will restrict other aspects of your design, because you don't want the main page content pushing your navigation off the bottom of viewers' screens. Many people will read just the first few lines of a webpage, then realize it's not quite what they're looking for. If you haven't got a nearby link to take them somewhere else on your site, they'll be off.

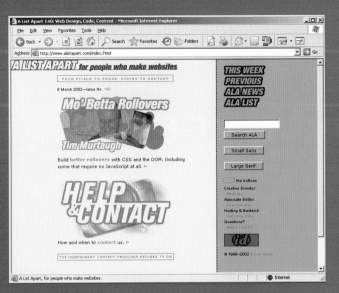

3 Likewise, placing your navigation down the right-hand side of the page can make for a refreshing change, like here at *www.alistapart.com*. But you need to put some thought into the design, or the nav may get chopped off for anyone viewing your site on a smaller screen

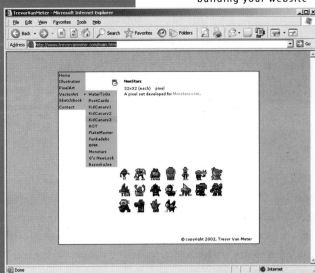

5 Another solution if you have a lot of links is to go for a two-tier navigation system, or to combine your content into fewer sections and use submenus to guide people around,. See *www.trevorvanmeter.com*.

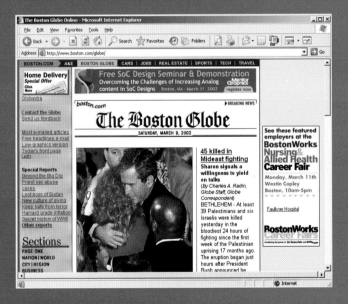

4 Across-the-top navigation has a strong appeal for designers, because it leaves a space free for the main content of your pages. But if you want to get a lot of links in your navigation, you're pretty well restricted to a vertical navbar. Take *www.bostonglobe.com*, for example: there isn't enough room width-wise for more than about 10 items, depending on your font and styling.

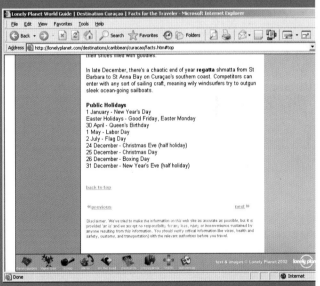

6 It's a good idea to include some navigation tools at the bottom of longer webpages too: give your visitors something to click on when they've finished reading an article or looking at pictures, like at *www.lonelyplanet.com*.

CREATING
ROLLOVERS

ROLLOVERS ARE A POPULAR FEATURE ON NAVIGATION BARS AND ELSEWHERE ON A
WEBSITE. A ROLLOVER IS THE NAME OF THE EFFECT WHERE A BUTTON CHANGES AS YOU
MOVE YOUR POINTER OVER IT, THEN CHANGES BACK WHEN YOU MOVE THE POINTER AWAY.
OR, AS WEB DESIGNERS SAY, ONMOUSEOVER AND ONMOUSEOUT. SOMETIMES THE IMAGE
CHANGES WHEN YOU CLICK (ONCLICK) OR JUST WHEN YOU DEPRESS THE MOUSE BUTTON
(ONMOUSEDOWN)...

Rollovers are quick and easy to set up using either your graphics or your Web authoring software. You can create a simple mouseover/mouseout rollover using two separate graphics files. One shows the normal button, the other shows the button as it appears when you mouseover. The HTML in the webpage contains a snippet of code that effectively says, "When the user puts their pointer over this graphic, swap it for that other graphic instead—and then swap it back after." The language used for this is JavaScript, which we'll

look at later on. But in the meantime, your software should be able to create the effect for you.

Some effects you can use for your rollovers are obvious: change the color of the graphic or increase its drop shadow so it appears to lift off the page. Others are more inventive: how about having a blurred graphic come into focus, or some additional information about the link appear beside it? Experiment and see what you can come up with. But as with everything in design, settle on a style and use this for all buttons of the same type on your site.

USING IMAGEREADY

There is more than one way to create a rollover, but the easiest is with Adobe's ImageReady, which comes bundled with Photoshop. You simply design your ordinary, off-state button in the usual way, or copy and paste it from your page design into a new document…

HOW TO//USE IMAGEREADY

1 Then using new layers, or duplicating and editing existing ones, create a design for how you want the mouseover state to look. You can hide layers used for the off-state design—just click the "Eye" icon next to them in your *Layers* palette—but don't delete or amend them in any way.

3 Click the *Normal*, (off-state) thumbnail to select it, then hide the layers you used for your over-state design, and show the ones for your off-state. The two thumbnail images in your rollover palette (below) should now look different, reflecting your button states.

2 Now open your Rollover palette from the Window menu, and click the little New State icon at the bottom, which looks like a folded page. You'll see a new thumbnail appear in the palette, representing your mouseover button.

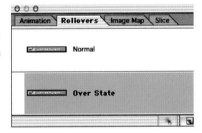

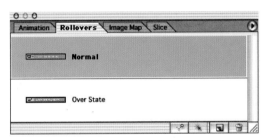

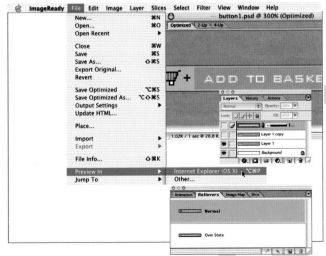

4 Before you export the rollover, you can see how it looks using the *Play* button at the bottom of your *Rollover* palette, or with the File>*Preview In* menu, which should have a list of installed browsers you can choose from.

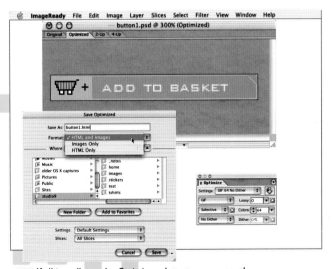

5 If all is well, use the *Optimize* palette to compress the graphics in the usual way, then choose File>*Save Optimized*. In the *Save* dialog, make sure the *Save As Type* option is set to *HTML and Images*. ImageReady will automatically create the rollover code for you.

ROLLOVERS & SLICES

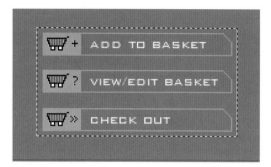

1 You can easily combine the *Rollover* tools with slicing to quickly create several buttons at once, and this is ideal for navigation bars, or our mini-basket navigation on this T-shirts page. Start by drawing up your slices as before...

2 Again, create the designs for your over-states on new layers. Use different layers for this for each button, like in the picture. When you're done, hide all the over-state layers.

3 Using your *Slice Select* tool, select your button slices one by one, then set up their rollovers using the palette, just as before. Use the *Play* option to check you've got it right...

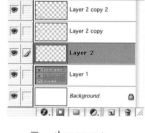

4 ...then export everything and check it in your browser.

ROLLOVER SPEED

There's one important issue with rollovers: download speed. Because each button now needs two or more graphics files, they're going to take about twice as long to download. If you've got a lot of buttons, this is going to have a serious impact on your overall page-loading speed. There is nothing you can do about this directly, except keep a close eye on the file size of your buttons, and try not to go over the top. Think simple, compact and effective.

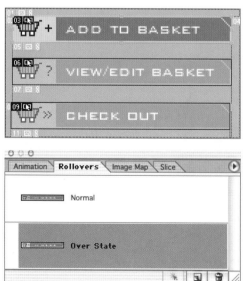

ROLLOVERS IN FIREWORKS

1 Rollovers in Fireworks work in a similar way, but here you have a dedicated button-creating window. Start by selecting an individual button.

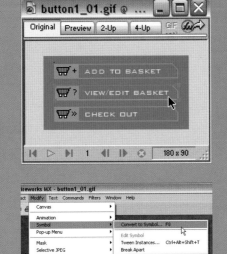

2 Then choose the Insert>*Convert to Symbol* command. In *Options*, set the *Type* to *Button*. A slice is automatically created for the button.

3 To create the different states, you need to edit the symbol. To do this, double-click on the slice, and it will open in a new window. You can now use the tabs across the top to copy, paste, and amend your graphics for the different buttons states. Then export your buttons as normal.

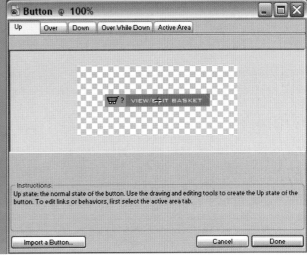

ROLLOVERS IN DREAMWEAVER

1 Another way to create rollovers is directly in your Web authoring software. These mostly work in the same way, but we'll take Dreamweaver as our example. Click the *Insert Rollover Image* tool in your toolbox…

2 In the dialog that appears, browse to the image files for your button states.

3 Do this for each button, and that's all there is to it!

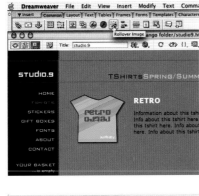

EVERYTHING ABOUT LINKS

WE'RE GETTING CLOSE TO A COMPLETE DESIGN TEMPLATE NOW. WE'VE GOT LAYOUT, GRAPHICS, ILLUSTRATIONS, AND INTERACTIVE BUTTONS. WE'RE NEARLY READY TO ADAPT AND APPLY THESE TO REAL-LIFE PAGES IN A WEBSITE. WHAT WE DON'T HAVE YET, HOWEVER, ARE LINKS. THESE ARE WHAT GIVES THE WEB ITS UNIQUE QUALITY, BECAUSE THAT'S HOW PEOPLE GET FROM A TO B TO C.

It's tempting to create all your pages before you set up your navigation links, simply because you want to know what their Web addresses are. In practice, though, it's wise to do the links first, otherwise you'll have to keep changing all the pages you've created, and that's a hassle. So we'll take a look at this here.

It's absolutely paramount that you get your links right: Web browsers aren't forgiving of a typo here or accidental space character there. This is all it takes to give your viewer a nasty "404—Page not found" error, and they will never get to see what you've put so much work into.

Like a space character between words, "/" denotes the end of one file or folder name, and the beginning of another. A name without an ending, like "*recipes*," denotes the name of a folder, while "*index.htm*" denotes the name of a file. You simply follow the path written in the address. The address of an image file in your navigation might be: "*/images/navigation/homebutton.gif.*"

ABSOLUTE LINKS

A good way to organize the files in your site is to have one folder for each of the sections, plus one for images and other media. You want to put all the HTML files, or webpages, for a particular section in its own folder, and call the main hub page for that section "index.htm." The address within your site, or local address, of a main recipes page could be "*/recipes/index.htm.*" The external address will be "*www.yoursite.com/recipes/index.htm.*" For the main page of a subsection about salsas, it could be: "*/recipes/salsas/index.htm.*"

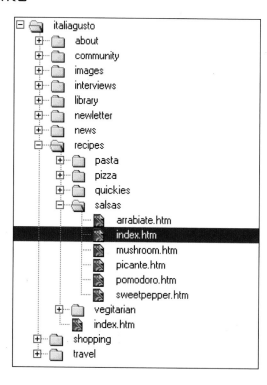

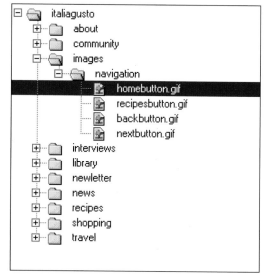

RELATIVE LINKS

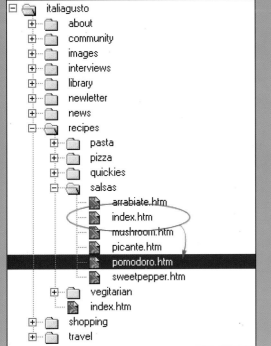

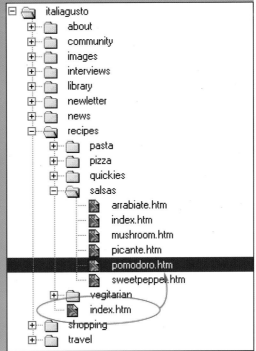

From the recipes index page, you could use "*salsas/pomodoro.htm,*" which looks for the subfolder called "*salsas,*" then the file called "*pomodoro.htm*" within this.

In relative links, "../" means go up one level to the folder that holds the current one. So the relative link from the Salsa Pomodoro page back to the main recipes index page is *../index.htm*.

Those are called "absolute addresses": they always point to the same place. Starting a local address with / means "follow that path from the top-level folder of my site" (called the root). But you can also have relative links. Just typing the "address *pomodoro.htm*" will look for a file with that name in the same folder as the webpage that asks for it—so this would work linking from the salsas index page.

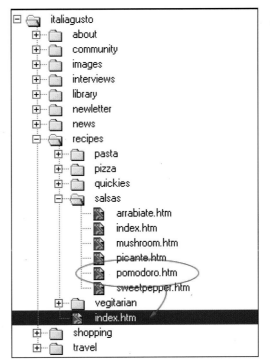

LINKING TO OTHER SITES

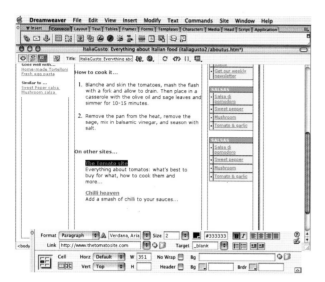

1 If you are linking to external websites, you need to use the full path, including the domain name, of course. You also need to be 100% sure to include the http:// prefix: without this the link will not work. If you just put *www.anothersite.com* (for example), the browser will look for a folder with that name within your own site.

1 If you want to link to a file that downloads when someone clicks on the link—a Word document or PDF, for example—just give the address to the file, and it will automatically start to download. Some types of files, like GIFs and JPEGs, will open in the browser window. Here you need to instruct your users to right click on the link and select the "*Save Target As*" option in the context menu. Mac users without a right-click button should click and hold until the menu appears.

2 You may want links to other people's sites to open in a new window. Your Web authoring software should have a *Target* setting beside the link field. Setting this to "*_blank*" opens the link in a new window. The other options are to do with frames, which we look at later on in the book.

2 You may want to put download files on an FTP server, for faster downloads. In this case, upload them using your usual FTP software, then set up the link with the file's address as before. With FTP you must use the *ftp://* prefix, just like using *http://*.

EMAIL LINKS

3 You can also give your users an email link. In the link field of your Web software, type "*mailto:*" followed by the address you want to give. For instance, if you type "*mailto:me@mysite.com*," when your user clicks on the link, this will directly open a new message window with their email software, addressed to "*me@mysite.com*."

4 If you also want to specify a subject line for the email, add on the end "*?subject=*" followed by your subject line. So the whole address could be mailto:me@mysite.com?subject=Enquiry from website."

5 If you have trouble with this, try to avoid any unusual characters or punctuation in the subject line, and replace spaces with a +. This is called URL-encoding, which you can see here in HTML code. It's a complex technology for including special characters in Internet addresses; your software *should* do this automatically, but not all apps do.

ItaliaGusto: Everything about Italian food (italiagusto2/aboutu

Title: ItaliaGusto: Everything abc

```
able>

align="top">
  width="128">
    <img src="side.gif" width="128" height="281"></p>
178     <p><font face="Verdana, Arial, Helvetica, sans-serif" size="1" color="#009900"><a
"ftp://ftp.italiagusto.com/pdfs/salsas/pomodoro.pdf"><font color="#CC0000"><b><img src="/in
border="0">Download
179        this recipe in <br>
180        PDF format</b></font></a></font></p>
181           <p><font face="Verdana, Arial, Helvetica, sans-serif" size="1" color="#00
182              <a href="mailto:comments@italiagusto.com?subject=Salsa%2BPomodoro"><fon
"/info.gif" width="11" height="8" border="0">Contact
183              us </b></font></a></font></p>
184        </td>
185        <td width="351">
186           <p><font face="Verdana, Arial, Helvetica, sans-serif" size="1"><b><font color="#00
187              time:</font></b> 5 minutes</font> </p>
188           <p><font size="2" face="Verdana, Arial, Helvetica, sans-serif" color="#333333"><b>
189              simple sauce is served with pasta, with a knob of fresh butter and grated
190              parmesan.</b></font> </p>
191           <h5><font face="Verdana, Arial, Helvetica, sans-serif" color="#CC0000">Ingredients
192           <ul>
193           <li> <font face="Verdana, Arial, Helvetica, sans-serif" size="2" color="#333333">
194              fully ripe tomatoes</font></li>
195           <li><font face="Verdana, Arial, Helvetica, sans-serif" size="2" color="#333333">
196              tbsp extra virgin olive oil</font></li>
```

TEMPLATES AND LIBRARY ITEMS

So you've created a template HTML page for your website, and you've planned ahead how you're going to structure the site, and you've learned how to set up links to other webpages. Now you're going to turn all this into a website. And it can be quite a task...

CREATING INDIVIDUAL WEBPAGES

Before you begin, draw up a list of all the pages you want to include, using a tree structure. Even if it's just a few, it helps to keep track of where you're at, and you can cross the pages off as you go.

Turning your template into a real webpage is simply a matter of duplicating it, renaming the copy, and putting it in the right folder. Now open this page, change what's in the main content area to what you want for the content of the page, adjust the navigation

and any section headings as appropriate, then finally check all the links and fix any that are broken. Before you move onto another page, test this one thoroughly in as many different browsers as you can, otherwise any mistakes you've made will be replicated to other pages in your site, and then you've got a much bigger job fixing them.

USING TEMPLATES

One of the problems in creating webpages like this is that if you later want to add a new button to your navigation, or change something else about your design template, you've got to do it to each and every page of your site, which can be a long and tedious task. Most good Web design apps include special template features, which allow you to set up your site up so that any changes you make to your design template are automatically reflected on every page. How you do this depends on your software...

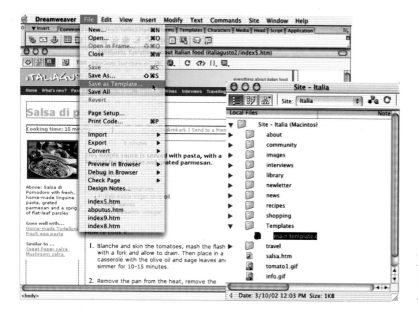

1 In Dreamweaver, you simply open your template design, then choose File>*Save as Template*. The file is saved in a special *Templates* folder, with the ending ".dwt."

2 Now you need to specify which bits of your template are going to be fixed for every page in the site, and which are allowed to change for different pages. Dream-weaver assumes that everything is fixed unless you say otherwise, which you do using Modify> Templates>*New Editable Region*.

3 Now give the region a name.

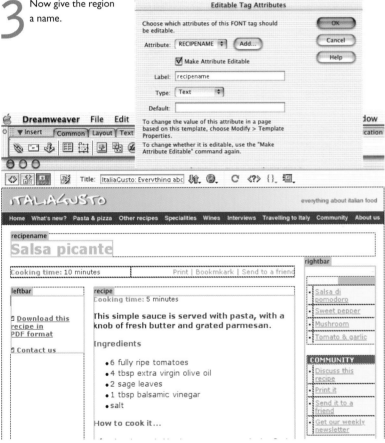

6 If you later decide to change the background color, for example, you simply change the template and hit *Save*. The individual pages are updated automatically.

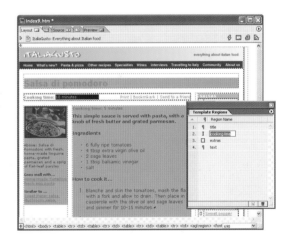

7 In GoLive, you use the Template Regions to set up editable areas of an HTML page you want to use as a template. Then choose File>*Save As...* and select Templates from the Site Folder menu at the bottom of the dialog. To create a new page based on this template, choose File>*New Special>Page From Template*.

4 You might need several editable regions: here we've set four, which you can see outlined in red. These are the only bits you will be able to change individually for pages in your site that use this template.

5 To create these pages, choose File>*New from Template*, and update as appropriate.

LIBRARY ITEMS

1 Using library items is a similar, time-saving technique. Here you are dealing with the elements that you put into a page, rather than the fixed outer shell of a template. Take for example a box of links that you want to appear on all the pages of a particular section in your site.

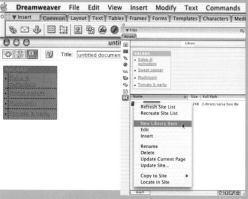

2 You can create this as a mini webpage by itself, then in Dreamweaver select Window>*Library* to open the *Library* window, and in the menu at the top-right corner select *New Library Item*. You should see it in the *Library* window. Give it a useful name.

4 Alternatively, you can double click to open and edit it. When you save it, Dreamweaver gives you a dialog that allows you to update all the relevant webpages automatically.

3 You can now drag and drop this item into any page.

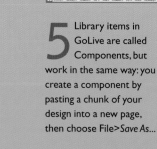

5 Library items in GoLive are called Components, but work in the same way: you create a component by pasting a chunk of your design into a new page, then choose File>*Save As...* and select Components in Site Folder menu before you save. You can now drag this component into a new page from the Site Extras section of your Objects palette.

THE STUDIO 9 TEMPLATE

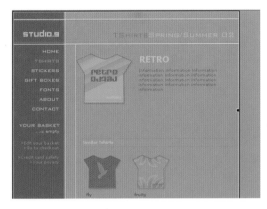

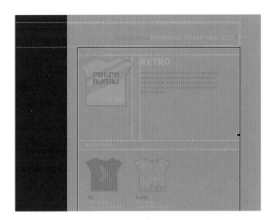

3 The main content area uses a much more relaxed, free-flowing table, just to outline the main areas of content.

1 Let's take a look at the design template for the Studio.9 T-shirt site, because we haven't done this yet. It begins with page margins all set to 0, and a 3x3 table. Here you can see it with the design faded in the background.

4 To create the lined edge of the nav bar, you can use the tiled background image technique we discussed earlier in the chapter. This is easier than doing it with tables, and the GIF is tiny.

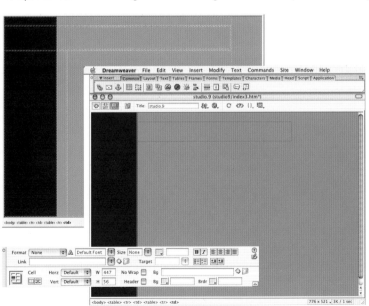

2 To create the lines around the title area, you can use a 3x3 table with the row-and-spacer technique from earlier in the chapter, which you can see here with and without table edges. This makes for a quicker, download than doing it all as a graphic. To be on the safe side, we set the exact width and height for every set in the table.

5 Finally, add in the logo, sliced graphics, heading, text, and so on.

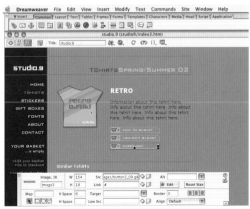

THE STUDIO 9 TEMPLATE 2

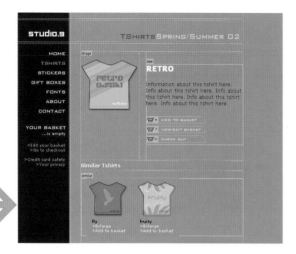

6 Next, save it as a template that will serve for all T-shirt pages, and then create three editable areas: one for the T-shirt picture, one for the text, and one for similar T-shirts at the bottom.

8 This looks pretty messy in Dreamweaver, but when you preview it in the browser window, it looks great.

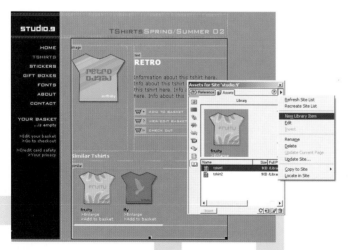

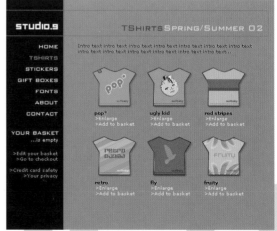

7 Finally, turn each of the T-shirt thumbnails in the "similar" section and on the home page into a library item, so that if you decide to change one later, all the pages will update automatically.

9 For the main hub page of the T-shirt section, amend the template slightly, to show all the *Library* item thumbnails in a tabular format, as you can see in our initial design. Copy and paste your template file, then open it to do some editing.

10 This begins with a two-row, single-column table with no padding or spacing. The top row holds the intro text, while the second will show off the thumbnails.

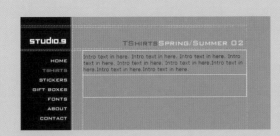

11 In the second, add a 100%-wide table with plenty of cell spacing, and enough rows and columns to hold all the thumbnails.

12 Next drag in some sample thumbnails from the Library to check everything's working fine. Watch out that these don't push out the width of the table, because this will make a mess of your design.

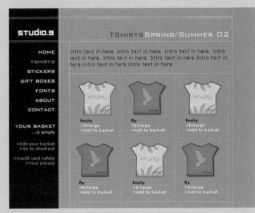

13 All being well, turn the rest of your T-shirt thumbnails into library items if you haven't already, and copy them in your template. Then just turn the central area into an editable region, create the actual hub page from this template, and link it all up. It's useful to use a template for this, even though you only have one T-shirt hub page, because at some point you might want to create more hub pages based on the same template, for different types of T-shirt, different colors, and so on.

DECIDING ON A HOME PAGE

We've looked at two different types of page design you will usually need in a site: hub or index pages, which link your viewers to different content within your site; and item, product or article pages, which will hopefully satisfy whatever it is your user is looking for. Of course, the differences between these aren't so great that you can't mix and match to keep the pace up. There are other types of page, including functional pages, such as forms, which we'll look at later. But one that is invariably unique within your site is the home page. It is also often the hardest to create...

A brief yet direct introduction at Mango tells users instantly what the site is about, and outlines the available features. On the left, the Latest Releases section puts the most important content on the site upfront.

The most important aspect of the portfolio site is visual, so it kicks off with a big image, and the text opens with an instruction on how to see more. The headings immediately indicate what you can find in the portfolio.

TARGETING YOUR HOME PAGE

If you get comprehensive visitor statistics with your website package, you will probably find that 50% or more of your visitors make it no further than the home page. But this depends heavily on various factors like, who they are, what they were expecting at your site, what they are looking for having logged on, and of course… how well your home page meets its remit.

So, job one is to figure out its precise remit. First, remember who your webpage is aimed at, and what you want to get out of them. People will come to your website for many different reasons, and many of these will not be what you've got in mind. Maybe they saw you on a search engine, and popped by looking for something entirely different. These people aren't important to you: they're simply eating up your valuable bandwidth. How many megabytes of Web files does your host allow you to send down the line before you have to pay extra?

First and foremost, the job of your home page is to make sure people who are important to you know they're in the right place as soon as they get there. They may have already looked at five or 10 sites with no luck. So, you've nothing to gain from holding your story back or being coy about who your site is for, and why. Tell it straight and do it with pride.

CONTENT

The next purpose of your home page is to indicate what content is available on your site, so people can get to what they want quickly. Again, you've got nothing to gain by delaying your visitor. There are many ways to do this, from the extended animated intro to the jam-packed links index, and you should be able to work out which method is best from the purpose of your site and the way you expect people to use it. Let's take a look at some of the options…

SPLASH OR STRAIGHT-IN?

"Splash" intro or trailer screens have been popular in the past, and yes, they look great. But if you're into this idea, you've really got to ask yourself, what purpose does it serve? If your site is purely there for information or shopping, it's probably not a good idea: just let your users get in quick, like at *www.theonion.com*. There are only three types of site that generally benefit from a

splash screen. The first is highly visual sites, where viewers come to enjoy pictures. In this case, why not kick off with a picture of the week, like you'll find if you log on to *www.surfstation.lu*?

Highly branded sites can also benefit from a splash screen—but only if it strongly represents and pushes home the message of the brand. Think of this as advertising or entertainment—and make it good, like at *www.nike.com*.

In the third case, they play a more practical role. For example, sites that use a lot of plugin technology, like Flash or Shockwave (see the next chapter for more on these), involve large file sizes, so it's good etiquette to let people know, and offer links to the technology if they don't already have it. Another example is where designers prefer to open the main site in a new window with controlled size and appearance, in which case a functional splash screen is again necessary. Check out *www.guinness.com*, pictured.

HOME PAGE

2

WHAT INFORMATION AND HOW MUCH?

1 For the home page proper, your first question is this: How much information do I want to show? You should be able to figure this out in large part from the style, function, and audience of your site. It also ties in with whether or not you want the page to scroll or not. If your site is about information or selling products, you probably want to get as much as you reasonably can on your home page, unless you are really going for the lean-and-clean look. Try *www.mtv.com* for size.

2 How much content you can "reasonably" include is hard to gauge, of course. You need to weigh up these factors: how do you expect people to use your site?; how "visual" do you want it to be?; what is the balance of text versus images?; and what about the file size? Nike USA, at *www.nike.com/usa*, manages to squeeze a lot into a small space, relying on strong visual cues and short sentences that tell it straight. There are no less than 20 links on this page.

4 As for the rest—there are several approaches you can take. One is to provide a descriptive and/or visual guide to the different sections on your site, like at *www.laperla.com*. This has the advantage of giving people a complete overview of what's on offer, which they can use as a starting point to dig deeper.

3 You also need to think about what content you want to put on your home page. As a rule of thumb, this gets harder the bigger your site is. But one dead cert is this: unless you're already well known, a 2-line introduction saying what the site is and what it does will do you no harm. *www.wineonline.com* uses this to great effect with a witty but clear message…

5 Many sites start deeper: they show you the latest or greatest content straight away, whether it is news, top-selling products or the latest features. This is almost always the best approach for maximising traffic. If you're selling products, think of this as a shop window: show off the best you've got. Take a look at *www.shockwave.com*.

USING FRAMES

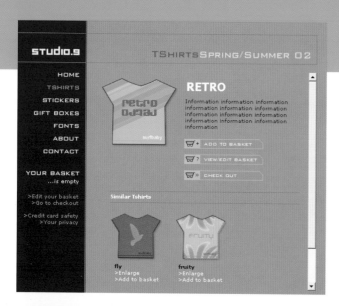

Using frames, we can display scrollbars in the flow of the designs of these pages, so users can scroll key content while the rest of the page stays put.

Our design for the Mango site includes a feature that, so far, we haven't looked at. It has a scrollbar right in the middle, rather than at the side. This has the advantage of making it possible for you to combine the attractions of a webpage that fits entirely within one screen, but still have lots of content and a scrolling mechanism. Like everything in Web design, an abundance of technical problems and design issues are part of the process, but you might decide it's worth it, especially when you need to strike a difficult balance between presentation and content.

The most common and easiest technique for creating this effect is to use frames. These effectively divide your browser window up into several smaller windows, each holding a complete webpage. By controlling whether or not they have borders between them, by setting which of these sub-windows (or "child windows") have scrollbars, and by carefully designing your webpages to line up, you can give the illusion that your design is a single webpage with a scrolling section in the middle.

DECIDING WHETHER TO USE FRAMES...

The decision about whether or not to use frames is a tough one: frames have their advocates and their opponents. News sites tend to avoid them, for example. But like most aspects of your design, you should balance technical issues with functionality.

Let's take a closer look. Frames look good, but you can also design a page so that as your user scrolls one part of it to see more content, another part stays

FRAMES ARE GOOD FOR...

	Small, presentation-oriented sites
Pros	Wow factor
	Attractive presentation with more content
	Navigation or other key design features always visible
	If you want to change the navigation, you only need to update one file
	Can speed up page loading

FRAMES ARE BAD FOR...

	Large-scale commercial sites
Cons	Uses lots of files
	Can't easily link people to particular pages
	Reduces value of search engine listings
	Can't bookmark particular pages in Netscape
	Difficult to set up in complex designs
	Distorts site visitor statistics

immobile, and still in view in the browser (or "parent window"). This is ideal for navigation, branding elements, and so on.

MANY PAGES, ONE PAGE

The other benefits derive from the fact that each frame or window contains a separate webpage, meaning a separate HTML file. When your user clicks on a link, you only need to change the file in the content window, not the other windows. Your navigation, for example, might have an HTML file all to itself, but you can use this one file across your whole site—and if you need to add a new button, that's easy. Also, your user may be downloading less new HTML every time they click a link, because the new file only needs to contain the content, and not the navigation and other code.

Nevertheless, you'll need to have at least one file for every frame in your design, and this can get complicated, especially if you have a tricky design where things all need to match up properly, like in the Mango site.

PROBLEMS WITH LINKS

There are worse drawbacks, though: unless you get into seriously technical ground, there is no way to link your users to individual pages within a framed site. This is because at the hub of the site is a file that contains information about the frames, and how they appear, plus links to the files that should load into the child windows. This is called the frameset, and that's the page you need to link people to—it should be

your *index.htm* page; if you link people directly to the other pages, they will simply see them as they are, without all the other frames surrounding them.

This in turn makes it harder for your site to benefit from search engines, because much of the value these offer is in linking people to specific pages in a site.

And finally, in the same way that you cannot link to individual pages, you can't theoretically bookmark individual pages. Internet Explorer has a technical solution to this, and it works well; but in Netscape, it is simply the frameset that gets bookmarked, and people coming back will always end up at your homepage.

ALTERNATIVES

There are two alternatives to using frames, and both have their pluses and minuses. The first is to use the <iframe> tag, which simply creates a frame of specific dimensions inline, or in the flow of, an ordinary webpage. You can specify the name of the file it should show, whether it scrolls, and so on. This won't work in Netscape 4, and it won't solve many of your frame woes, but it will make creating your frame-based page much easier. Using a separate frameset for each section of your site is workable enough to allow you to link people directly to these pages, rather than always the home page.

The other, and much better, alternative is to use the <div> tag together with cascading style sheet (CSS) clipping and overflow settings. This is much harder to set up, however; we'll take a look at CSS and layer techniques in chapter 7.

SETTING UP FRAMES

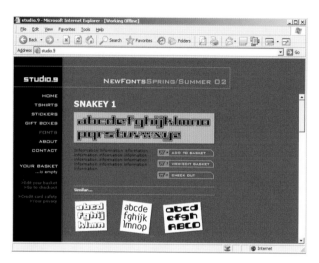

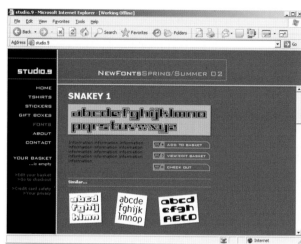

1 The easiest frameset to create is for the Studio.9 design, which we've adapted here for the section on fonts. But to make things even easier, first off…

2 We'll put the scrollbar right at the edge as usual, but not right up to the top of the page.

3 This design will need three frames, which we've marked out here: one for the navigation, one for the page header, and one for the scrolling content. This overall combination is called a frameset, and will be the *index.htm* file for the fonts section of the site. We'll also need to create a file for each of the individual frames.

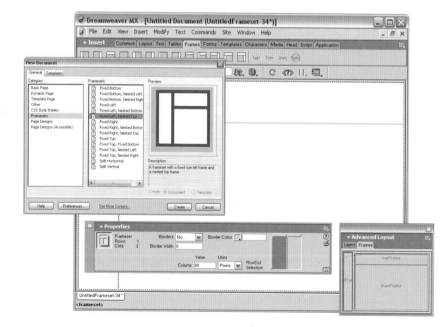

4 Your Web authoring software should have tools for creating frames. Both GoLive and Dreamweaver have readymade drag-and-drop framesets in the toolbox, which you can use as a starting point. Then using your *Frames* and *Properties* palettes together, you can adjust the settings. Add a left and top frameset. Like tables, you can nest frames to create more complex arrangements.

5 As with tables, you can set frame widths and heights in pixels or as percentages. *Relative* is an option that indicates whether a row or column should take up any remaining space in the browser window, or share it with other rows and columns. Other settings include *Border Width and Color*, *Margins*, and an option allowing your user to resize frames.

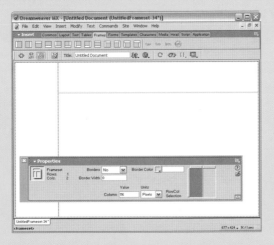

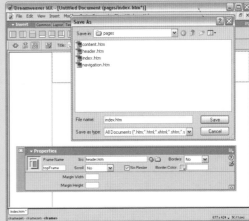

6 Particularly important are the *Scrolling*, *SRC*, and *Name* properties for frames. We set scrolling to *No* for the left and top frames, while the content frame is set to *Auto*—scrollbars appear only if they are needed.

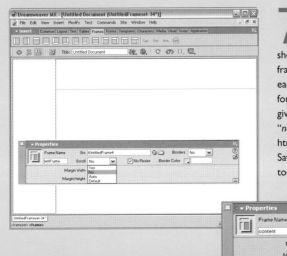

7 A frame's *SRC* property gives a link to the webpage that should be loaded into that frame. Save the pages in each of these as blank files for the time being, but give them the names "*navigation.htm*," "*header. htm*," and "*content.htm*." Save the overall frameset too, as "*index.htm*."

8 You also need to give each frame a name—preferably an obvious one. This is so that when you set up a link in one of the pages, you can use the name to tell the browser which frame to load the new file into. We'll look at this more in a moment…

CREATING THE PAGES

1 The HTML for each of the frame pages can be quickly adapted from the 'No-frames' template we created earlier. Make sure that your frame sizes are matching up exactly, and check they work fine as you resize the window.

2 Here we add new colors and graphics for the fonts section.

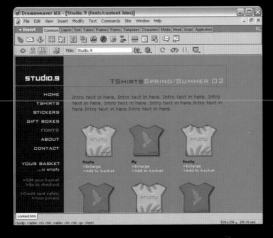

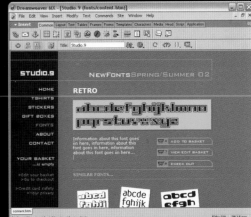

SETTING UP FRAMES

2

LINKS WITH FRAMES

1 When your user clicks one of the similar font links at the bottom, all that needs to change is the content page. The rest stays the same. Set the link up in the usual way, but to be clear which frame the link opens in, set the *Target* option to the name of the frame. If you want to open the link in any other frame, it's just the same: give its name.

2 Some links, like the check-out link, you might want to open without the frameset, or using a different frameset. Again, you provide the link in the usual way, but set target to '*_top*'. '*_parent*', meanwhile, signifies the parent window—but beware. This can be confusing if you have used nested frames. '*_self*' signifies the current frame.

3 Sometimes people will come to a page in your site via a search engine. Without complex code, it's hard to instruct the page to pick up the frameset automatically. Your best bet is to always make sure you've got a link to the main home page on every page, even if it's just at the bottom, so a lost surfer can click their way to comfort.

ADVANCED FRAMES

1 In our original design, we didn't want the scrollbar to float in the page. One solution is to use nesting to create extra frames around the content. You can do this by dragging new frame borders from the edge of the page (but first double-checking that they aren't hidden).

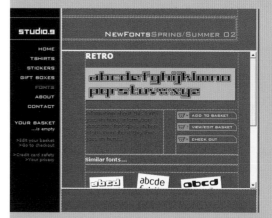

2 Then create a single, empty page with the right background color, and put this in these "silent" frames.

5 …then click to the code view, and type this, all on one line:
`<IFRAME SRC= "somepage.htm" NAME="framename" WIDTH=430 HEIGHT=380 FRAMEBORDER=NO MARGINHEIGHT=0 MARGINWIDTH=0 NORESIZE></IFRAME>`
Change "somepage.htm" to the link to the page you want to appear in the frame, choose a name, and set the width and height you want for the scrolling area.

```
Arial, Helvetica, sans-serif" color="#E0393C">Text
43        in here text in here text in here text in he
text in
44        here</font></td>
45        <td align="right" width="7%"><img src="Untitl
width="6" height="192"></td>
46      </tr>
47    </table>

48
49    </td>
50    <td width="5%"> </td>
51    <td width="70%">
52      <IFRAME SRC="salsahome.html" NAME="contentframe
FRAMEBORDER=NO WIDTH=430 HEIGHT=380 MARGINHEIGHT=0 MARGIN
NORESIZE></IFRAME>
53      </td>
54    </tr>
55    </table>

56
57    </td>
58  </tr>
59  <tr>
60    <td width="603"> </td>
61  </tr>
62  </table>
```

3 The frame for Mango World Music would be particularly complicated. Combine this with the scale planned for the site, the number of files used, and the color coding of the sections… and you'll see that the whole thing is getting out of hand. The *<iframe>* tag is a much better option—while Netscape 4.x users will simply see an ordinary, scrolling webpage.

6 If you haven't done so already, create the HTML page to go in the scrolling inline frame…

7 …and that's it, you're done!

4 Dreamweaver up to version 4 doesn't support iframes. If you have an earlier version, you're going to have to type in the code by hand. But don't worry, it's a breeze. For this, you can use a normal, no-frame page, like the ones already created. First, clear out the area where you want your iframe to appear, and put your cursor into it…

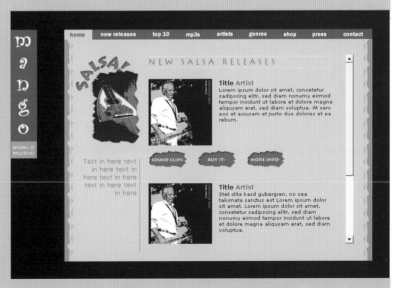

JUST AS ANIMATORS PUSHED BACK THE BOUNDARIES OF FILM IN THE 21ST CENTURY, SO ANIMATION IS BRINGING LIFE, MOVEMENT, AND COLOR TO THE WEB. BUT ANIMATIONS ARE NOT JUST ABOUT CARTOON CHARACTERS; ANIMATION TECHNIQUES CAN ADD A MUCH MORE SUBTLE AND PROFESSIONAL GLOSS TO YOUR INTERNET PRESENCE.

5

ANIMATION

INTRODUCTION TO ANIMATION

Animation has always been a popular addition to the Web designer's repertoire, but with the advent of faster Internet connections and improved technologies for delivering high-octane animated graphics in just a few kilobytes, the medium is really taking off. Today you can realistically post animation on your website that is of a higher quality and resolution than you see on your TV, with interactive features, research tools, ecommerce, downloadable resources, and more...

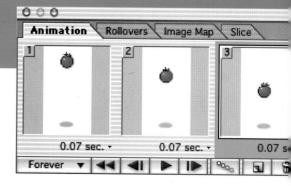

Slight changes in position combined with rapid playback create the illusion of motion —this is the underlying principle of animation.

You create animation for the Web in the same way as you create static graphics. At its simplest level, animation is just a series of slightly different static images, played back at high speed to give the illusion of smooth movement. Like their celluloid counterparts, these static images are called "frames" (confusingly for a Web designer), and the rate at which they change is measured in frames per second (fps). While films play at 24 frames per second, you can get a decent enough impression of motion with just 12, or even 9, fps. But there are no rules, and for some types of animation you don't need to create the illusion of smooth movement; you just want a graphic to change.

GIF ANIMATION

The traditional file format for delivering Web animation is one you already know about: the GIF. It also remains one of the best. An animated GIF works in exactly the same way as an ordinary GIF file, it just contains more than one image. You create, optimize, and add it to your webpage in exactly the same way. When you load the page, the animation should start to play back automatically.

One of the numerous advantages of the animation method is that rather than setting a single, overall frame rate, you can allocate timing in milliseconds to each individual frame. For instance, you could have frames one, two, and three changing quickly, then hold frame four for half a second, then move more quickly again for frames five, six, and seven. You can also include in your GIF file information about whether your animation should loop and play from the beginning again when it finishes, and if so, for how many times, including an infinite loop.

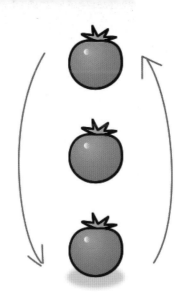

In many cases, you can also use the same Web graphics software to create your animated GIF. This should have a *Frames* or *Animation* palette, or a *Timeline*. Clicking through the different frames here, you can create or adapt the graphic for each individual frame, and then apply your animation settings.

Small is effective with GIF animation. Use looping to make short animations seem much longer.

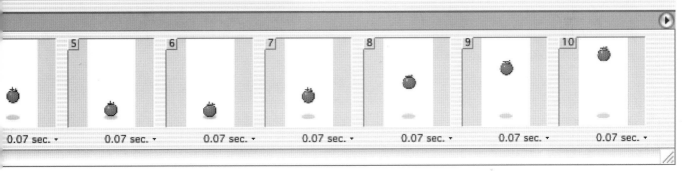

GIF animation in ImageReady: this bouncing tomato is really just a series of static GIF images compiled as frames into one file, with information about how quickly each one should play.

FILE SIZE

But there are problems with GIF animation, the most serious one being download time. Because the file needs to include one image for each frame of your animation, the file size escalates rapidly. And because a GIF animation needs to download completely before it can begin to play, or even display the first frame, this can really slow down your webpages. The animation is likely to be one of the last things to appear on the page as the other graphics download; and this becomes a very real problem if the animation contains important information.

There are techniques you can use to keep your GIF animations slim, fast, and effective—we'll take a look at these in depth over the next few pages. But the chief consideration is this: keep it simple, use as few frames as possible, and try to use GIF animation in small but effective ways. Remember, in Web design you can achieve as much with subtle details as you can with big statements.

FLASH AND VECTOR GRAPHICS

There is an alternative to the GIF format, and it is one that enables you to create large, extended animation features in a realistically small file size. This is Macromedia's Flash format, which has been developed over the last few years to become one of the world's favorite platforms for presenting seriously groundbreaking, entertaining, and experimental Web design.

This is possible because Flash takes an entirely different approach to animation, in two ways. First, it uses vector, rather than bitmap, graphics technology. A bitmap graphic is one that contains information individually describing the color of each and every pixel in a file. Most graphics formats are bitmap, including GIF and JPEG. A vector graphic, on the other hand, contains mathematical descriptions of the image's components, its lines, and curves. Many graphics can be summed up in this way in just a few

ANIMATION BASICS 2

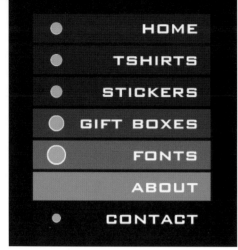

Flash uses vector graphics to offer fast-loading, intensive, and extended animation sequences. It is also completely scalable.

short lines—particularly those that are made of simple shapes and discrete areas of line and color—which makes for miniscule file sizes. Other vector formats include Encapsulated PostScript (EPS), and TTF, the format used for TrueType Font Files. The Portable Networks Graphic (PNG) format is a crossover one: traditionally it is a bitmap format, but it is also used by Fireworks as its native, editable file format supporting vector technology—and much more besides.

Ordinary vector file formats are, of course, practically useless for photos and similar continuous tone images. But there are two further advantages to vector technology. First, because it describes shapes rather than details, you can resize a vector graphic as much as you want without losing quality: you can blow it up to 100 times the size if you like.

And second, it's always easier to go back and edit vector graphics, because the vectors of the shapes in your graphic aren't fixed in the way that pixel colors are in a bitmap.

Because vector graphics are completely scalable and based on mathematical descriptions (which you don't need to know about), the visible dimensions of your Flash animation make no

difference to the file size. By comparison, take a 200 x 200 pixel bitmap animation with four frames. The file needs to describe 40,000 pixels for each frame, or 160,000 pixels in all. The same bitmap animation at 800 x 800 pixels needs to describe 2,560,000 pixels in all. In reality, the GIF format uses special techniques to reduce this, but you get the idea.

In addition to the reduced file size of vector graphics in Flash, the medium supports streaming, which means the animation can begin to play as it downloads, rather than wait for the entire file to be loaded before beginning.

TWEENING

The second feature of Flash animation that enables you to create sophisticated animations with just a few kilobytes is called "tweening." This is a feature used in most animation software to make it quicker and easier for you to create your work. In the case of Flash, the benefits of tweening are also transferred into the final animation file, which has the suffix .swf (Shockwave Flash), making for a faster download.

Tweening, a contraction of the words "in between," is a technique that allows you to set the position or appearance of a graphic for one frame, then set a different position or appearance for a later frame, and rely on the software to calculate all the frames in between.

Let's take an example: your animation features a falling leaf. You draw the leaf, and on frame 1 put it at the top of your canvas. On frame 6, you put it at the bottom of the canvas, then ask the software to work out the position of the leaf for the in-between frames. This is tweening, and the frames at either end of the tween, 1 and 6, are called keyframes. You can also use this technique with rotation, transformation, color changes, opacity and other properties of a graphic. In better software you can even set the motion to "ease in" or "ease out."

Flash includes sophisticated interactive features, which make it ideal for complex graphics and animations that respond to user input.

◄ BACK   Title of image 2 - 2002   NEXT ►

With tweening, you can speed up the creation and, with Flash, delivery of animation. Using this technique, the software calculates all the in-between frames for you.

The advantages of tweening are all too obvious: at 12 frames per second, a one-minute stretch of animation equates to 720 frames. Five minutes of animation, therefore, uses 3,600 frames. If you have to draw the graphics for each and every one of these frames by hand, it's going to be a draining job—and expensive, too, if you're in business. Using tweening, you can automate huge swathes of your animation in three short steps, freeing you up to focus more time and energy on being creative.

But in the case of Flash, there is more to it. While the GIF format needs to store all the visual information for every frame of the animation, an SWF file only needs to store the keyframes and tweening details. The actual tweening is carried out after your viewer has downloaded the file into their browser, with the in-between frames being calculated on the fly. In other words, rather than trying to shove 720 frames of graphics down a phone line for just one minute of animation, you can deliver a mere 10 keyframes, then rely on your viewer's software to do the rest of the work. In this way, you can see that the savings on file sizes are going to be immense; this makes Macromedia's Flash format uniquely practical for serious animation work on the Web.

INTERACTIVITY

There are other advantages to Flash, which in its recent versions offers more than just animation. The software also has powerful tools for interactivity, sound, and other media. You can create buttons and rollovers in Flash, just as you can with normal graphics, and again you can achieve these in far smaller file sizes. And you can include Flash within an ordinary webpage—it's not a case of choosing between Flash and HTML.

But there are some disadvantages to the medium. Most importantly, it's a plugin technology. This means that in order to see Flash content in your webpages, your viewer must have the Flash plugin for their Web browser. This isn't a huge problem, however. Reliable statistics are hard to come by (some claim 90% of users have it, which is unlikely), but the plugin comes bundled with Internet Explorer as a standard and soon most Web users *will* have it installed. You can also use special JavaScript codes to check if users have the plugin, and deliver an alternative for those that don't, or link them through to *www.macromedia.com*, where they can download it in just a few MB.

There are other disadvantages to using Flash: first, it is harder to maintain and update than ordinary HTML, simply because of the way the software works. Second, and more seriously, search engines cannot currently index the content of Flash SWF files, as they can with ordinary HTML, which means Flash-only sites don't figure well in the search engine listings. The Flash community is working on solutions to this. Although Flash files can contain ordinary text, the medium simply isn't as practical as HTML for purely information-oriented purposes.

ANIMATION BASICS 3

DHTML lacks the graphical possibilities of other animation formats, but it is fast loading, and offers powerful features for interacting with HTML-based design. This is ideal for news tickers, menus, and the like.

Shockwave is similar to Flash, but catering more for the multimedia design. This is the medium to use for Web-based games and visually rich chatroom environments. Take a look at *www.shockwave.com* to see samples of some of the best Shockwave creativity.

SHOCKWAVE

A format closely related to Flash, called Shockwave, is also created by Macromedia. The two are easy to confuse, as Flash used to be known as Shockwave Flash, and is sometimes still called that, but the formats are different in several important respects.

Shockwave is designed specifically as a multimedia format. So it includes many of the same features as Flash—animation, interactivity, sound, tweening, vector graphics, and so on—as well as stronger support for bitmap graphics, a 3D engine, and more.

The line between Flash and Shockwave can seem a little blurred, but making a choice between the two should be no trouble. If you can achieve what you're after with Flash, go that route. It generally offers faster downloads, it's easier to use, the software is less expensive to buy, and more people have the Flash plugin installed than the Shockwave one. But if you want to create games, interactive 3D stuff and more multimedia-oriented content, you may be better off with Shockwave.

DHTML

There is a third realistic alternative to GIF and Flash for Web animation: DHTML, or Dynamic HTML. This is an extension of ordinary HTML that throws JavaScript and cascading style sheets, or CSS, into the mix, enabling you to add sophisticated animation and interactive features directly to the elements in your webpages. The everyday rollover button is a very basic application of DHTML, which you can develop into increasingly complex ways in which a webpage changes as your user interacts with it.

DHTML can be very difficult to work with—particularly when you try to get your effects to work in the same way across all browsers—but it offers the same benefits as ordinary HTML does over using image files for your design: it's fast to download and easy to update.

Because of the difficulties involved, we'll take a deeper look at using DHTML in chapter 7, but if you want to press ahead, your Web authoring software should have some tools to help you get started. Increasingly, these apps include one-click or drag-and-drop DHTML objects, often called *Behaviors* or *Actions*, which deal with all the code in the background while you concentrate on the design. Combine these with a *Timeline*, which you will find in both Dreamweaver and GoLive, and you can create animation.

Like HTML, DHTML is not the most intuitive of technologies to design with, and the animation tends to be more than a little shaky, so it's not suitable for serious animation, but you can use it to add some neat features to a webpage.

QUICK GUIDE//ANIMATION FORMATS

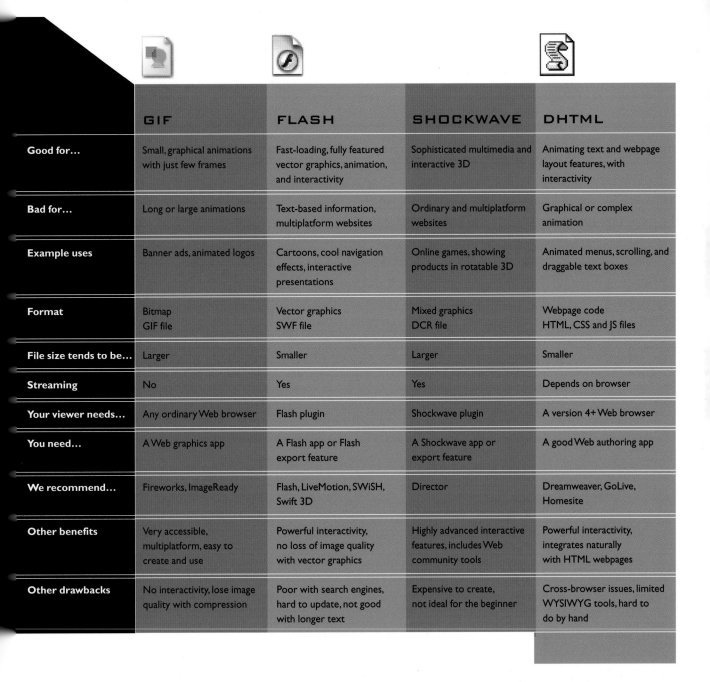

	GIF	FLASH	SHOCKWAVE	DHTML
Good for...	Small, graphical animations with just few frames	Fast-loading, fully featured vector graphics, animation, and interactivity	Sophisticated multimedia and interactive 3D	Animating text and webpage layout features, with interactivity
Bad for...	Long or large animations	Text-based information, multiplatform websites	Ordinary and multiplatform websites	Graphical or complex animation
Example uses	Banner ads, animated logos	Cartoons, cool navigation effects, interactive presentations	Online games, showing products in rotatable 3D	Animated menus, scrolling, and draggable text boxes
Format	Bitmap GIF file	Vector graphics SWF file	Mixed graphics DCR file	Webpage code HTML, CSS and JS files
File size tends to be...	Larger	Smaller	Larger	Smaller
Streaming	No	Yes	Yes	Depends on browser
Your viewer needs...	Any ordinary Web browser	Flash plugin	Shockwave plugin	A version 4+ Web browser
You need...	A Web graphics app	A Flash app or Flash export feature	A Shockwave app or export feature	A good Web authoring app
We recommend...	Fireworks, ImageReady	Flash, LiveMotion, SWiSH, Swift 3D	Director	Dreamweaver, GoLive, Homesite
Other benefits	Very accessible, multiplatform, easy to create and use	Powerful interactivity, no loss of image quality with vector graphics	Highly advanced interactive features, includes Web community tools	Powerful interactivity, integrates naturally with HTML webpages
Other drawbacks	No interactivity, lose image quality with compression	Poor with search engines, hard to update, not good with longer text	Expensive to create, not ideal for the beginner	Cross-browser issues, limited WYSIWYG tools, hard to do by hand

ANIMATION SOFTWARE

THERE IS A DIVERSE RANGE OF TOOLS YOU CAN USE FOR ANIMATION, AND GETTING THE RIGHT ONE FOR THE JOB IS ESSENTIAL. FIRST YOU NEED TO ESTABLISH WHAT TYPE OF ANIMATION YOU WANT TO CREATE, AND WHICH FORMAT IS BEST FOR IT. THEN CHOOSE YOUR APP BASED ON WHETHER IT HAS THE RIGHT FEATURES, AND WHETHER YOU FEEL COMFORTABLE USING IT.

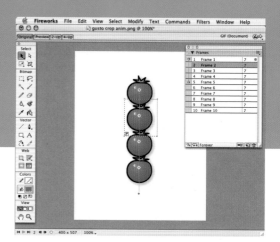

FIREWORKS

As simple GIF animation goes, this is probably the best tool on the market. You just draw your starting animation graphic in the normal way, then using the *Frames* palette (via the *Window* menu) you can duplicate into as many frames as you need, and make adjustments on each to complete your animation. Fireworks includes sophisticated tweening tools for position, rotation, opacity, and more, and you can export your completed animation in the same way as an ordinary GIF file. In particular, Fireworks' vector graphic toolset makes it easy to incrementally edit graphics for your individual frames.
www.macromedia.com

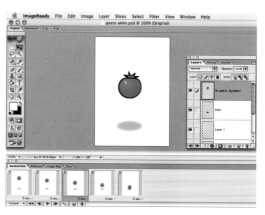

IMAGEREADY

Your other best bet for GIF animation is this companion tool to Photoshop, (it's bundled on Photoshop CDs). It has many of the same tools as Fireworks, revolving around an *Animation* palette, which includes thumbnail previews of your individual frames. You can tween a great variety of layer properties, including effects and envelopes, while close integration with Photoshop and GoLive makes ImageReady ideal for anyone using these apps.
www.adobe.com

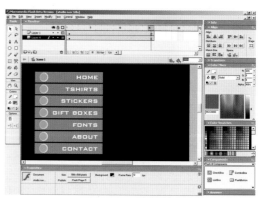

FLASH

If you want to create Flash animation, Macromedia's own Flash tool is the industry standard, and by far the most powerful application for the job. Here animation revolves around the *Timeline*, rather than a *Frames* or *Animation* palette, but the principle is similar. On the left are your layers, while across the top, each notch represents a frame.

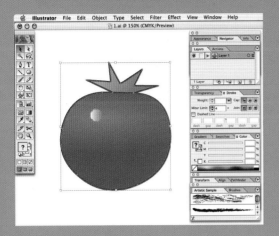

Flash has sophisticated onboard vector drawing tools, as well as easy-to-use *Actions* for creating interactivity and a complete one-click tool for preparing your animation to post to the Web. The only real disadvantage is that Flash, as an extremely powerful bit of software, can be somewhat overwhelming at first.
www.macromedia.com

OTHER FLASH TOOLS

Depending on what type of animation you want to create, there is an increasingly wide range of other tools out there that you can use to produce Flash SWF files. Fireworks, Adobe Illustrator (pictured) and Macromedia FreeHand, for example, all have SWF export options, which are useful if you want to create quick, simple Flash animation, but less ideal for more complex work, because the software just isn't designed for the job.

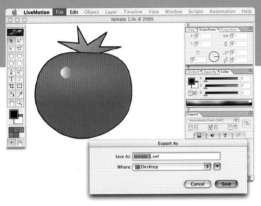

For more complex animation, on the other hand, there are plenty of dedicated applications, many of them specializing in specific types of Flash animation and effects. You can find links to many at *www.macromedia.com*.

LIVEMOTION

LiveMotion is Adobe's contender to Flash, offering SWF export, as well as the company's own SVG scalable format. It lacks access to many of the key advanced features the Flash format has to offer, but makes up for it with an interface that will be familiar to Photoshop, GoLive and Illustrator users—plus close integration with these. It also includes a good variety of instant onboard styles and effects, which has made it popular with some beginners.
www.adobe.com

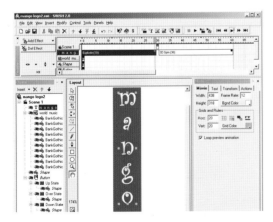

SWISH

SWiSH (Win only) brings impressive, yet easy-to-use text effects to Flash, making it an excellent option for beginners looking for something to spice up webpages. It's currently fairly limited in what it can do, and it's not ideal for cartoon animation, but again, try the demo and see if works for you.
www.swishzone.com

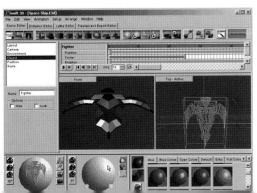

SWIFT 3D

Another effects-fueled, easy-to-use Flash app, Swift 3D enables you to create high-impact wheeling, swirling, and rotating 3D animations, including text, and export them to SWF format. This is great fun, and although it's a good option for beginners, Swift 3D has made its name in a number of professional designers' armories too. Definitely one to try.
www.swift3d.com

GIF ANIMATION

GIF ANIMATION IS BASICALLY ABOUT CREATING A NUMBER OF ORDINARY STATIC IMAGES, AND COMPILING THEM INTO A SINGLE, ANIMATED GIF FORMAT FILE. TO DO THIS, ALL YOU NEED IS SOFTWARE THAT SUPPORTS EXPORTING ANIMATED GIFs, WHICH MANY GRAPHICS APPS DO NOWADAYS. THE STATIC IMAGES ARE CREATED USING A FRAMES OR ANIMATION PALETTE IF YOUR APP HAS ONE, OR ON SEPARATE LAYERS.

More sophisticated software, including ImageReady and Fireworks, offers more powerful features such as tweening and redundant pixel removal. These are important tools for reducing the file size of your animation, and place aspects of your animation that don't change at all—say a background image—in a single frame that stays visible throughout.

Download time is the key issue in GIF animation: combining so many images into a single file quickly escalates the file size, and by the time an animation appears on your webpage, your user may have decided to click a link, or go somewhere else. You've just got to shave those kilobytes off! A good technique is to use simple, looping animations where the end matches the beginning, and the appearance of continuous motion belies how few frames you actually used.

Without further ado, let's have a go at this, creating a bouncing tomato for the ItaliaGusto site.

SIMPLE ANIMATION

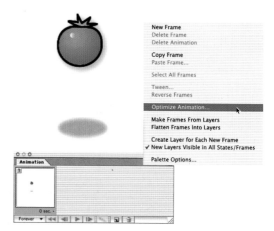

1. Here's a quick sketch of the animation we want to create. There's two ways you can do it: either position the tomato by hand for each frame, or just create the top and bottom frames, then use tweening so your software calculates the animation. We'll try both.

2. First, you need to draw your tomato: it's just a distorted circle and a star shape (top), with gradient fills and a softened highlight.

3. Add in a soft shadow on the "ground" below the tomato, for added realistic detail. This doesn't change, so put it on a separate layer. In ImageReady, choose *Optimize Animation* from the *Animation* palette menu, and tick both boxes in the dialog. In Fireworks, choose the *Share this Layer* option from the Layers palette menu.

STEP BY STEP

4 Using your *Frames* or *Animation* palette, create 9 new frames the same as the first...

5 ...and then step through them, moving the tomato down a little further for each frame, until at frame 5 it is resting on the ground. For frames 6 to 10, make it bounce back up.

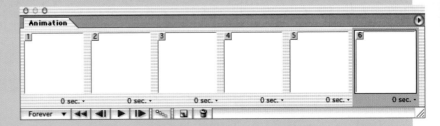

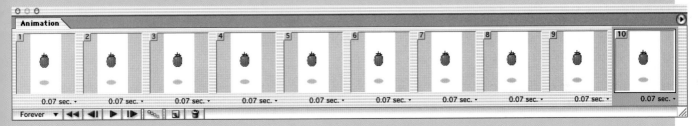

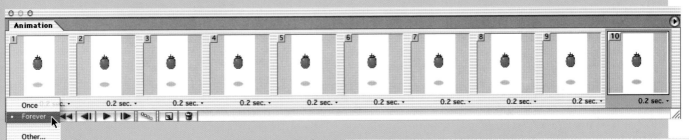

6 Use the options by the frames to control how quickly they play, and the menu at the bottom of your palette to control how many times the animation repeats. Ours is a looping animation, so set this to *Forever*.

7 Finally, crop your animation as close to the content as possible, then optimize and export it in the usual way. In Fireworks you need to choose the *Animated GIF* option from the *Format* menu in your *Optimize* palette.

8 You add an animated GIF file to a webpage in the usual way. It will start playing in the browser as soon as it has loaded. Our final file is just under 3K—less than a second to go through your average 56K modem!

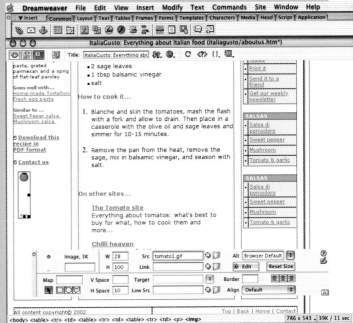

TWEENING

TWEENING IN FIREWORKS

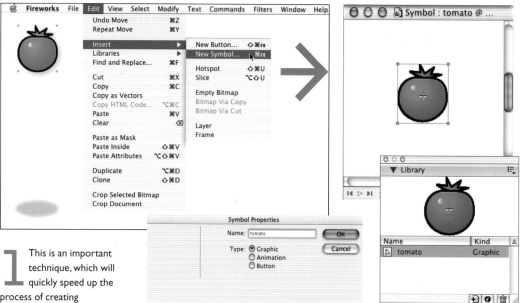

4 Now if you open your *Frames* palette, you should see six frames showing your tomato moving downward. Just repeat this process to create an upward motion after the last frame.

1 This is an important technique, which will quickly speed up the process of creating animations. It works differently in different software packages. In Fireworks select your graphic, choose Insert>*New Symbol*. Set the *Symbol Type* to *Graphic* in the dialog and name your symbol.

2 Now paste your graphic into the symbol dialog window. Your graphic is then stored in the library so that it can be re-used.

3 Drag two instances of the tomato symbol onto the workspace into desired positions. Next, select both tomatoes, and choose the Modify>Symbol>*Tween Instances* option. In the dialog that appears, set the number of steps to 3, and check the *Distribute to Frames* box.

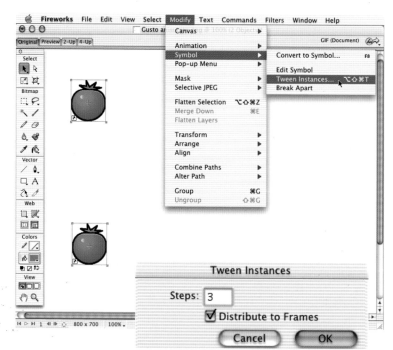

TWEENING IN IMAGEREADY

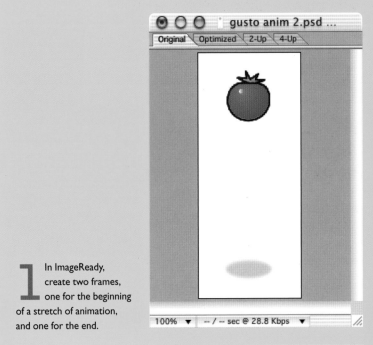

2 Then click the *Tweening* button at the bottom of your *Animation* palette (the four small circles), and select your options in the dialog that appears. As you can see, you can tween effects and opacity as well as layer position.

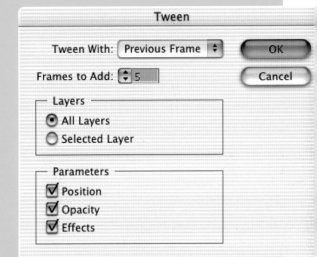

1 In ImageReady, create two frames, one for the beginning of a stretch of animation, and one for the end.

3 The in-between frames are automatically created for your animation; now all you need is to create the "upward" frames, then crop and export.

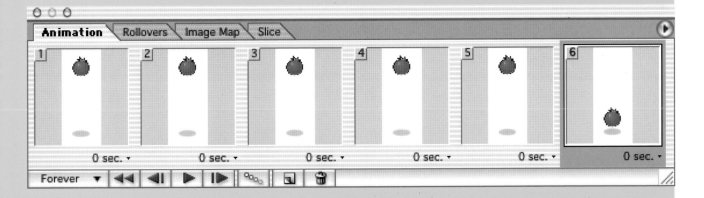

SWISH
TEXT EFFECTS

In terms of file size and the quality of the result, Flash would almost certainly be a better medium for creating the bouncing tomato animation on the previous pages—and, indeed, most animations. Over the last few years, Flash SWF has become the definitive format for animated graphics on the Web, and today it's hard to think of a visual website that doesn't use it in some way or other. One area it really excels in is for extended interactive text effects, which we're going to create in this project.

Flash, the application, is the definitive tool for creating content in Flash format—no surprises there. But it's also a very advanced bit of software, and not always the easiest to use if you're looking for a particular result. There are many apps out there that specialize in creating specific effects, or undertaking "niche" tasks with Flash. One of these is SWiSH, an app dedicated to the fun and funky. You can download a free, fully functional trial from *www.swishzone.com*.

One attraction of SWiSH is it's incredibly easy to use, and in just a few minutes you can knock out something to be proud of. As your ideas get more complex, you'll need to use more diverse tools, but as a starting point with Flash, nothing could be better. Even as a professional, you could use this to create effects sequences really quickly that would take ages using the Flash application itself.

THE PALETTES

Like other design software, SWiSH uses tabbed palettes, which can click through to quickly edit and adjust different aspects of your animation and the objects in it. Like all the interface elements in SWiSH, you can click and drag these to anywhere you like on your interface.

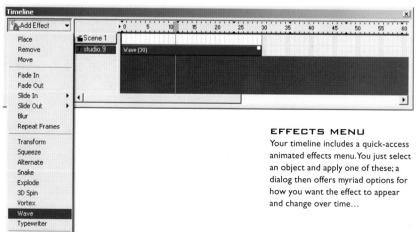

EFFECTS MENU
Your timeline includes a quick-access animated effects menu. You just select an object and apply one of these; a dialog then offers myriad options for how you want the effect to appear and change over time…

THE SWISH INTERFACE

SWiSH might seem a bit confusing when you first open it, but take a moment to look it over and things should start to fall into place. Flash's interface is very similar to this…

THE CONTROLS

You can use the controls to preview and play through your animation. You can also just click and drag the red bar at the top of your timeline.

THE INSERT TOOLBAR

Here you have buttons to insert text, images, buttons, sprites, and scenes quickly into your movie. A sprite is a self-contained object, a minimovie of its own within your main movie. A scene is a new stretch of animation, with a fresh timeline—you can use scenes to organize your work when you're creating more complex works.

THE TOOLBOX

This holds your key drawing and editing tools, just as in other design software. Flash is a vector technology, so you can always edit what you've created.

THE TIMELINE

As opposed to the *Animation* or *Frames* palettes of ImageReady and Fireworks, SWiSH (like Flash) has the *Timeline*. It's basically the same, but shows 100 frames or more at once. It also acts as your layers palette, showing layers and/or objects down the left-hand side. This is where you control, and create, the animation aspects of your design.

THE OUTLINE WINDOW

This acts a little like a layers palette, listing all the scenes and objects in your animation. To select an object, just click its name in here, or select it in your main workspace.

THE CANVAS, OR STAGE

In the center is your main workspace—the canvas, or stage, as animation applications often call it. The background rectangle represents the boundaries of your animation, known as a "movie" in Flash. You can move objects outside this, but they won't appear in your final animation, depending on the output settings.

ACTIONS PALETTE

Use this palette to add special actions and interactive behavior to your animation. These can either happen at particular frames, or when a user interacts with part of your animation, by rolling their mouse pointer over or out, or by clicking on it.

MOVIE PALETTE

Use this to control the size, background color and playback speed of your animation.

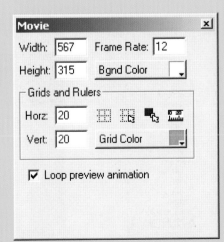

OBJECT PALETTE

This palette changes according to your currently selected object. Use it to type in text, change color, appearance, shape, and so on.

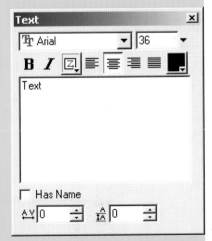

SWISH//A SIMPLE EFFECT 2

1 We want to create a fun, yet simple and fast-loading logo effect for the Mango World Music site. At the beginning, the characters of the text fly in from different directions; when you rollover, they fade out, then fly in again.

2 The easy place to begin is with your existing logo. If your software offers the option to export graphics in Flash SWF format, this is a good bet, because you can import the SWF files into SWiSH and skip a few steps. Fireworks, Illustrator, and CorelRAVE all offer this. When you import the graphic, check the text that you want to animate is a single text field. If not, delete it, and recreate it as a single text item.

3 Otherwise, import your existing logo file, and use the drawing and text tools to recreate it as accurately as you can. When you're done, delete the original graphic to save on file size.

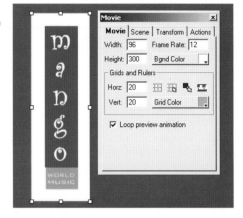

4 Before you begin to animate, quickly drag in the edges of the background to match exactly the space taken up by the content.

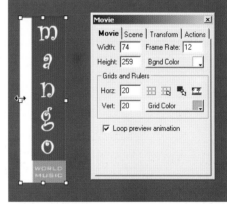

5 To begin your animation, select the text you want to create an effect for, and choose one of the options in your timeline's effects menu. Explode is a good option.

STEP BY STEP

6 The dialog that appears offers a variety of options; experiment with different settings here, and drag the slider at the top of your timeline to see how it looks.

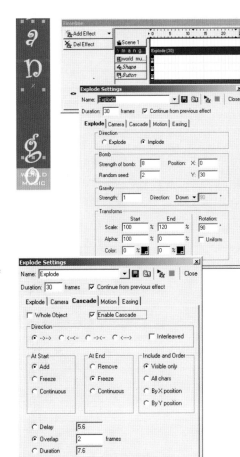

7 On the *Cascade* tab, tick the *Enable Cascade* box to make the effect work through one letter at a time.

8 Now close the dialog, and add another effect immediately after—here we're going for *3D Spin*, again with cascading. Close the dialog again, and play your animation right through. Pretty cool.

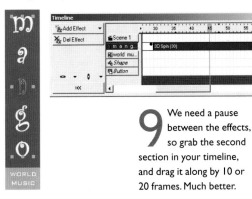

9 We need a pause between the effects, so grab the second section in your timeline, and drag it along by 10 or 20 frames. Much better.

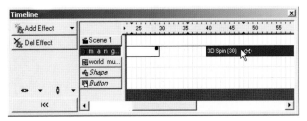

10 Select the graphics behind your animated text, or if you have none, draw a rectangle with the same color as the background, and drag it below the text in your timeline. Then open your *Actions* palette, and use the *Add Event* menu to add an *On Press* event. Use the *Add Action* menu to add a *Goto URL* action, and set the URL to the address of your homepage, or wherever you wish. Don't forget to use *http://* as a prefix if your link is to a complete *www* address.

11 Now click File>Test>*In Browser* to test your work. You should find your animated logo shows a hand cursor when you roll over, and links to your home page.

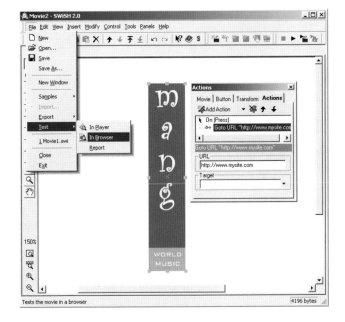

1 In Flash format, you create interactivity using *Actions*. These are simply instructions on what the Flash player should do at certain times, or in connection with certain user events, like mouseover, mouseout, and so on. Setting up a link in your *Actions* palette was itself a simple action.

3 In your *Actions* palette, select *At Frame* from the *Add Event* menu. This should default to the frame you have selected. Then use the *Add Action* menu to add a stop action here. The animation will always stop now when it reaches this frame, and wait for further instructions.

2 We want the animation to stop after the first effect, and immediately continue when the user "rolls over." So, select Scene 1 in your timeline, and select the frame at the end of the first effect.

4 Select the background graphics, which have the *Goto URL* action, and add a new *On Rollover* event. Set the action for this event to *Play*. The animation will now continue playing whenever you rollover it.

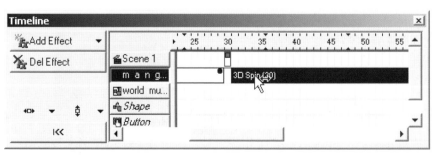

5 Finally, drag the frames for the second effect back, so the animation plays it immediately when you rollover, without a pause.

ADDING FLASH TO A WEBPAGE

1 To create your Flash-format movie for the Web (it needs to be an SWF file), choose File>Export>*SWF*. You can use the *Export* palette in your *Window* menu for a variety of specialist options.

2 To add Flash technology to a webpage, you need to use HTML code for embedding plugin objects, which is quite complex. But many Flash apps, including SWiSH and Flash itself, will automatically create the HTML for you. In SWiSH choose File>Export>*HTML*.

3 Then open the HTML file in your Web authoring app, select the plugin object, and copy and paste it into the appropriate webpage.

4 Alternatively, Dreamweaver and GoLive both include easy Flash objects in the toolbox. You can use this to add Flash content to your webpages in the same way as you add images.

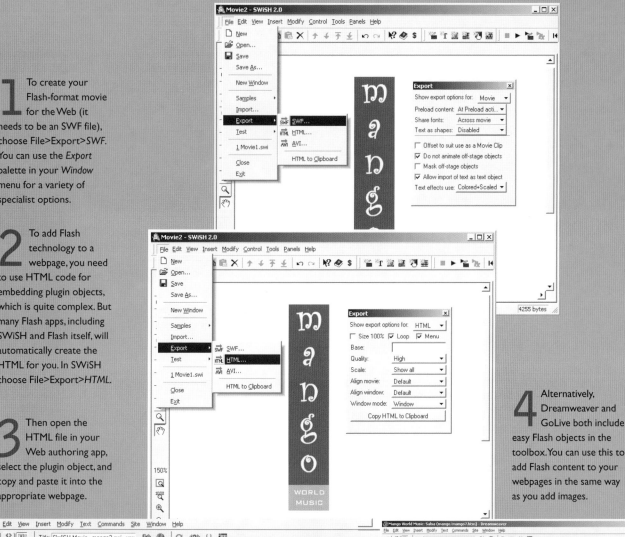

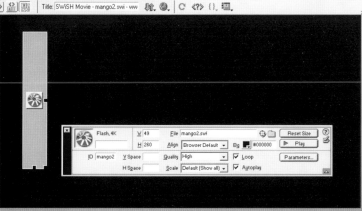

USING FLASH

SWiSH IS GREAT FOR CREATING FUN, ANIMATED EFFECTS IN FLASH FORMAT, AND INCLUDES SOME USEFUL TOOLS FOR ADDING INTERACTIVE FEATURES TO YOUR ANIMATION. BUT FOR SERIOUS ANIMATION WORK AND MORE COMPLEX INTERACTIVE IDEAS, YOU REALLY NEED TO USE FLASH ITSELF. APART FROM A SOPHISTICATED INTERFACE AND POWERFUL CREATION TOOLS, IT IS THE ONLY APP THAT OFFERS ACCESS TO ALL THE FEATURES THE FLASH FORMAT HAS TO OFFER.

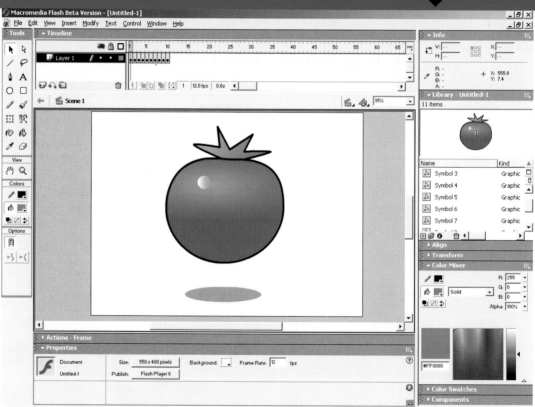

THE FLASH INTERFACE

If you tried out SWiSH, the Flash interface will be familiar because it is very similar. Some of the ways in which it behaves are slightly different, and you'll find many more tools and palettes at your disposal.

PUBLISHING YOUR FLASH MOVIE

Adding your Flash animation to a webpage works in exactly the same way as with SWiSH. In Flash, you can use File>*Export Movie* to create just the SWF file, or File>*Publish Settings* and then the *Publish* button to create HTML as well as the SWF. This offers a variety of extra options.

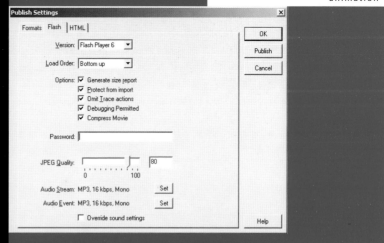

SYMBOLS

A key feature of Flash is symbols. Flash's Library, pictured, is a list of all the symbols in your animation.

Like *Symbols* in Fireworks and *Sprites* in SWiSH, these are self-contained graphics, which you can edit on their own and embed in your movie as many times as you like. Change one, and every copy you have used of that symbol changes to reflect this. This is very useful for speeding up your work, as a well as saving on file size. If you use a particular graphic several times, turning it into a symbol means it only has to be stored in the file once.

Flash uses symbols for just about everything, including animation and buttons. If you want to tween a graphic, you need to turn it into a symbol first. If you want a graphic to behave like a button, turn it into a button symbol. If you want it to contain its own, independent animation sequence, you can turn it into a movie clip symbol.

You can also use Flash actions to dynamically adjust other aspects of movie clip symbols, including *visibility*, *color*, *transparency*, *position*, and so on. You do this using Flash *Actions*, which are written in ActionScript—a language very similar to JavaScript. This is moving into more advanced territory than we will cover in this book, but the application's friendly drag-and-drop *Actions* palette makes it easy to learn if you are intent on pressing ahead.

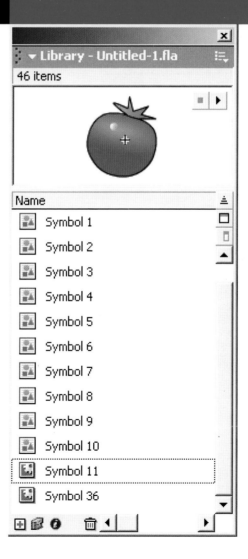

SIMPLE FLASH ANIMATION

1 If you remember, we said the simple bouncing tomato animation for the ItaliaGusto site would be much more efficient using Flash, so we'll take a look at redoing this. If you drew your tomato using Fireworks, Illustrator, or similar, you can export the static drawing in SWF or EPS format, and import this directly onto the first frame of your Flash movie. If not, you'll have to draw it again, to take advantage of vector graphics.

2 Before you can animate this graphic, you need to turn it into a symbol, using Insert> *Convert to Symbol*. Set the *Behavior* to *Movie Clip*.

3 Now put your tomato symbol at its "top" position, then go to frame 20 in your timeline, and use Insert>*Keyframe* to add a keyframe here.

4 At frame 10, add another keyframe in the same way, and here move your tomato to the bottom of its bounce.

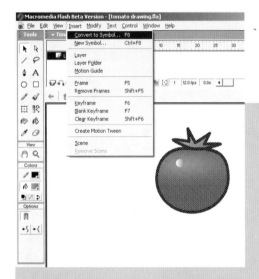

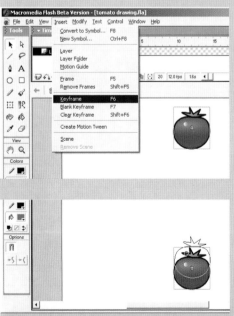

5 Now right-click frames 1 and 10, and for each select *Create Motion Tween* from the *Context menu*. In Flash MX, tweens are in *Properties*.

6 Now you can select *Test Movie* from the *Control* menu to see how your animation will look in the browser.

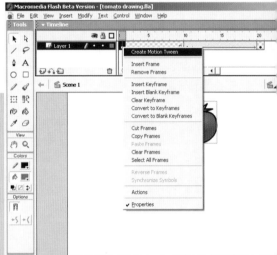

REALISTIC ANIMATION

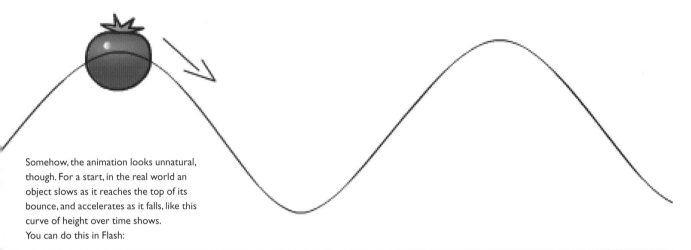

Somehow, the animation looks unnatural, though. For a start, in the real world an object slows as it reaches the top of its bounce, and accelerates as it falls, like this curve of height over time shows.
You can do this in Flash:

1 Select frame 1, and in your *Properties* palette, move the *Ease* slider down to –100 (in). At frame 10, move it to +100 (out). Now preview your clip and you'll see a more natural bounce.

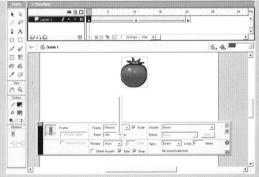

2 Secondly, bouncing objects tend to oscillate a little, in a different rhythm to the bouncing movement. For this we need a secondary animation within the tomato movie clip. Double click to the clip to edit it...

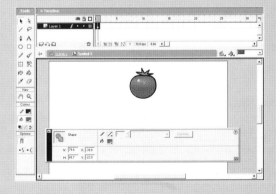

3 Then select all the graphics in turn and turn each into a *Movie Clip Symbol* again, in the same way as before.

Convert to Symbol

Name: tomato clip

Behavior: ● Movie Clip   Registration: ▦
         ○ Button
         ○ Graphic

OK   Cancel   Advanced   Help

4 Use the *Transform* tool to rotate the graphic a notch to the left, then create a new keyframe some way along the timeline—say at frame 64; and another halfway between, at 32.

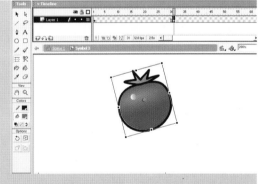

5 At the midpoint keyframe, rotate your tomato two notches to the right; then set up motion tweening at this and the first frame. Double click on the stage (canvas) to get back to your main timeline, and test your movie.

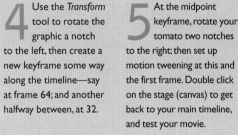

FLASH NAVIGATION

Flash offers high-impact, fast loading graphics of a kind that just aren't achievable with GIFs and JPEGs. One of the best applications of this on your site is in the navigation. After all, this is going to be on practically every page you create, so why not give that little bit of extra oomph?

Creating buttons and rollover effects is a breeze in Flash, and combined with a bit of animation, you can come up with something really impressive. The possibilities are limited only by your imagination and understanding of the software. Part of this is due to the fact that you can easily embed buttons within animation, animation within buttons, and animation within animation in Flash—an ability that opens many doors for the creative thinker.

Here we use these techniques to create a simple but effective fading navigation system for the Studio.9 site...

CREATE A SIMPLE NAVIGATION

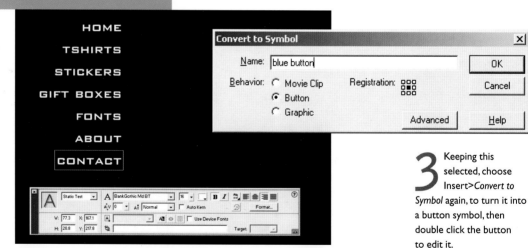

1 The idea of this navigation is that a button turns blue when you roll over it, and then fades back to black when you rollout. We start by recreating the navigation text in a new Flash document. Avoid using bitmap graphics wherever possible in Flash.

2 Next, create a new layer in your timeline, and drag this below the text layer. On here, draw a colored rectangle outlining the first link, and up to the vertical edges of your navigation bar. Turn this into a graphic symbol.

3 Keeping this selected, choose Insert>*Convert to Symbol* again, to turn it into a button symbol, then double click the button to edit it.

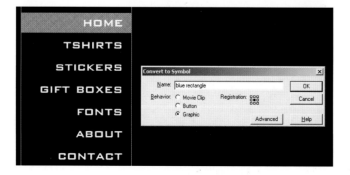

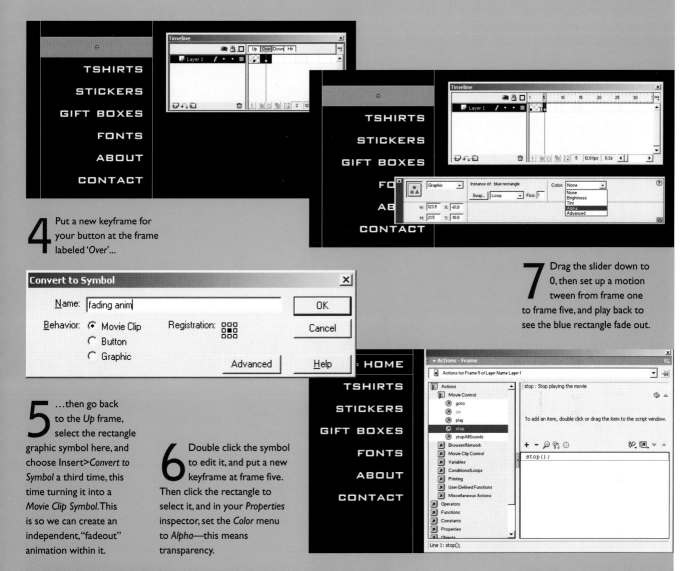

4 Put a new keyframe for your button at the frame labeled 'Over'...

7 Drag the slider down to 0, then set up a motion tween from frame one to frame five, and play back to see the blue rectangle fade out.

5 ...then go back to the *Up* frame, select the rectangle graphic symbol here, and choose Insert>*Convert to Symbol* a third time, this time turning it into a *Movie Clip Symbol*. This is so we can create an independent, "fadeout" animation within it.

6 Double click the symbol to edit it, and put a new keyframe at frame five. Then click the rectangle to select it, and in your *Properties* inspector, set the *Color* menu to *Alpha*—this means transparency.

8 The final step for this clip: click frame five to select it, then open your *Actions* palette. Here we need to add a *Stop* action, so the fade animation doesn't loop. Open the Actions>*Movie Control* folder on the left, and double click the *Stop* action to add it. Hit Control+*Enter* to test your movie—the button should be working fine for the top link. If all is well, you can move on.

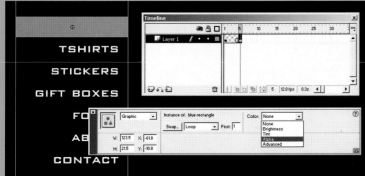

FLASH NAVIGATION 2

9 Now we just need to add this effect to all the links. Double click your stage twice to get back to the main animation area, then copy, paste, and move the blue button rectangle behind each of your links.

10 If you test your movie, you should see the effect clearly now. All you need is to add links to the buttons, then crop and export your interactive animation.

11 Select the blue button symbols one by one, and using your *Actions* palette attach an Actions> Browser/ Network/*getURL* action to each. Use the URL field to enter the Web address to which the button should link.

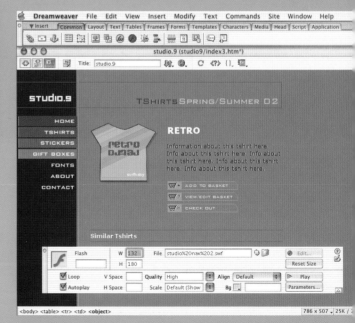

12 Finally, use the *Document Properties* to get your animation to the right dimensions, then export and embed it in your website template page.

ADDING ANOTHER EFFECT

1 To add a little extra character to our effect, we're going to combine a "retro" bubble-style effect with the fading button animation. Double click the top button, and then again on the "fade" animation movie clip (on the *Up* frame).

4 Now test your movie: you'll see shrinking circles appear in tandem with the "fade" effect.

2 On a new layer, draw a simple circle near the edge of the blue rectangle, and then turn this into a graphic symbol.

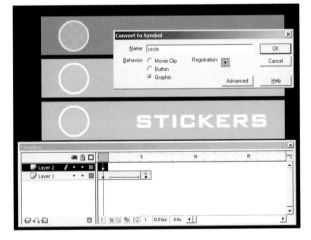

3 Create a new keyframe at frame five, and here shrink the circle symbol to a small dot. Then set up a motion tween from frame one.

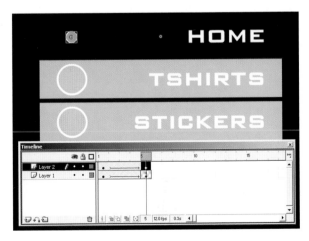

CREATING A
FLASH GALLERY

The last of our Flash projects is to create the slideshow gallery for the home page of our sample portfolio site.

An attractive feature of Flash is that, in the browser, you can dynamically load images and other animations over the top of the current animation, in the same way as HTML loads graphics files. But you can also superimpose and animate these on the fly.

Let's decide the slideshow is to include five images. To load all these at once would really slow the whole page down; but instead we can set up it up so only the appropriate image loads when your user clicks the *Back* or *Next* button to view it. We can even show a "Loading…" message so they know what's going on…

SETTING UP THE SLIDESHOW

1 First off, size and save your first image for the slideshow as a JPEG, then import this into a new Flash document. Set the size of the movie to match. At the end, we'll be loading this dynamically, but it helps to have it here while we set things up.

2 On a new layer, add in your button designs. We've put them on a semi-transparent black background, just to make sure they're readable, whatever the image. To do this, you need to make the black rectangle into a symbol first. Put your image title on a third layer.

SETTING UP THE SLIDESHOW

3 Back to the image: select this and convert it into a Movie Clip Symbol. In the registration grid here, click the top-left corner to set this as the registration point of the movie clip.

4 Then, using your *Properties* inspector, give this the name "image" in the *Instance Name* field. We'll use this name to send ActionScript commands to the clip.

5 Add new frames—not keyframes—up to frame five for all the layers. Then on the image title layer, turn all these into keyframes. On each frame, add a title as appropriate for each of your five slideshow images.

6 Before you move on, save your Flash file into a sub-directory of your website, and save the five images for your slideshow here too. Have them ready-compressed, and in JPEG format. Make sure they are exactly the same dimensions as the test image you added to your Flash file.

CREATING A
FLASH GALLERY 2

ADDING ACTIONSCRIPT

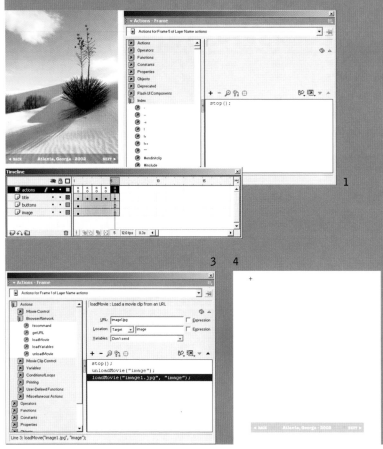

1 Back in Flash, add a new layer to your movie called "actions," and put a keyframe at each frame. We can attach actions to each of these keyframes, sending instructions to the movie clip to load a new image. But first, add a *Stop* action to each.

2 On frame one, add an Actions> Browser/Network/ *UnloadMovie* action. Change the *Location* dropdown for this to *Target*, then delete the 0 in the *Location* field next to it. Instead, type "image"—the Instance name of your movie clip. This removes any existing content from that clip.

3 After this, add a *LoadMovie* action from the same actions folder, and again set the *Location* dropdown to *Target* and type in the name of your movie clip— "image." In the *URL* field, type in the file name of your first image, including the ".jpg" ending.

4 Now double click the image movie clip to edit it, and delete the image that's in there. This might seem odd, but the image was only there for working with. In practice, we want it to load dynamically, and that's what the previous ActionScripts will achieve. Test your movie to check it works.

5 Now repeat this for each keyframe in your *Actions* layer, changing the URL of the image as appropriate.

SETTING IT IN MOTION

1 The final stage is to set up the buttons so they take us from frame to frame. Turn your two button designs into button symbols, and give them a *Rollover* style. For text buttons, it's worth putting a transparent rectangle in the background so your pointer still shows as a hand when it's over a small gap between characters.

2 For the *Back* button, add an Actions> MovieControl>*Goto Action*, and simply use the *Type* dropdown to choose the previous frame. For the *Next* button, do the same, but set it to *Next Frame*.

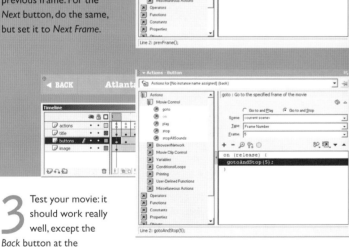

3 Test your movie: it should work really well, except the *Back* button at the beginning, and the *Next* button at the end. You need to put a keyframe at frame two of the buttons layer. At frame one, change the *Back* button's Goto action to send the animation to frame five, so it loops to the end of the movie.

4 Do the same for the *Next* button on the last frame, setting its Goto action to loop to the beginning of the movie— frame one.

5 As a final touch, add a little loading message on a layer below the image layer. Although the changeover will be very quick on your own computer, there will be a delay over the Internet as users wait for the image to download. You can preview this for yourself using the View>*Show Streaming* command when you test your movie.

6 Here are the final frames from the slideshow.

With the increasing uptake of broadband communications, it's not just animation that's bringing the Web to life. Video, sound, and music add extra dimensions to the online experience, and careful use of these mediums can bring an extra touch of class to your website—with a little imagination and knowhow

6

SOUND & VIDEO

WHY USE SOUND & VIDEO?

SOME SAY THAT SOON WE WILL BE ABLE TO WATCH FULL-SCREEN, FULL-RESOLUTION, FEATURE-LENGTH MOVIES STREAMING AT 24 FRAMES PER SECOND OVER THE INTERNET. THIS MAY BE TRUE, BUT FOR THE MOMENT IT IS MORE THAN A LITTLE AMBITIOUS!

Show off your travel clips—here's a Windows Media clip from Verona, to go with an article on the ItaliaGusto site. News sites like the BBC (*www.bbc.co.uk*) and Discovery (*www.discovery.com*) have made a feature of clips like this.

on a financial backer, a producer, or a distributor. Equally, small companies, magazine sites, and even hobbyists who would previously have considered video inaccessible, can now benefit immensely from a little multimedia razzmatazz in their online presence. This is particularly true since digital video, music, and sound-processing hardware is getting more affordable all the time. Our Mango World Music site could offer album sound clips as a teaser, along with snippets of interviews with artists and live performances.

Less obvious, but no less valuable in terms of generating traffic, ItaliaGusto can give users brief TV-style cooking movie clips, or moving pictures from Rome, Verona, and Venice. Studio.9 can show people wearing their Tshirts, while your portfolio could include a clip of yourself at work.

There are subtler ways you can use sound and video as well. Flash sites, in particular, often use sound effects alongside interactive features, in just the same way your computer beeps at you when you click in the wrong place, or boot up. Others opt for a constant, ambient backing track to provide additional atmosphere and branding. And if you're creating a story-based animation, then sound is essential.

High-speed Internet access and cheaper phone calls—not to mention increasingly sophisticated delivery technologies—mean sound and video can come into their own on the Web. If you are in any doubt about this, stop by *www.atomfilms.com* and see.

The appeal is twofold. On the one hand, for budding musicians, filmmakers, and multimedia artists, the Web offers a powerful, inexpensive means to get your work to a global audience, where other people can share it, and where you don't need to rely

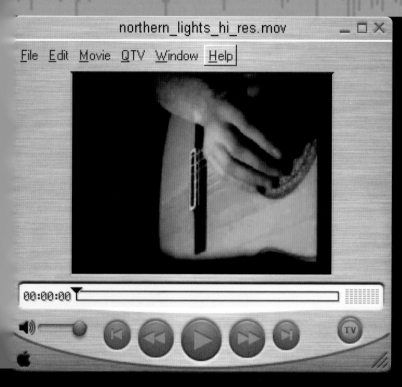

northern_lights_hi_res.mov

File　Edit　Movie　QTV　Window　Help

00:00:00

We can also use a visual interface format to present a range of MP3 preview clips, which users can check out as a taster before they buy an album.

Here we've created an exciting graphical interface in Flash for showing off Mango movie clips. We'll do this project step by step at the end of the chapter.

For Mango World Music we can show QuickTime clips of artists live in concert, or interviews. These are lengthy, so they've got to be well compressed!

MANGOMP3

ARTIST››	TRACK
Joey Bluegrass	Way Out West
Joey Bluegrass	Way Out West
Joey Bluegrass	**Way Out West**
Joey Bluegrass	Way Out West
Joey Bluegrass	Way Out West
Joey Bluegrass	Way Out West
Joey Bluegrass	Way Out West

▶ PLAY　■ STOP　◀◀ REWIND

One of Joey's own all-time favourite tracks, 'Way Out West' combines the best of old-school American blues with a bouncy west coast country melody.

MANGO HOME　　　MORE MP3S

Macromedia Flash Player 6

File　View　Control　Help

MANGOMOVIE

PLAY　STOP　REWIND

ARTIST: JOEY BLUEGRASS

ALBUM: LIVE IN DALLAS

TRACK: WAY OUT WEST

CREATING SOUND & VIDEO

OF COURSE, BEFORE YOU CAN PUT SOUND OR VIDEO ON YOUR WEBSITE, YOU NEED SOME SOURCE MATERIAL. THIS COULD EITHER BE RECORDED FROM THE REAL WORLD (WHICH MEANS YOU NEED TO TRANSFER THE SOUNDS ONTO YOUR COMPUTER SOMEHOW); MATERIAL CREATED DIRECTLY ON YOUR COMPUTER; OR A MIXTURE OF THE TWO.

SOFTWARE GUIDE

Most music today is created and/or prepared using a computer or some other form of digital recording technique, so in the case of Mango World Music we already have the sound files we need. But if you don't, you simply need to plug a sound source into the In jack of your sound card, and use some recording software to convert and save it as a digital file.

Video is more complex. If you want to transfer footage from a camera to your computer, you're best off using a digital video camera together with a Firewire port for plugging it in. This offers an extremely high data transfer rate—which you need, because video files can be very, very large. You also need software to handle the transfer process, and then edit your raw material into a meaningful story. Remember, short is good, so you should aim to make your point in a scene or message quickly, then move on.

If you're originating video on your computer, this might be in the form of 3D animation. For 2D animation and showy effects sequences, consider using Flash instead—it's much less burdensome to download. Nevertheless, there are a number of tools out there offering moving picture design and effects, which you can use with a blank canvas, or—more likely—to enhance existing video material.

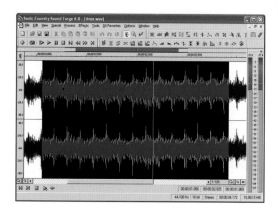

RECORDING AND EDITING SOUND

There are plenty of good apps for recording and editing sound, and they're not too expensive. Try SoundForge (*www.sonicfoundry.com*) or CoolEdit (*www.cooledit.com*) for starters on the PC, or Cakewalk Metro SE for the Mac (*www.cakewalk.com*). These include all the tools you need to digitize audio, edit your recordings, and prepare samples, as well as basic effects.

SOFTWARE GUIDE

CREATING SOUND

A great deal of music today is created entirely within computers, and there are literally hundreds of apps out there to help you. For synthesizing sounds, take a look at ReBirth (*www.propeller heads.se*), which emulates the legendary and influential Roland 303 drum machine; or Acid (*www.sonicfoundry.com*) for working with samples.

THE NEXT STEP...

The more serious sound designer will want to get hold of a complete MIDI and audio sequencing and effects system, like Logic Audio (*www.emagic.de*) or Cubase (*www.steinberg.net*). These can integrate with external keyboards, synthesizers, and other sound equipment, and form the basis of many modern sound recording studios.

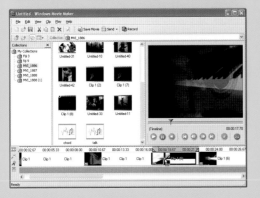

RECORDING AND EDITING VIDEO

Getting footage onto your computer in manageable portions, and then paring it down into a succinct storyline is quite a task. Windows MovieMaker (pictured) and Apple iMovie are fine for basic work, while Discreet's Cinestream (*www.discreet.com*) is a more powerful option for beginners, and Adobe Premiere is ideal for more serious work (*www.adobe.com*).

CREATING VIDEO AND ADDING EFFECTS

Many animation apps offer export to video formats, including Flash, Photo-Paint, and so on, although the value of this may be limited. 3D animation tends to benefit from using a video format; if you're interested in this, good starting tools include Vue d'Esprit (*www.eonsoftware.com*) and Cinema 4D (*www.cinema4d.com*). Many editing tools include simple 2D video effects; if you want to step it up, give Adobe's After Effects (*www.adobe.com*) a whirl.

PREPARING MEDIA FOR THE WEB

Once you've completed your sound or video masterpiece, you need to prepare it for the Web, which we'll look at over the page. Windows Movie Maker and Apple iMovie include basic tools for this, but for more involved work you'll need to invest in the detailed controls offered by Discreet's Cleaner (*www.discreet.com*), RealSystem (*www.real.com*), or similar. Macromedia Flash also offers excellent support for sound and video.

PREPARING SOUND & VIDEO FOR THE WEB

THE WEB IS A WORLD OF CONSTRAINTS, AND NEVER MORE SO THAN WITH SOUND AND VIDEO. YOUR SINGLE BIGGEST PROBLEM HERE IS FILE SIZE: THESE MEDIA EAT UP AN AWFUL LOT OF BYTES— JUST A FEW SECONDS OF WEB-PREPARED VIDEO CAN EASILY CLOCK INTO MEGABYTES—SO YOU'VE GOT TO MAKE THE PAYBACK GOOD. BUT THERE ARE A NUMBER OF TECHNIQUES YOU CAN USE TO CUT DOWN THE TIME LAG FROM WHEN YOUR VIEWER CLICKS ON AS VIDEO LINK TO WHEN THEY ACTUALLY SEE SOMETHING HAPPEN ONSCREEN.

The single quickest way to reduce the size of a video file is to reduce the size of the video itself, both in dimensions and length. You can also dramatically cut down on kilobytes by reducing the frame rate of your video: 12 frames per second means half the number of images as 24 frames per second.

As with graphics, you need to compress video for the Web. The tools and techniques to do this offer you the same straight trade-off between file size and quality. There are a number of formats you can use for this, and different compression methods that you can use within these, which are known as codecs. Just as with choosing between GIF and JPEG for static images, you should choose the codec that is most appropriate for the nature of your video.

All the popular video formats now support streaming, which, like Flash, means the file can begin to play before it has finished loading. You can take advantage of this by using a very simple, fast-loading introductory scene at the beginning of your movie clip, so at least your viewers have something to look at almost immediately.

In the end, your choice of format for video is going to hinge on this: do you have the software to create and deliver it? And do the majority of your users have the technology installed to view it? You should always offer a link for viewers to download what they

need, but many simply won't bother. The standard Microsoft Media Player is, of course, the most widely installed media player out there, and supports all the popular formats (although not always the latest versions of them).

PLAYERS, PLUGINS, AND MEDIA FILES

All sound and video files need a player or browser plugin to play back on. If you have the player, you usually also have the plugin, and vice-versa. Most Windows users will automatically have Windows Media Player installed; while most versions of MacOS include the QuickTime player. Both are also available for their "opposite" platforms—see *www.microsoft.com* and *www.quicktime.com*.

There are other players and plugins you can download for free, including RealPlayer (*www.real.com*), and Flash Player (*www.macromedia.com*).

Increasingly, these players are offering cross-format support, so, for example, you can view Real files through the Windows Media Player. However, you'll hit problems if you're using new or earlier incompatible versions of any of these formats. But it's not just about you: aim to ensure that most of your users can view your multimedia. And for those that can't, offer links to download the technology they need.

GUIDE TO FILE FORMATS

Audio   Real   Windows Media   Flash   QuickTime

SOUND-ONLY FORMATS

MP3

Famous for taking the music industry by surprise, MP3 is now the definitive format for music on the Web. It's the audio-only version of MPEG, and offers good sound quality with small file sizes. You can also compress it massively, while the audio remains acceptable for the Web. *http://mpeg.telecomitalialab.com*

WAV, AU, AIFF

WAV is the traditional Windows audio file format, used for music samples and recordings, computer beeps and noises, and so on. It's ideal for storing and working on high quality sound, but the file sizes are high, and compressed WAV sounds terrible, so it's not good for Web delivery. AU and AIFF are similar formats. *www.microsoft.com, www.sun.com,* and *www.apple.com*

MIDI

MIDI is to WAV as vector graphics are to bitmaps. It doesn't contain actual sound information, but instructions to a synthesizer or any MIDI device on what note to play, using what voice, on what MIDI channel, plus a host of more subtle instructions. Most soundcards include a basic MIDI synthesizer, called a Wavetable, which generates the sound. As an instruction set and interface, MIDI is very fast loading. But results vary according to the user's soundcard. *www.midi.org*

SKD

Sseyo Koan Design. A format used by "generative" music software Koan. Like MIDI, Koan files contain instructions to the computer's soundcard, and are therefore very small. Generative software creates music "on the fly," according to parameters set by the "composer." The Koan engine can also drive "generative" Flash animations via a plugin. *www.sseyo.com*

VIDEO AND SOUND FILE FORMATS

Windows Media

This is the new, standard Microsoft format for streaming video, usually with the ending WMV, or WMA for audio-only. Naturally, it's particularly effective for delivering to

Windows, and integrates well with the standard Windows Media Player. It's a good option for low-bandwidth, or modem delivery. *www.microsoft.com*

QuickTime

The QuickTime MOV format's forte is in high-quality, broadband streaming, and has become especially popular with the film industry. You can stream it from an ordinary Web server, or use a QuickTime server for advanced controls. *www.apple.com*

Real

The streaming Real format is one of the most popular on the Web, and especially where sound is important. Files usually have the RM ending, for RealMedia, although you may come across RV for RealVideo, RA for RealAudio, and others. The formats offer good picture and sound quality in return for small file sizes. You need to be conscious that a lower proportion of users will have the RealPlayer installed compared to the Windows Media Player. *www.real.com*

Flash

The Flash SWF format has full support for MP3 sound, and in version 6, video too. It has far more advanced interactive capabilities than the other formats here, and the Flash plugin is so common as to make this a no-brainer if you're already using Flash. *www.macromedia.com*

MPEG

Standing for Moving Picture Experts Groups, MPEG comprises a variety of formats, ideal for anything from DVD to Web delivery. These include MP3, which is used for sound, and MPEG-4, on which Microsoft's Windows Media format is based. *http://mpeg.telecomitalialab.com*

AVI

Microsoft's Audio Video Interleave is a popular format for storing video at medium to high quality. It used to be common on the Web, but has now been replaced by Windows Media. *www.microsoft.com*

DV

This is the standard format used by Digital Video cameras. It's not designed for use on the Web: use DV to edit and store footage, then export your movie to another format for streaming. A good reference is hard to come by, but try *www.dvcentral.org.*

TIPS FOR CREATING VIDEO

When you're creating video for use on the Web, consider carefully how well it's going to work in context. Streaming video is small, short, and highly compressed, which means subtleties are lost. Be obvious about your subject; use strong, clear lighting, and shoot closer up than you would normally. If you are using actors, encourage them to be obvious in their actions and expressions. But most importantly, get your message across quickly. Web surfers aren't as patient as movie audiences.

BASIC EDITING

1 Before you prepare video footage for the Web, you'll need to edit it down to capture the best moments, or tell a meaningful story. To do this you need software with video editing tools—see page 149 for some pointers. Windows Movie Maker, pictured, is an easy place to begin. We're creating a short "gig-and-interview" video for the Mango Site.

2 Begin by importing your raw materials— video clips, sound files, images, and so on. Windows automatically splits video files into clips wherever there is a sudden change in the picture; or you can do this yourself, using the Split button.

3 You can also record material directly— use this to transfer footage from a video camera, or record sound for your video.

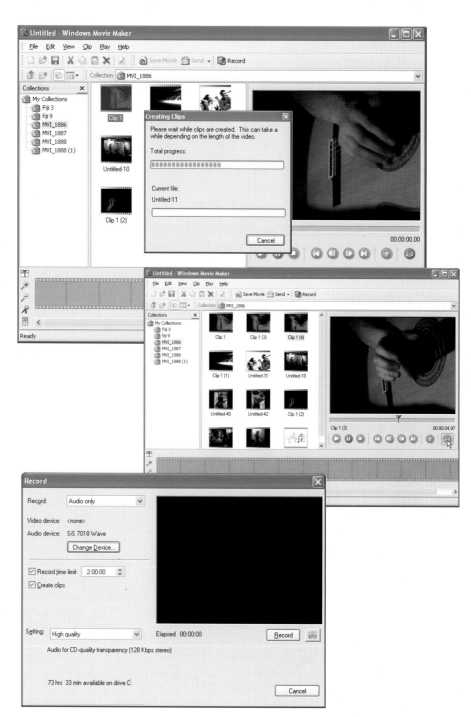

BASIC EDITING

4 You build your video using the storyboard at the bottom. Just drag the media clips in, change their order, and so on. We're cutting between live concert and interview footage.

5 Switching to the *Timeline* view, you can precisely control the start and end points of individual clips, and add in sound files, for narration or a backing track.

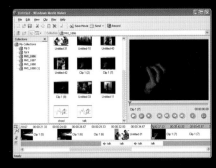

6 Zooming in to the timeline, you can add smooth, fading transitions between clips, for extra effect. You just grab the second clip, or it's trimming points, and overlap it with the first. Use the *Play* menu to preview your movie.

7 Finally, choose *Save Movie* to export your final file. Windows Movie Maker includes optimization tools for the Windows Media format—just select one of the presets from the menu (*Low* is best for most Web video), and the software will handle resizing, frame rate, compression etc.

8 The *Other* setting in your *Save Movie* dialog allows more specific choices. Use this if you want to compress your video using other software—perhaps because you want a different delivery format. In this case, choose one of the high quality DV-AVI settings in the *Profile* menu.

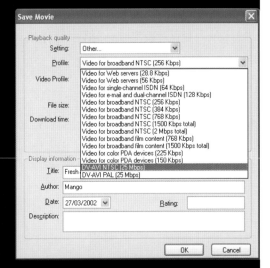

ADDING VIDEO TO A WEBPAGE

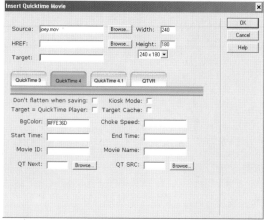

1 There are two ways of giving users access to your online videos. The easiest is to link to the video file, as if it were another webpage or a download. As long as your user has a compatible player installed, this will automatically open and begin to play.

3 To do this, you need to use an embedded plug-in object. Dreamweaver and GoLive include these for some formats (look in your toolbox), and you can download others from their respective websites. We'll deal with extending your software in this way in the next chapter.

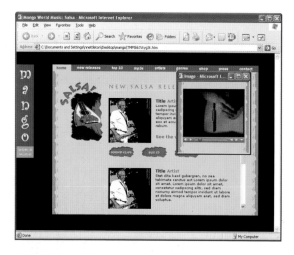

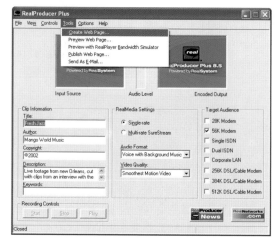

2 You may prefer to show the video within your own webpage, however. This is called an embedded, or inline, video. This gives viewers less control over how they see the work, but you can present it within a branded interface, serve advertising, and so on.

4 Some Web video apps will automatically create the basic HTML for you, including RealProducer and Cleaner, which we're going to look at next…

REALMEDIA & REALPRODUCER

1 RealMedia is an excellent alternative to Windows Media for fast-streaming video, and offers excellent sound quality. Real's dedicated tool for this, RealProducer, is a breeze to use, and offers more in-depth settings than Movie Maker, although it only has basic editing features. You can even serve live broadcasts, using its startup wizard.

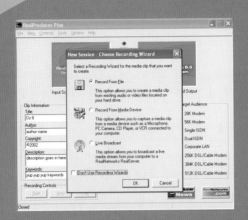

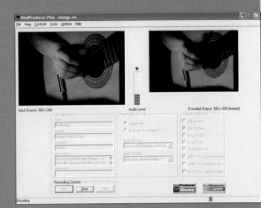

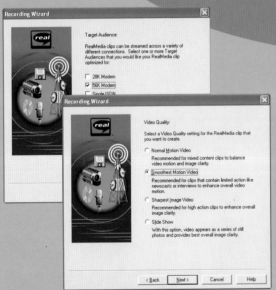

3 In the main window, you can now check your settings, then hit *Start* to create a Real file ready for the Web, and watch its progress.

4 Using the *Create Web Page* option in the *Tools* menu, you can have RealProducer automatically create a webpage linking to or embedding your RealMedia movie…

2 Using the *Record From File* option, you can import a finished movie clip for converting to Real format. The wizards take you through a number of screens where you can select easy options that are appropriate to your video. For the Mango piece, we put an emphasis on strong sound and smooth images with low action.

5 To transfer this into a page using your website design template, just copy the HTML from the <! HTML INSERT BEGIN /!> tag to <! HTML INSERT END /!>, and paste this into your own page code.

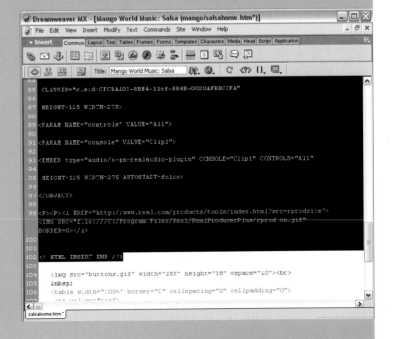

DISCREET CLEANER

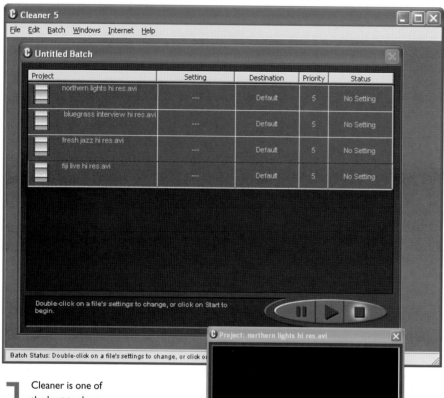

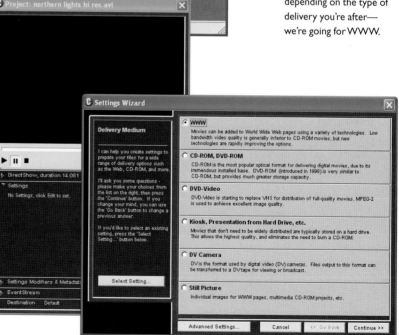

2 After dragging your source clips into the *Batch* window, double click on the first clip, and in the *Preview* window that then opens, click the *Edit* button under *Settings*. This opens a wizard with a range of options depending on the type of delivery you're after— we're going for WWW.

1 Cleaner is one of the best tools on the market for preparing Web video, and it's used by professionals and amateurs alike. You can use it to create Windows Media, Real, and QuickTime content. The software combines in-depth settings with excellent compression standards. But most importantly, it enables you to make compression settings for a number of video clips, then leave it to do the job while you get on with something else.

DISCREET CLEANER

3 Cleaner's wizard is much more detailed than RealProducer—after choosing the format you want, you can make decisions about streaming, sound and picture quality, smoothness of motion, and so on. Note that you need to make sure your server is going to work with the streaming option you choose—advanced streaming features usually need a dedicated server to work properly.

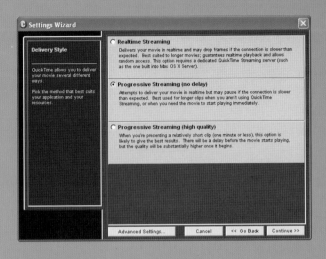

4 This done, using the *Edit* button under the *Settings* tab of your preview window, you can adjust lighting, cropping, and other features of the video image, rather like in Photoshop. Choose Windows>*Dynamic Preview* to get a split "before and after" view of your clip.

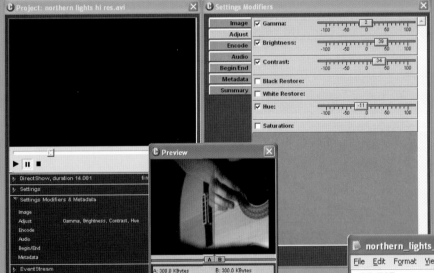

5 Once you're happy with all your settings, just click the *Play* button at the bottom of the *Batch* window, and Cleaner will get to work on the clips. You can watch the progress in a monitor window, while you grab a coffee. Cleaner will make a record or a log of any errors if things go wrong.

6 Cleaner automatically creates the HTML to display your videos—just copy and paste it into a webpage in your site.

```
<OBJECT
CLASSID="clsid:02BF25D5-8C17-4B23-BC80-D3488ABDDC6B"
WIDTH="240" HEIGHT="196"
CODEBASE="http://www.apple.com/qtactivex/qtplugin.cab">
<PARAM NAME="src" VALUE="northern_lights_hi_res.mov">
<PARAM NAME="autoplay" VALUE="true">
<PARAM NAME="controller" VALUE="true">
<PARAM NAME="loop" VALUE="false">
<EMBED SRC="northern_lights_hi_res.mov" WIDTH=240
HEIGHT=196 AUTOPLAY=true CONTROLLER=true LOOP=false
PLUGINSPAGE="http://www.apple.com/quicktime/">
</EMBED>
</OBJECT>
```

SOUND & VIDEO
WITH FLASH

FLASH INCLUDES EXCELLENT SUPPORT FOR MP3 SOUND, AND VIDEO FROM FLASH MX. IT OFFERS ONE OF THE EASIEST—AND MOST OVERLOOKED—WAYS TO GET THESE MEDIA ONTO YOUR SITE. AND BECAUSE THE SOUND AND VIDEO INTEGRATE SEAMLESSLY WITH FLASH GRAPHICS AND INTERACTIVE FEATURES, YOU CAN VAMP IT UP WITH CUSTOM INTERFACE FEATURES TO MATCH YOUR SITE DESIGN, OR ADD YOUR OWN HAND-DRAWN ANIMATIONS, ROGER RABBIT-STYLE!

ONE SHOTS

You'll need to edit and prepare your sound and/or video first. In particular, you should top and tail sound files to remove silent time. Then save it uncompressed in a common format supported by Flash (AVI, QuickTime, WAV, and so on—there are plenty of them). Flash includes the compression features you need.

Now you can import your sound or video file into Flash, in the same way as you import bitmap graphics, and place it on the timeline.

We'll do three quick Flash projects here. First, we simply add incidental sounds that play when you click buttons in a navigation. In the second, we'll create an MP3 player, where users can select a track and click a *Play* button to hear it. In the third, we'll look at using video.

1 You can't edit sound in Flash, so you need to do this first using SoundForge or similar (see page 147). Edit out silences at either end of the file, then save it in uncompressed MP3 or WAV format. Flash includes the compression tools you need. It's not a good idea to recompress media!

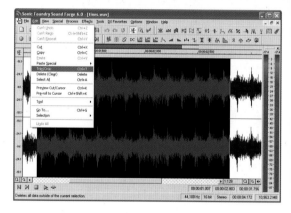

2 We've created some simple sound effects for the buttons on the Studio.9 navigation bar. This comprises a series of buttons, which are all exactly the same (they're different "instances" of the same symbol). In Flash this means that by changing one, we can change them all (the button labels are superimposed). Begin by importing the sound files, using File>*Import*.

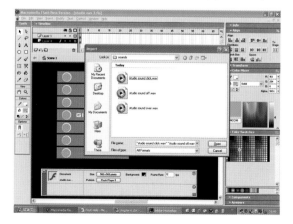

ONE SHOTS

3 Your sound object will then appear in the *Library*, which you can open from the *Window* menu. You can drag things from here to your workspace, to add them to your Flash movie.

4 But here we want to add sounds to the button events, so double click one of the buttons to edit the symbol, and add a new layer in the timeline, called "sounds."

6 Add keyframes to the "over" and "down" frames for the button, and set up sounds for each of these in the same way…

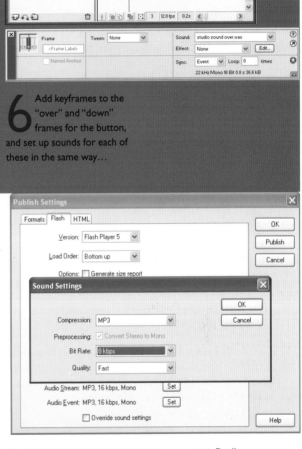

5 Select the first frame of this layer, then use the *Properties* inspector to select a mouseout sound effect for this frame. Set *Sync* to *Event*—this is suitable for a movie that must complete after it's begun, regardless of other changes. You can have several instances of an event sound playing at once.

7 Finally, use File>*Publish Settings* and go to the *Flash* tab to choose compression settings for event sounds— MP3 is a good bet. Test your Flash movie using Control>*Test Movie*.

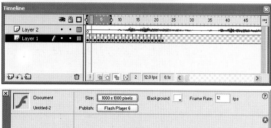

1 Event sounds have to download completely before they begin to play. If you want to use extended backing music—say for an intro sequence—or record an animated character's voice, streaming sound is a better bet—it can begin to play after just a few frames' worth have loaded. If the movie stops, the sound stops too, and animation is forced to synchronize with it as it plays.

2 For sounds that you want to start and stop at particular frames or user events, use the *Start* and *Stop Sync* settings in the *Properties* inspector. You can have only one instance of a particular sound playing at once with this setting.

3 Sound synchronized in this way has to load completely before it begins to play. But as a major advantage, you can use the loop option with short stretches of music—2 bars, say—to create a continuous backing track that has a very small file size. Avoid looping streaming sounds, because this increases the file size.

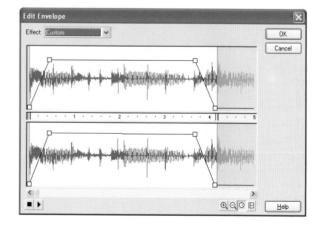

4 Using the *Effect Edit* button, you can adjust the volume and balance of sounds, to add fading, variety, or to match a sound stereophonically to the position of its apparent source in your animation.

VIDEO IN FLASH

1 The advantage of using Flash for your video is that you can easily create your own playback interface, and, providing you have Flash MX, add interactive features as part of the presentation. Here's a simple design for presenting movies on the Mango World Music site, which we've created in Flash. The viewport is a "hole" in the interface, with a dummy image behind it, where we'll put the movie clip.

3 Don't add extra keyframes if asked, but instead, when the movie has completed importing, turn it into a movie clip symbol, this time adding the required frames.

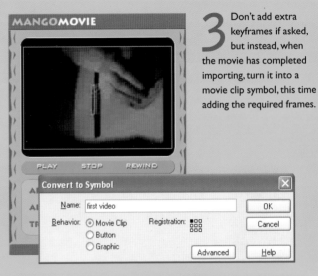

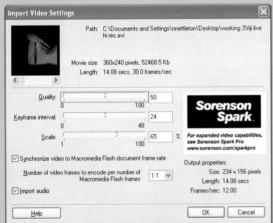

2 As with sound, you need to edit your video beforehand, and save it uncompressed, then import it into Flash using File>Import. The Import dialog gives you several options, including quality and scaling for the movie. Adjust these as best you can—you may need to practice a few times— then hit OK.

4 The symbol should open automatically— if not double click to edit it. Add a new layer called "actions," and on the first frame add a "stop" action. Turn the last frame into a keyframe too, and here add a "goto" action, sending the clip back to frame 1.

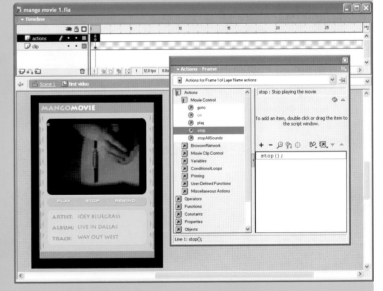

5 Double click the workspace to go back to your main movie, and here use the *Properties* inspector to give the video symbol the instance name "video"— this is important for the control buttons.

VIDEO IN FLASH 2

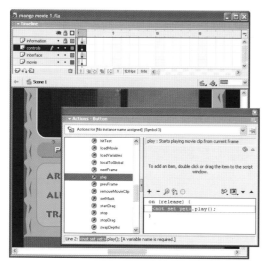

8 This opens a dialog listing your named movie clip instances—select the one that contains your imported video, then hit *OK*. You've built a simple command that tells that clip to start playing when you click the *Play* button.

9 Now do the same for the *Stop* button, but use the Objects> Movie>MovieClip>Methods >*stopAction* instead; and for the *Rewind* button, use the Objects>Movie>MovieClip >Methods>*gotoAndStop*, putting "1" in the Parameters box, meaning frame one—the beginning of the video.

6 If you haven't already, turn your control graphics into button symbols, then select the *Play* button, and open your *Actions Editor*. In the tree menu on the left, browse to the folder Objects>Movie>MovieClip>*Methods*, and in here, double click the *Play* action.

10 Finally, test your movie in the usual way, then publish and add it to a webpage…

7 The *Editor* will automatically add the "on release" event we need; select the middle line, and put your pointer in the *Object* box above, and click the *Target* icon just above the code window.

Now we've covered the basics of good planning, design, and functionality, plus the technologies you need to make it all work, you're probably ambitious to get ahead. So, in the final sections of the book, we're going to look at how you—the power user—can really give your Internet presence that professional boost. And once we've done that, we're going to examine some of the ways you can aim to make money online. If you want to avoid the mistakes of the dot-com crash, and bring in revenue from minimal expenditure, you'd better read on!

So far we've covered both the basics of website building and design. And some of the elements that bring color and movement to the online experience. But what are the intermediate elements that encourage visitors to interact with your site, as opposed to just sit back and be entertained?

THE POWER USER'S TOOLBOX

FORMS →
GETTING USERS TO JOIN IN

ONE OF THE MOST POWERFUL ASPECTS OF THE INTERNET IS THE MECHANISMS IT OFFERS FOR PEOPLE TO INTERACT WITH ONE ANOTHER, AS WELL AS WITH THE GRAPHICS AND INFORMATION THEY SEE ON A PAGE. WITH ALMOST ANY WEBSITE YOU CREATE, AT SOME POINT YOU WILL WANT TO ADD FEATURES LIKE THIS—FOR INSTANCE TO GET FEEDBACK ON YOUR WEBSITE, OR ENABLE USERS TO SIGN UP FOR A MAILING LIST. THE SIMPLEST WAY TO ACHIEVE THIS IS USING A FORM.

Forms are a special area of HTML that offer the designer a range of interface elements like text fields, dropdown menus, and file upload fields. These enable the user to turn the ordinary flow of information on its head: when they click the "submit" button at the bottom, the data gets sent back over the phone line, via their connection server and to the hosting server. What happens to it here depends on the instructions in the form.

Usually, the data needs to be dealt with by a server-side script. This is a piece of code, like a mini program, which lives and works on the server (at no point does your user need to download it). The script contains commands for dealing with information sent from a form. This will usually have an ending like .cgi, .asp, or .php and it's the address of this file that you provide in the HTML of the form.

Server-side scripts can be used to do almost anything. In connection with forms, they are often used to send an email containing the form data, which is ideal for small feedback operations; adding information to a database; for use as an automated guestbook; or to pull information out of a database and put it in a webpage. Search engines are the obvious example of this.

More sophisticated user-oriented features like the last two can be incredibly complex and time-consuming to create, and you're not likely to do this yourself. But most Web-hosting companies offer at least a couple of prefabricated server-side scripts, which you can use to create simple, interactive features at the drop of hat (or, rather, the click of a mouse). All you need to know is the address of the file and any special HTML requirements for the form.

FORM BASICS

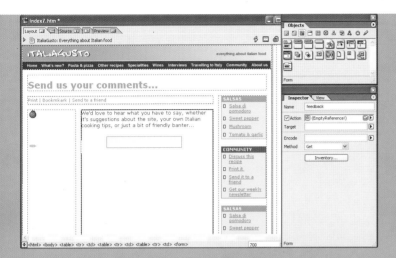

1 Here's the starting point for a simple feedback form on the ItaliaGusto website. The first part of any form is the `<form>` tag itself, which marks the beginning of your Web form, and `</form>`, which marks the end. Some software adds this automatically, but do check because it's important. This tag includes settings for a name, action, and method. Give your form a sensible name without spaces, dots, or unusual characters.

2 The *Action* is the address of the server-side script that will deal with the data, while the *Method* setting controls how the data is sent over the Internet—either GET or POST. Sometimes this doesn't matter, but check to make sure. You will usually find a list of scripts available to you on your Web host's site, together with the details you need and some instructions.

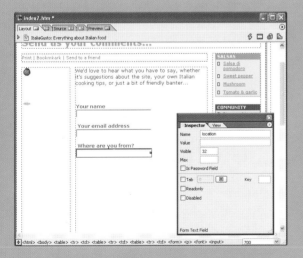

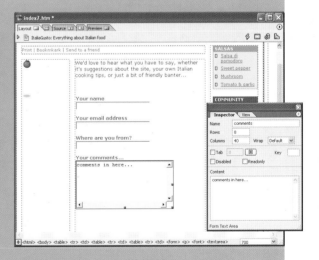

3 All other elements of your form need to go between the `<form>` and `</form>` tags. The most obvious is the simple text field, where users can type their name, email address, or whatever you request. You can use the size settings and your normal font properties to control how it appears—but beware, things can look very different depending on the browser. As with the form itself, you should give each element a different name, and avoid spaces, dots, and special characters.

4 For longer text, like a message, use the multiline text area element. In Dreamweaver, you use an ordinary text field and set it to *Multi Line*. In GoLive, pictured, use the *Text Area* object.

FORM BASICS//2

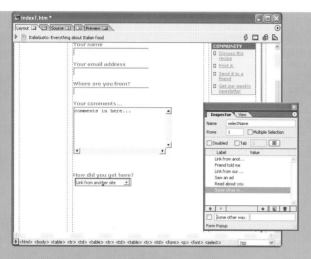

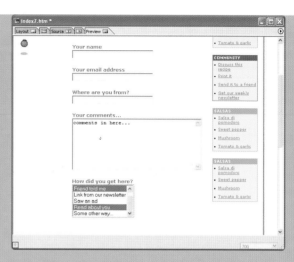

5 The *Select* element—a popup or dropdown menu— is a great addition to any form where you want to offer one of a number of options.

6 Alternatively, you can offer a multiline list box, where users scroll through the options and use *Control* or *Shift* to make multiple selections.

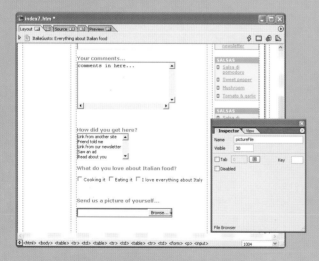

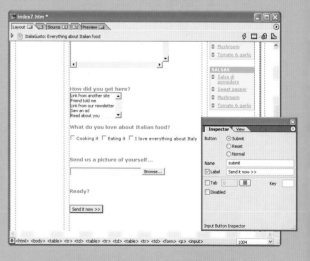

9 Another useful element in forms is the file upload field, but you need to check if this will work with your Web host—many disable these because of the risk of viruses. Where enabled, this allows your user to select a file from their computer and send it to you or upload it to a database.

10 Finally, and most importantly, your form needs a *Submit* button: when your user presses it, the information from the form is sent to the server-side script named in the form's action. You can use the standard *Submit* button, giving it your own label…

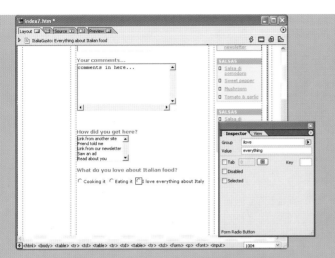

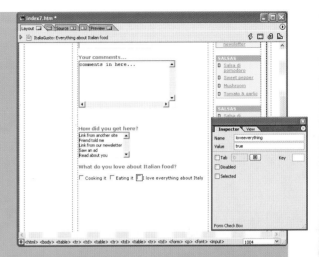

7 If you have just a couple of options from which you'd like users to choose, consider using radio buttons instead. Give the same name to all your radio buttons in the same group, and use the value setting to change the meaning of each button. Add a label for the button as normal text next to the button.

8 With radio buttons, your user must choose one, and only one, option. Checkboxes, on the other hand, allow multiple choices, or none at all. With these, you should give each checkbox a different name.

11 Or you can use your own graphic. For this to work, you need to use the *Input Image* element, and not the normal image object. It works in much the same way, but the HTML code is different, and you don't need to give it a link—this is already given in your form tag. You might also want to add a *Reset* button, which simply clears all the form entries.

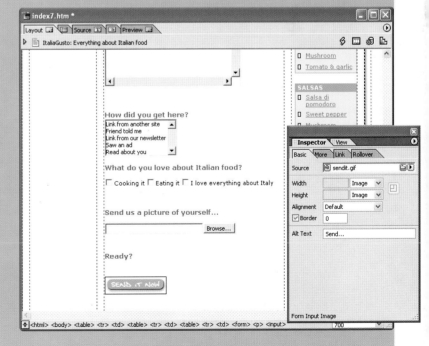

DESIGNING A FORM

One of the main difficulties with forms is getting them to look attractive on the page, not to mention making them easy to use. Often the spacing is awkward, and you may get some nasty surprises when you take a look at your work on another platform or browser. Here you can compare the same page in Internet Explorer 6 and Netscape 4.

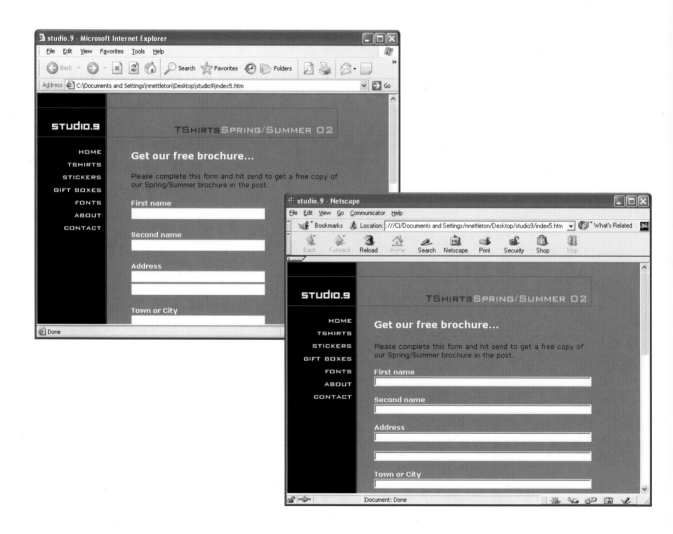

STEP BY STEP

3 You should aim to make form fields' sizes roughly match the amount of content you expect to go in them. If there are a number of short items, try using nested tables to put related fields next to each horizontally.

1 The first solution is to put the whole lot in a table within the form tags, using a new row for each item or group of items in your form. This gives you much better control over the spacing.

4 If your form is quite long, consider breaking the fields up into several groups, and adding a big, clear heading at the top of each. Don't be afraid to include instructions or short explanations of why you're asking for a particular bit of information. (Put yourself in the visitor's shoes!)

2 Try using a two-column table with all the labels on the left, and the form fields on the right. Then align all the labels to the right. Now you have an attractive, shorter layout with a central point of alignment, which makes it much easier for the visitor to use.

5 If you are asking for someone's personal details, such as their email address, you need to be aware of their privacy and your legal obligations. Include a clear statement of what you will and won't do with their information, and offer an opt-in or opt-out box for anyone who would prefer not to be contacted by you or your associates.

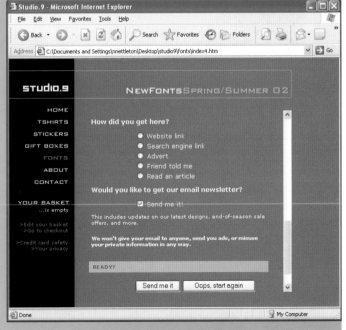

THE JUMP MENU

1 One feature you can offer with forms, which has nothing to do with user communication, is the jump menu. It's a simple dropdown menu with a list of items on your site; when a user clicks on one of these, it takes them to that item. This is just like a list of links, but here you can squeeze a lot of options into a small space, which makes it ideal for a site index, or a complete list of your products.

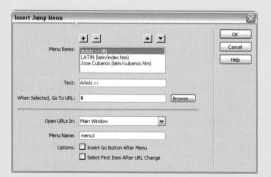

2 Dreamweaver and GoLive have easy objects from which you can create *Go* menus. In Dreamweaver, use the *Jump Menu* object in the *Forms* section of your toolbox. Then just add in your menu items; if you have an entry that you don't want to behave as a link, just type "#" instead of a URL.

3 In GoLive, you need to use the *URL* popup in the *Smart Objects* section of your toolbox. In the *Inspector* palette, you can then add in your various options.

4 If you want to do this by hand, start by adding an ordinary *Select* (popup) menu form element to your webpage, then add in the entries you want to appear. For each entry, put the address it should link to as the value.

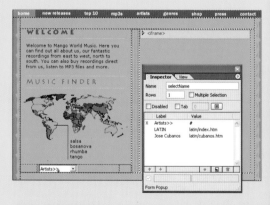

5 Then open the code, and where you see "<select … >," type this before the closing ">": onchange=' location.href=this.options[this. selectedIndex].value"

Be sure to get the capital I in "selectedIndex," and that's all there is to it!

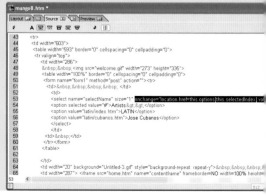

A SITE SEARCH

1 Creating your own effective site search is quite a task, and should not be undertaken lightly. We'll take a look at what you'd need for this later on in this chapter; but an excellent alternative is Google's search engine (*www.google.com*, pictured). You can adapt this and use it on your site for free, in return for hosting advertising—or pay a little for no ads.

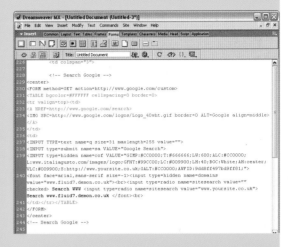

3 At the end of the registration process, you get a number of lines of copy-and-paste HTML code which you simply add to your site where you want the search box to go. If you want this to appear on every page, it's probably best to set it up as a *Library* item.

4 And here's the finished result—much quicker and less expensive than trying to create your own search engine!

2 You can get details of the various programs available at *www.google.com/services*—we're going for the Free Search option. You will need to get your site online and indexed by Google first (see our tips for search engines in the next chapter), and then sign up for the program. As part of this, you can customize the colors of the results page Google creates. Don't forget to include your own logo.

USING STYLE SHEETS

THE SECOND TOOL IN OUR POWER USERS' TOOLBOX IS CALLED CSS, OR CASCADING STYLE SHEETS. BY WAY OF INTRODUCTION, STYLE SHEETS HAVE BEEN USED FOR CENTURIES IN DESIGN, AS A WAY OF SETTING DOWN HOW A PARTICULAR BOOK OR SERIES OF PAMPHLETS SHOULD LOOK. WHAT FONTS AND COLORS DO THEY USE? WHAT ARE THE SPACING, MARGINS, AND COLUMN SIZES LIKE? AND SO ON.

stylesheet.css

More recently, style sheets were introduced into some design software—especially DTP—as a way of laying down rules that you could quickly apply to different parts of the design. For instance, you might have the rule "Heading 3 means 18 point bold type in red Helvetica, with a 9 point space beneath it." Now whenever you have a heading that you want to appear in that style, you just select it and set it to Heading 3. No need to run through all those settings over and over again.

Moreover, if you later decide all your Heading 3 headings should be blue, and not red, the theory is you can just go back to your style sheet and make the change there. All the headings in your document update accordingly.

FAST WORKING, EASY TO UPDATE

CSS, the Web designer's equivalent, works in much the same way. As with library items and templates, you can put all the style rules for your site in a single, separate file. Then when you decide to change something, it reflects site-wide, and that makes it easy to maintain continuity and update your webpages quickly.

There is a difference, however—one that is particularly attractive if you're working on a larger site. When you update a CSS file, your Web app doesn't have to then update all your webpages, because the Web browser itself loads the external file as part of the webpage, rather like an image file, based on a single line of code near the top of your HTML. All your style rules are then applied on the fly.

DESIGN CONTROL

Using CSS you can completely dispense with messing with all your font sizes, colors and so on individually. But there is another appeal: it offers much greater control over the size, appearance, positioning, and other properties of your design elements.

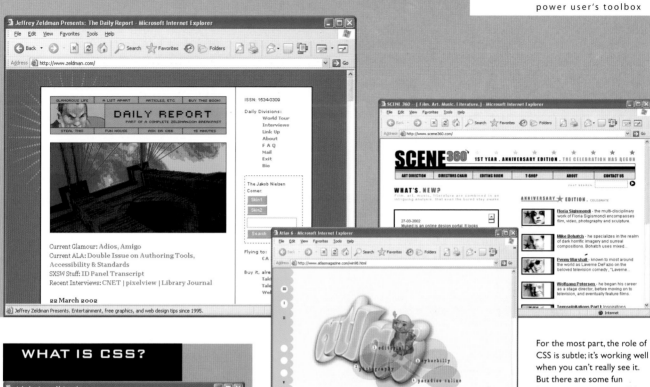

WHAT IS CSS?

```
stylesheet.css - Notepad
File  Edit  Format  View  Help

body { margin: 0; padding: 0; background-color: white; }

p { color: black; font-family: Verdana, Arial, sans-serif }
.subhead { font-weight: bold }

a { color: blue; text-decoration: none }
a:hover { color: red; text-decoration: underline }
```

CSS stands for Cascading Style Sheets, the language that is used to define style sheets for the Web. It can either go direct in your HTML within a special <style> tag, or you can put it in a separate file with the suffix ".css." Like HTML, a CSS file is a simple text file that you can drag into any ordinary text editor. It's very easy to understand:

P { font: 11px Verdana; color: black; line-height: 15px;}.subheading { font-weight: bold; color: blue }

This simply means, anything that's within a <p> tag—meaning a paragraph—has the properties defined on that line, while anything that is specially labeled as a subheading—called a class—is bold and blue. To specify that a particular paragraph is a subheading, you would then add class="subheading" into the p tag, like this:
<p class="subheading">This is your subheading</p>

For the most part, the role of CSS is subtle; it's working well when you can't really see it. But there are some fun features you can create: A List Apart (*www.alistapart.com*, far left) and Zeldman.com (above left) offer users a choice of site skins, based on special CSS techniques, while Atlas Magazine (*www.atlasmagazine .com*, left) uses an interesting CSS styling for text, and Scene360 (*www.scene360 .com*, above right) changes the scrollbar appearance of the news frame.

For instance, you may have found the settings for font sizes—1, 2, 3, and so on—a bit limiting. Maybe 1 is too small, and 2 is too big. And anyhow, they don't come out quite the same size on different browsers, and any viewer can make a mess of your intricate design just by fiddling with the text size options in their browser's *View* menu.

You can quickly overcome issues like this using CSS, which enables you to specify font sizes (and the spacing between lines) in exact pixels, control the size of form elements, and throw in some fun effects too. You can put color into your dropdown menus, set up rollover styles for ordinary text links, and change the pointer that appears for different parts of the design.

STYLE SHEET BASICS

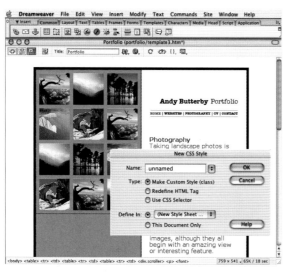

1 Most good Web authoring apps include some sort of palette or dialog for creating style sheets. In Dreamweaver, this is the CSS palette from your *Window* menu. Start by removing all your font and size settings, then click the *New* button in this palette, which looks like a little page with a + symbol, at the bottom of the palette.

3 If you opt for an external style sheet - which is a good idea— you'll need to save the currently black CSS file now somewhere in your site. Put in a folder called "library" or something similar. Then you get a dialog where you can specify a great many properties for all your p tags—most are obvious, but we'll take a look at some in a moment.

4 To create a style rule that applies only when you want it to, you create what is called a class. Choose the Make Custom Class option in Dreamweaver, and give it a name—which must begin with a "."—such as ".subheading."

2 A good place to begin is with the <p> and <td> tags, which will outline almost all the body copy in your site. Choose the *Redefine HTML Tag* radio option, and select "p" from the dropdown menu. The *Radio* options at the bottom of the dialog allow you to choose whether the style rule goes in an external file, or directly within the HTML of the page.

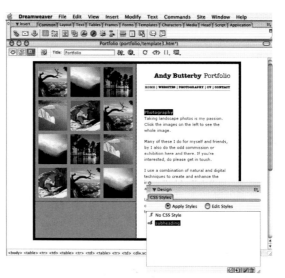

5 The outcome, when we head back to the page, is a much more attractive text size for the paragraphs. To apply a class to something in your web page, first select it, then click its name in your CSS Styles palette.

GOLIVE

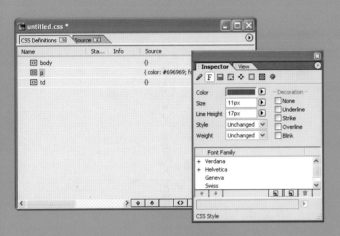

1 In GoLive, your best way it is to choose the File>New Special>*Cascading Style Sheet* option. This opens a window listing the rules in your style sheet—empty entries have already been added for the body, p, and td tags. Select the p tag, and you can use the buttons across the top of your *Inspector* palette to access the different properties you can set.

3 Now save the style sheet in your website folder, then open a webpage and click the CSS icon at the top-right corner—it looks like a staircase. From the corner menu of the window that opens, choose *New Link to External CSS*, and use the *Inspector* to set up the link to the CSS file you just created.

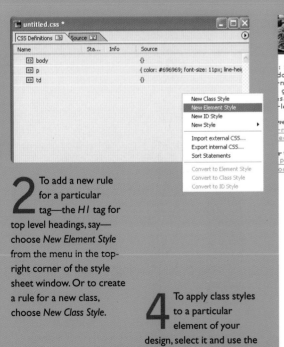

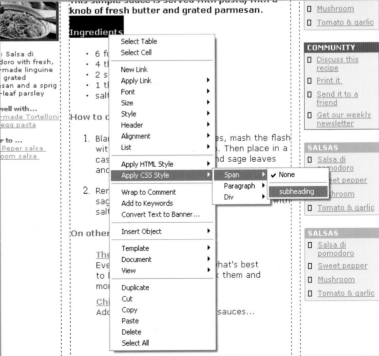

2 To add a new rule for a particular tag—the *H1* tag for top level headings, say—choose *New Element Style* from the menu in the top-right corner of the style sheet window. Or to create a rule for a new class, choose *New Class Style*.

4 To apply class styles to a particular element of your design, select it and use the *Apply CSS Style* option from your right-click menu.

DESIGN WITH CSS

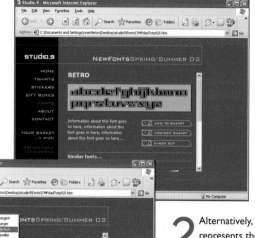

1 One advantage of CSS is that it helps you to separate styling from content, and if you make good use of this, you can easily change design aspects of your whole site in just a few clicks. This is particularly useful if, like many designers, you're always tweaking things. But you can also use CSS to gain greater control of your design. For instance, you can set the p tag—for paragraph text—to always show 11-pixel text in Verdana, Arial, or Helvetica, with 17 pixels line-height for extra spacing between lines. This is more attractive, and a level of design you can't achieve without CSS.

2 Alternatively, you can use the "em" unit, which represents the width of an m character. Here, users can still adjust the size of the character using their browser's *View* menu, which is useful if someone has trouble reading small text.

3 Many designers prefer to remove the underline that automatically appears on links. You can do this by redefining the tag, setting its text-decoration property to none. You can also use this to set link colors, and make them all appear in bold, or with a particular background color.

4 By defining a style for "a:hover," you can also control how your links' appearance changes when a user rolls over them. In Dreamweaver, choose the *CSS Selector* option, or in GoLive just type "a:hover" as the name of your new element style. For instance, they can change to white and be underlined.

5 Finally, you can develop your style sheet with rules for different types and levels of headings, links, and other elements in your design.

CSS & FORMS

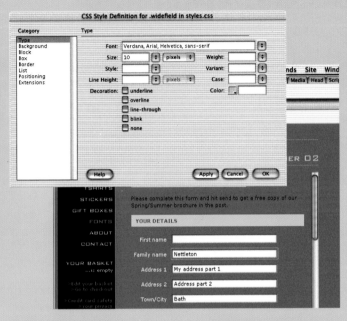

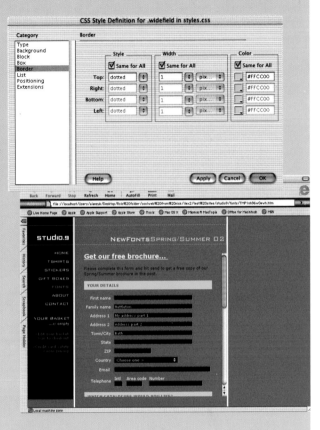

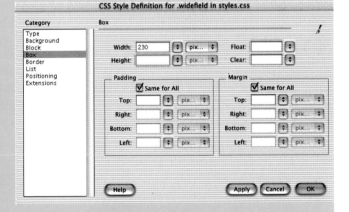

1 CSS is particularly useful in connection with forms, which are difficult for the designer to control. While not all CSS properties work with all CSS elements, you'll find that some key options work well with forms. By defining the input and select tags, you can get better control of the font size and face.

2 The color, background color, and border settings work in newer browsers, which you can use to particularly great effect. Why not try a 1px dotted white border?

3 But one of the most useful CSS settings for forms is the width attribute. Ordinarily, the size of form fields depends closely on your user's platform and interface settings, and they vary wildly. But by setting up a couple of classes with different pixel widths and applying these to the appropriate fields, you can take control.

CSS AND BACKGROUNDS

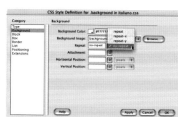

1 Another powerful feature of CSS is its ability to control the appearance, positioning, and scrolling properties of background images. We might want to add a background image for the ItaliaGusto site. You can do this using the *Page* or *Document* properties, but you'll get better control if you use CSS…

2 To do this you need to redefine the body tag. Use the *Background* options to browse to the file you want to use for your background. The *Repeat* option allows you to control whether the background tiles, and in what direction. We set it to "no-repeat," so the image appears just once.

3 The *Attachment* property allows you to control whether the background image moves when your user scrolls the page—we've gone for the fixed option, so it stays put. This is a great effect, and makes the page appear to be "floating" over the image.

SCROLLING AND WINDOWS

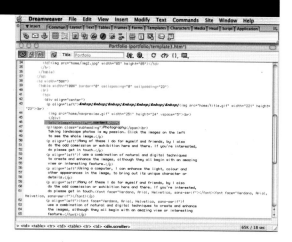

1 While we're on the subject of windows, CSS offers an excellent solution to the frames problems we spoke about earlier—problems with managing files, search engines, and so on. For this you need to remove the frames of iframe from your document, and open the code where you want the window to go. Then type this:

```
<div class="scroller"
>content</div>
```

2 "div" in itself doesn't mean very much, but we're going to define the class "scroller" to turn it into a floating, scrolling box, and replace the word "content" with actual content. Head back to the design view, and create a class called "scroller."

TWO QUICK EFFECTS

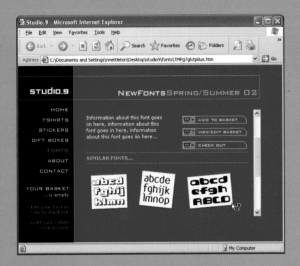

1 The CSS language is always expanding to offer new possibilities for designers. One is the cursor attribute, which works best with links and enables you to choose what type of cursor appears when your user rolls over a particular element. You'll find these in Dreamweaver's *Extensions* section, but in GoLive you'll need to add it yourself in the *Source* tab. Just type:

```
cursor: crosshair;
```

in the line for the `<a>` tag. There are number of values you can go for, including default, pointer, move, crosshair, wait, and help.

2 For Internet Explorer users, you can also control how their scrollbars appear, to match your site design—but you will have to type in the code for this yourself. You need to redefine the body tag, like this, adding in your own color codes:

```
body {scrollbar-face-color: #ffcc00; scrollbar-
shadow-color: #ffcc00; scrollbar-highlight-color:
#ffcc00; scrollbar-3dlight-color: #ffff99; scrollbar-
darkshadow-color: #993300; scrollbar-track-color:
#fdf5dc; scrollbar-arrow-color: #000000; }
```

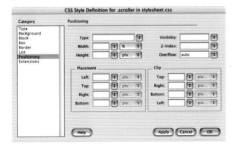

4 Now cut and paste the content for the box in place of the word "content" and preview the result in your browser. This won't work in older browsers—the content will just appear in the normal way—but it looks great for most users, and it's very efficient.

3 For this, the key CSS properties are width, height, and overflow. Set the width and height to the dimensions you want for the scrolling box, and set the overflow to "auto"…

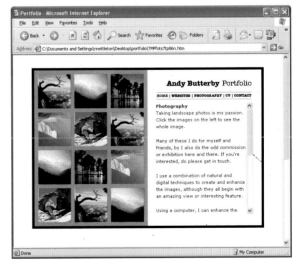

BEHAVIORS AND ACTIONS

You may remember back in chapter 5, on animation, DHTML was mentioned as an option open to you for creating Web animation, although we didn't look at it in detail. The D in DHTML stands for 'Dynamic', and although not suitable for graphical types of animation, the technology behind it enables you to add impressive features for interacting directly with HTML elements of a webpage.

The ubiquitous rollover button is a very simple example of Dynamic HTML, as is the dropdown Jump menu we created a few pages ago. Other examples are popup windows, news tickers, visual dropdown menus, collapsible tree menus, and HTML text that changes depending on where you put your mouse. You can find out how to do some of these over the next few pages.

DHTML isn't a language in itself. Rather, it's a combination of HTML, CSS, and JavaScript. The last of these is the lynchpin: a simple but powerful scripting language that contains the tools you need to create onmouseover, onmouseout, and other events, change the properties of elements in your page design, and perform logical and mathematical calculations. It's almost exactly the same as the ActionScript language used by Flash.

You can write JavaScript by hand directly into a webpage, but most Web authoring apps include a bundle of drag-and-drop behaviors or actions, which you can use to set up DHTML features quickly without knowing a thing about the code. For Dreamweaver and GoLive, you can also download new behaviors.

EXTENDING YOUR SOFTWARE

Both Dreamweaver and GoLive are fully extendible products, with online libraries where you can browse and download behaviors, actions, productivity tools, and other extensions created by the user community, and sometimes by developers themselves. It's well worth taking advantage of these—head to *www.macromedia.com/exchange* for Dreamweaver, or *http://xchange.studio.adobe.com* for GoLive.

The quality of the extensions varies wildly, from the indispensable to the utterly useless—quality control is kept at a minimum in these libraries, to ensure a good flow of creative ideas and experiments. But both include user ratings, reviews, and more, which should help you choose.

To use Dreamweaver extensions, you also need to download and install the Macromedia Extension Manager, which is quick and easy.

LEFT: The Adobe Xchange,
http://xchange.studio.adobe.com
BELOW LEFT: The Dreamweaver
Exchange,
www.macromedia.com/exchange

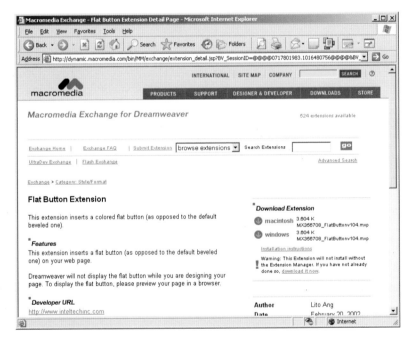

UNDERSTANDING JAVASCRIPT

JavaScript is a simple scripting language used in almost every webpage on the Internet. It is used to create rollovers, open windows, detect what platform you are using, create interactive HTML elements, and store simple pieces of information on your computer in the form of cookies. It doesn't, however, have access to personal information and system files, so it's perfectly safe for the user.

Like CSS, JavaScript can either go directly in a webpage, or in an external file with the ending .js. When in a webpage, it appears within the <script>…</script> tag. This would usually be in the head section of your HTML—a special area that doesn't display on the page, but instead contains supporting information for the document, including the title, description, links to CSS files, and more.

This simple JavaScript detects if the browser is Internet Explorer, and if so redirects users to another page, called "home_ie.htm":

```
if( navigator.appName == "Microsoft
Internet Explorer" )
{ location.href = "home_ie.htm" }
```

USING BEHAVIORS

A POP-UP WINDOW

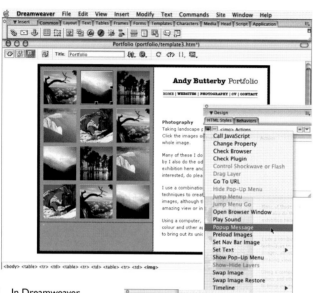

1 In Dreamweaver, you'll find a *Behaviors* palette. Simply select the object you want your user to interact with, add a link to it, then click the + menu in this palette and choose your behavior. A dialog may appear with options.

2 Afterward, your behavior appears in the palette with a little dropdown menu— you can use this to choose the event that sparks off the behavior.

3 In GoLive, you can use the *Actions* palette. Again, select your linked item, then click the *New Action* icon in the palette. Use the *Action* menu to select the action you want, and fill in the details.

1 One of the simplest and most popular uses for DHTML is the popup window. You don't want to go overboard with these, because they can be annoying, but the technique is ideal for showing off larger images in a gallery or portfolio, as well as product shots.

2 You need to add a normal link to the image first, to keep older browsers happy, and with this link selected, use the *Open Windows* or *Open Browser Window* action. Here you can choose a file to load into the new window, as well as its dimensions and other properties. In particular, you can choose whether it's resizable, and it shows scrollbars if needed.

3 Think carefully before you take away menubars, or resize handles and other features. What if someone wants to bookmark the page, or their computer settings mean the page in the popup window is smaller than the window itself?

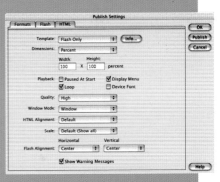

5 This is also the technique we want to use for our Flash movie interface on the Mango site. You can use Flash's File>*Publish* command to create the HTML file for the movie clip. In the *HTML* tab of the *Publish* dialog, set the width and the height to 100%, so the interface matches the size of your popup window.

6 Then open the HTML file and set all its margins to 0, to make the most of the space in your popup window.

4 Window size is a particular problem, because different browsers measure this in different ways, depending on scrollbars, titlebars, window borders, and so on. It's a good idea to make the window a little larger than the image or interface you want to show. Then when you create the page to go in it, give this a neutral background and center the image in the document.

7 Finally, set up the popup window in the usual way—it's probably a good idea to include resize handles here, so users can view the movie larger or smaller, depending on what they prefer.

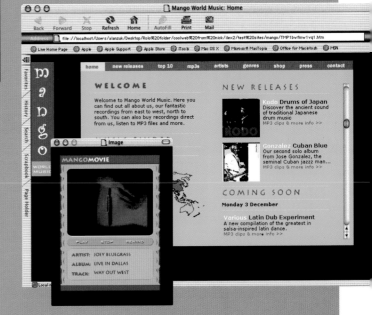

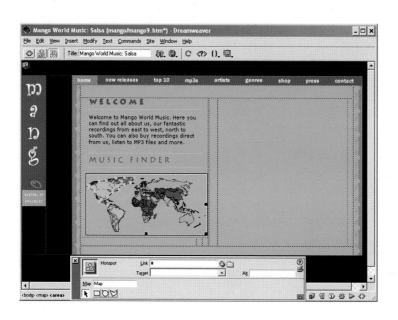

1 Another DHTML feature on the Mango site is the interactive map on the home page. When users roll over different parts of the map, it tells them a little about music from that area, and they can click to find albums to match. Using an HTML imagemap, you can define different links for different parts of a graphic, which is what we need. Using the imagemap tools in your Web authoring software, draw the shapes of the areas directly onto the image.

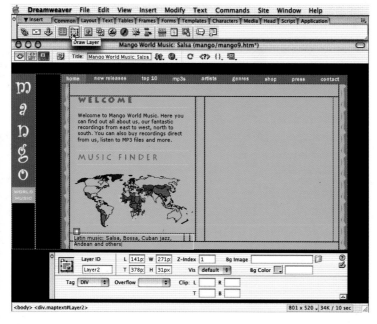

2 This done, use your *Layer* or *Floating Box* object to draw a layer where you want the changing information to appear, set its particular properties, and add in some dummy text.

5 Now repeat this for the same map area, but this time leave the text box empty and set the event to 'onmouseout'.

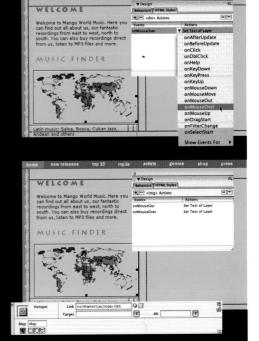

3 The best way to control the appearance of this text is using a CSS class applied to the layer, or <div> tag, itself. Set up the class in the usual way, then select the layer (rather than its contents), and apply the styling.

4 Now go back to your image map, and select the first link area. In Dreamweaver, use your *Behaviors* palette to add a *Set Text>Set Text of Layer* action. Choose your layer name in the drop-down, then type in the text for that area of the map, and hit *OK*. Make sure the event is 'onmouseover'.

6 This is a good time to check it's all working in your browser, before you move ahead. If all is well, simply repeat from step 4 for each of the areas on your map. Finally add links to the areas on your interactive map, remove the original dummy text from the layer…

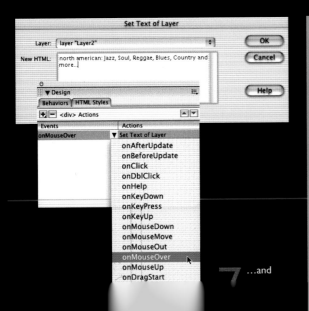

7 …and

SITE SEARCHES DATABASES
& UPDATING YOUR SITE

While DHTML and JavaScript open the door to interactive Web design without Flash, there are limits to what they can do. You can't, for example, use these to create a search engine for a site that has more than just a couple of pages, because JavaScript has no ability to look through the other files on your site. Neither can be used to automatically add form entries to a guestbook, or in any way change the files on your site. Activity like this needs to be performed by scripts on the server.

WEBSITE DATABASES

Increasingly, website developers are using databases to hold all the content of their webpages. The Web pages themselves are merely shells, containing the design, and empty spaces where the page-specific images and text should be. When you click a link to a particular article, special scripts on the website's server find the appropriate content in the database, place it in the HTML file, and then send this modified, complete webpage back to you.

Search engines like Yahoo! and AltaVista, for example, hold vast databases of websites and webpages on the Internet. When you tap in your keywords and hit 'enter', the search engine browses through its database to find entries that match, then dynamically assembles the HTML page on the server before sending it down the line. Guest books, mailing lists, and large content-oriented sites work this way.

The advantages are threefold. First, it's very easy to add new content to your site: you simply put it in the database. All the fuss over creating a new webpage, getting links right is done automatically. Second, if you want to redesign your site later, you only need to change a couple of template shell pages, and not the whole thing.

But most importantly, database-oriented sites like this enable users to interact more with the content, using site searches, or adding their own content to the database using forms, which is what happens with a guest book.

FROM EXPENSIVE TO FREE

The trouble with creating sites like this is that you need a great deal of knowledge about programming and the technologies involved, or you need to pay someone else to do it for you, and this can become very expensive. You also need your Web server set up specifically to run these technologies—which may also run up your bill!

But all is not over for the low-budget Web designer. Increasingly, companies that already have these technologies built are offering site search tools, guest books, mailing lists, and more for free, in return for selling advertising at the top of the page. It's a small price to pay if you consider what features like this can do for your website, but if you prefer many of these companies also offer a paid-up, no-ads alternative.

We're going to take a look at some of these, and how you can use them in your site, in the next two chapters.

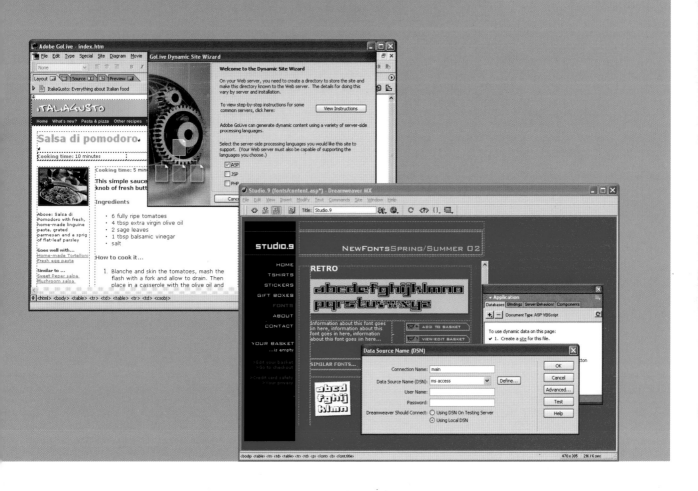

DYNAMIC WEBSITE TECHNOLOGIES

You'll need to install and run a basic Web server on your computer—both Windows XP and Mac OSX have this bundled in—as well as database software such as Microsoft Access, or the more reliable MySQL, which you can get free from *www.mysql.com*.

If you use GoLive or Dreamweaver MX, you already have the tools built in to create the scripts that connect webpages to your database. If not, you'll need to learn the scripting language yourself. There are several you can choose from, all fairly similar to JavaScript and ActionScript. The most popular is ASP, Microsoft's Active Server Pages technology, which works with VBScripts and Jscript. Head to *www.msdn.microsoft.com/asp* for more info. A better

option for beginners, though, could be Macromedia's ColdFusion technology, or CFML, which is quick, easy, and intuitive to work with. Find out more at *www.macromedia.com*.

A third popular option is PHP, an "open-source" technology—see *www.php.net*. Open-source technology means the source code is freely available for developers to enhance, add new functionality, or use it to develop new applications. Under a "public licence" agreement, developers agree to feed their work back into the open-source community.

Ultimately, however, your decision is going to be limited by what technologies your Web-hosting company is prepared to offer, and what they charge for it. Be sure to check this out before you embark on a time-consuming project!

HAVING MASTERED WEB DESIGN, GRAPHICS, ANIMATION, MOVIES, FORMS, STYLE SHEETS, AND A SMATTERING OF DHTML, WHAT ELSE CAN YOU DO? PUT YOUR SITE ON THE INTERNET, OF COURSE, AND—MORE IMPORTANTLY—GET PEOPLE TO VISIT. THIS MAY SOUND SIMPLE, BUT IT CAN BE FRAUGHT WITH DIFFICULTIES. IT'S THE POINT AT WHICH MANY SITES FALL DOWN. FOLLOW THIS GUIDE, AND YOU'LL BE ON THE RIGHT PATH...

GOING LIVE & GETTING VISITORS
↓

GOING...GOING... LIVE

IF YOUR WEBSITE IS A SMALL, EXPERIMENTAL HOME PROJECT AND YOU HAVEN'T TOLD A GREAT MANY PEOPLE ABOUT IT, THIS ISN'T SUCH A BIG DEAL. BUT IF, ON THE OTHER HAND, THIS IS YOUR BUSINESS SITE, OR YOU'VE ANNOUNCED A LAUNCH DATE, OR YOU'RE EXPECTING MORE THAN A HANDFUL OF LOST ODDBALLS TO STOP BY, THEN GOING LIVE WITH YOUR WEBSITE CAN BE A VERY STRESSFUL EXPERIENCE. IN PRINCIPLE, IT'S JUST A MATTER OF TRANSFERRING THE FILES FROM YOUR COMPUTER TO YOUR WEB SERVER. IN PRACTICE, THINGS RARELY GO AS SMOOTHLY AS THIS. OVER THE PAGE WE TAKE A LOOK AT THE TOP 10 PROBLEMS IN GOING LIVE WITH YOUR WEBSITE. BUT FIRST...

GOING FOR THE SOFT LAUNCH

Many of the problems in going live with a website boil down to this: you're transferring all this technology you've created from one environment (your computer) to another (your web server), and then onto hundreds of millions of other computers. And you can be 99% certain these won't be set up the same way.

Serious web designers go to great lengths to replicate server and user environments, but there's only so much you can do. The only way around it is to test your site extensively before you go live, whether you're talking five web pages or 500.

1 First off, upload your files to a test website, if you can—one that nobody knows about. If for whatever reason you can't get proper testing web space, then create a directory called "test" in your main website and use this—but beware this will play havoc with absolute links, if you've used them.

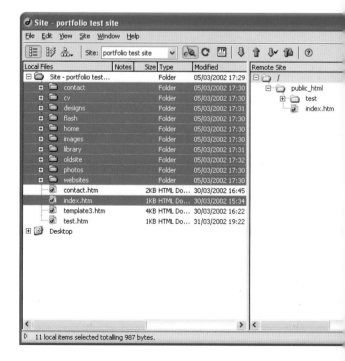

SITE LAUNCH

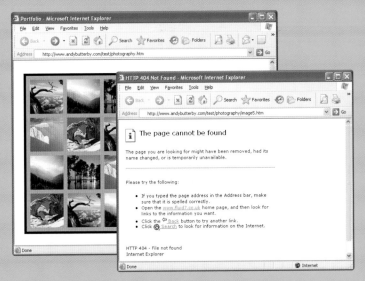

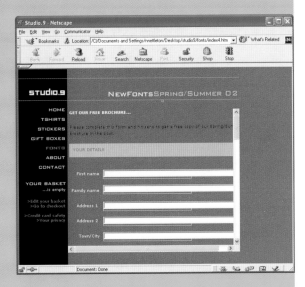

2 Your first task is to check and test all your links, images, and so on. A lot of software, including Dreamweaver and GoLive, has tools for doing this on your computer, but you should do it yourself on the web server, just to be sure. Problems associated with a change of directory structure are commonplace, as well as files that didn't upload properly, or you just had something in the wrong folder on your computer.

4 Next, borrow a friends' computers or head to a web café and test your site on as many different setups as you can—PC, Mac, Internet Explorer, Netscape, Opera… You name it, your best customer is probably using it. You especially need to double-check forms, for technical faults as well as design errors, like this little mess…

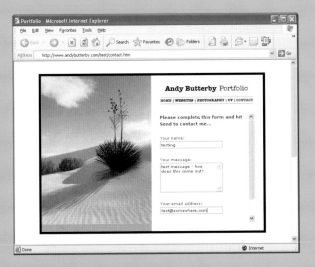

5 You should also check all your plugin objects—Flash, streaming movies, and so on. Different sound and video formats can be troublesome on different platforms, or may simply not play at all. And what happens if your user doesn't have the right plug-in installed? Does your page degrade gracefully, and offer clear instructions on where they can get the software they need?

3 Second, check any forms you've created to make sure they're working. If you're expecting to get an email back from the form, make sure you get one. If it's a jump menu, make sure it jumps you to the right places.

 Finally, when you're happy with everything—this is the time to go live properly with your website. If you've announced a launch date, do try to launch in advance. It's guaranteed you'll find further errors in the mean time, as well as details you'd like to improve.

TOP 10
GOING LIVE ISSUES

LAUNCHING A NEW WEBSITE CAN BE A COMPLETE NIGHTMARE, EVEN IF YOU TAKE THE SOFT ROUTE. PREPARE FOR THE WORST, AND YOU WILL ENJOY A SMOOTHER RIDE...

☐1 YOUR SITE ISN'T FINISHED

Almost comical, but so common as to be a serious issue in the Internet business: web projects have a habit of dragging on and on. This is only going to be a disaster if you've announced a firm launch date, but either way, you should plan and stick to a rigorous schedule for creating and completing a site. Remember, you can always add new sections and amend a site later on—the web is very much a living entity.

☐2 YOU JUST CAN'T GET YOUR WEBSITE TO UPLOAD

FTP is always a bit awkward to set up, particularly since you have to get the settings exactly right. This is the most likely cause if you're having trouble uploading your site—follow your host's FTP instructions to a T. Also, sometimes add-on FTP features in Windows Explorer, Dreamweaver, and so on are less reliable than a dedicated FTP app, so you might want to try this. If all else fails, your host may be having server problems— give them a buzz and ask.

☐3 YOUR SITE EXCEEDS YOUR WEB-SPACE MB LIMIT

This is unlikely to be a problem unless you are posting particularly big files online, such as a lot of large video clips. There are only three solutions: either increase your limit (you may have to pay), compress your files better, or rethink your content strategy.

☐4 YOUR SITE HAS UPLOADED, BUT IT DOESN'T OPEN WHEN YOU TYPE IN YOUR WEB ADDRESS

The usual cause of this problem is your home page having the wrong file name. You can check if this the case by trying the address www.yoursite.com/filename.htm. If this works, you know your web address is corresponding properly to your webspace folder. Home pages should usually be called "index.htm" or "index.html," and some hosts are quite specific about which, so read the instructions they give. In other cases—particularly database sites, home pages have the name like "default.asp." Alternatively, it is possible that your host hasn't set up your website properly to match the address with your web space—contact them to check this.

☐5 YOUR SITE DOWNLOADS AT A SNAIL'S PACE

For beginners, this is probably the most common of our top 10. When you're creating pages on your computer, everything loads instantly, so it's easy to get carried away with huge graphics and loads of bells and whistles. Now you're going to regret it! The only solution is to go back and rework your content ideas.

6
THE LINKS DON'T WORK

Usually, you'll have this problem if the directory structure of the site on your computer doesn't match what you've got in your web space—particular if one or the other is within another folder. You need to go back and match them up. Alternatively, if you've used absolute links, check that your web host supports this. Also, be aware that the same naming rules apply for the default hub pages in subfolders as for your main home page.

7
A FRIEND/CLIENT EMAILS YOU TO SAY THE DESIGN IS A MESS

Hopefully this isn't a comment on your aesthetics—it's just that your site isn't working on their platform. You must, must check your site on as many platforms as you can—but no matter how many, there will always be someone for whom something isn't working properly. The only solution is to go back, find the cause of the problem, and fix it.

8
YOUR FORMS DON'T DO WHAT THEY'RE MEANT TO

Another common problem here: forms can be a pain to set up until you get the hang of it. You need to follow your host's instructions to the letter, because the scripts they use require exact information.

9
YOUR SITE IS FULL OF TYPOS AND OTHER MISTAKES

Yup, this really does happen, even in a surprising number of professional sites. Designers tend to forget that spelling is important for a lot of users. Make sure you give all the content of your site a final, detailed proofing before you publish a word. Apps like Dreamweaver and GoLive now include spellcheckers, which you should use.

10
YOU'VE USED TECHNOLOGY THAT YOUR SERVER DOESN'T SUPPORT

This is unlikely unless you've gone for streaming media or database technology without checking you've got the right hosting package for the job. Do check this before you embark on time-consuming projects! If you have overlooked this, you'll either need to upgrade your hosting plan, or drop the fancy stuff.

DEALING WITH NETSCAPE 4

Web designers and developers have complained a great deal about differences between the major web browsers. After all, it makes their work a lot harder, and costs big companies a lot of money. The World Wide Web Consortium (*www.w3c.org*) has worked hard to impose standards in the last few years, but there remain a number of major cross-browser differences that could cause you endless trouble. This is particularly true if you care to look at your site in Netscape version 4.

This browser is clearly on the way out—it may account for 5 to 10 percent of web surfers, depending who you ask, although you should treat such figures with caution. In any event, this is still enough potential customers for companies to invest great time in making sure their sites continue to work, or at least, look okay, in NS4.

Some of the key problems you will face in this browser include limited and faulty support for CSS; table background images that repeat over from the top left corner of each table cell; and flat rejection of links that contain spaces (which you should avoid anyway).

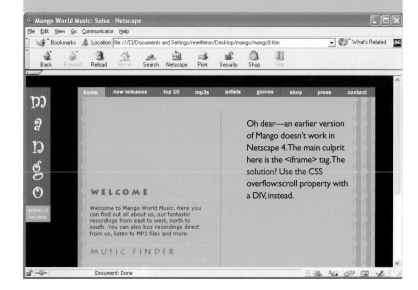

Oh dear—an earlier version of Mango doesn't work in Netscape 4. The main culprit here is the <iframe> tag. The solution? Use the CSS overflow:scroll property with a DIV, instead.

ATTRACTING VISITORS

OF COURSE, YOU COULD BE FACING THE OPPOSITE PROBLEM WHEN YOU GO LIVE WITH YOUR SITE—NOT WHETHER IT'S GOING TO WORK PROPERLY FOR EVERYONE COMING TO SEE IT, BUT WHETHER YOU'RE GOING TO GET ANY VISITORS AT ALL. IT'S A BIT LIKE THROWING A BIRTHDAY PARTY: IT'S HARD TO TELL IF YOU'VE GOT FIVE OR 50 PEOPLE COMING.

Microsoft's www.bcentral.com —get a free site counter, but try to avoid giving the game away if you've haven't had as many visitors as people might expect.

Worry not. While you may have seen a handful of sites with a bashful little counter boasting "This site has been visited 6 times" (mostly by the designer, no doubt), it really only takes a few simple initiatives to get the figures rolling. The first step, incidentally, is to avoid such counters at all costs. Do not tell users how many people come to your site, unless it's a very big number. Even then, think first: what do you have to gain from it?

HOW MANY PEOPLE VISIT YOUR SITE?

Nevertheless, knowing how many visitors you have, how long they stay for, and what they're looking at is key information in developing a successful Internet project. You can use this to tailor what you're offering, direct people quickly to the most popular features, and choose where to focus your marketing efforts.

Many sites offer free basic counters, which you can add to your home page with just a line of code (try Microsoft's *www.bcentral.com/products/fc* for instance). Be aware that these often entail some form of reciprocal marketing, or the figures aren't that useful.

As a better option, most Web hosts will offer basic stats for free or a small fee, and more detailed usage reports if you're prepared to pay. As your site grows, you may find this becomes a valuable resource. And if you ever want to sell advertising, it will be essential.

TOP 10 MARKETING TECHNIQUES

1

JUST TALK

The cheapest, and probably most powerful, way to get people to your site is simply to talk about it. Anyone, everyone—it doesn't matter who, just get the word of mouth going.

2

USE YOUR STATIONERY

If you have company stationery, you should update all this to include your Web address—business cards, letterheads, brochures, you name it. It's surprising how many companies miss out on this valuable opportunity to tell existing customers and partners about their website. Consider including your Web address as part of your company logo.

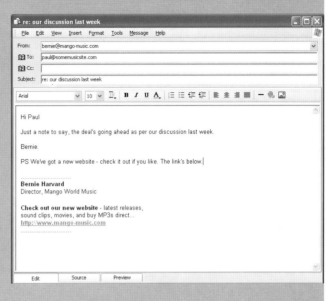

3

EMAIL

Email is particularly valuable to the Web marketer, because users can just click on the link, rather than remember and type in a Web address. You should include your Web address in every email you send, together with a line describing what's on your site. For older email software, include the http:// prefix on the front of Web address so they arrive as a live link.

4

REGISTER WITH SEARCH ENGINES

If you can get a good placement for particular keywords at a search engine like AltaVista (pictured), you will quickly find a lot of traffic coming to your website. There is a fine art to achieving this, and we'll take a deeper look over the page. A word of warning: search engines aren't patient with webmasters that abuse their rules.

TOP 10 MARKETING TECHNIQUES

⑤

ADD YOUR SITE TO DEDICATED DIRECTORIES

As well as search engines, there is a large number of directories on the Web covering almost every topic you can imagine. Popular directories attract a huge amount of through-traffic, including regular visitors. Use a search engine to find as many of these as you can, and submit your site—or better, individual pages—to their database. *www.sonicswitchblade.com*, pictured, looks like a good bet for Mango Music.

⑦

JOIN A LINK OR BANNER EXCHANGE

A more organized form of mutual marketing is the link or banner exchange: by joining an existing group of sites with a topic in common, you agree to host links of ad banners for the others, while they do the same for you. Try *www.ringsurf.com*, pictured, or tap "link exchange" into a search engine.

⑥

SWAP LINKS WITH RELATED SITES

Swapping links, page for page, is a standard deal on the Internet. Not all sites accept links, but if you do yourself, use the search engines to find as many sites of related interest as you can, and simply contact the webmaster with your proposal. They want traffic too, so you've got a good chance of getting a "yes". A number of sites offer a gauge of how many other sites link to you—try *www.linkpopularity.com* for one.

8

NEWS GROUPS AND DISCUSSION BOARDS

The Internet community is packed with communities using discussion boards, which are Web-based discussion areas, and news groups, which you access using your email software. These are invaluable as an opportunity not only to share ideas, but also get yourself (and thereby your website) known in your specialist field. Try *www.ezboard.com* for discussion boards, and use your email host's news server to access news groups (pictured). Later in this chapter, we'll show you how to create your own Web community features.

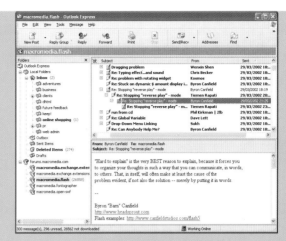

9

CREATE A FLIER

Depending on the type of website you have, you may find it effective to design and print a flier that you can use to attract traffic—particularly people who hadn't considered that you might have an online service. This also helps to establish your brand name outside the virtual realm, and reinforce the trust users need to spend money on the Web.

10

CONTACT THE MEDIA

And finally, don't be afraid to get in touch with magazines—both online and in print—as well as newspapers, local radio, and so on, to tell them about your website. Many journalists are always on the lookout for new, high-quality websites in their field of interest, so providing you target them carefully (that is, make sure your information is relevant), and send a concise, interesting press release, you've got a chance.

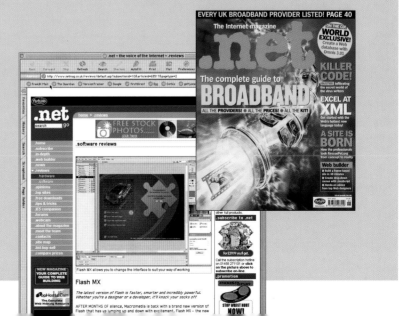

SEARCH ENGINES

REGISTERING YOUR SITE WITH SEARCH ENGINES SHOULD BE A KEY ELEMENT IN YOUR PUSH TO GET TRAFFIC TO YOUR SITE. FOR MANY, THIS IS THE PRINCIPLE SOURCE OF VISITORS.

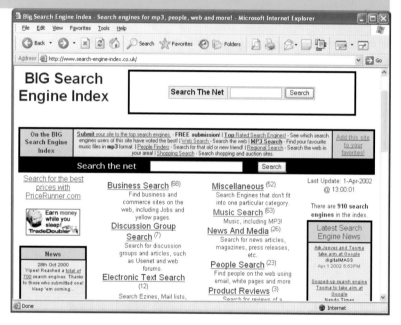

LEADING SEARCH ENGINES

Yahoo www.yahoo.com
Google www.google.com
AltaVista www.altavista.com
Excite www.excite.com
Lycos www.lycos.com
HotBot www.hotbot.com
Ask Jeeves www.askjeeves.com
alltheweb www.alltheweb.com
EntireWeb www.entireweb.com
Find more at www.search-engine-index.co.uk

The most important sites to register with include Yahoo!, Google, AltaVista, Excite, and Lycos, although this is by no means an exhaustive list. There are many other search engines that share a smaller but still significant portion of the market. There is also a rapidly growing number of specialist search engines dedicated to particular topics or media, such as MP3. These are well worth the extra time it takes to register with them, and *www.search-engine-index.co.uk* offers a comprehensive directory that should make a good starting point.

1 With most search engines, registering is a fairly straightforward process (although it often takes several weeks for them to respond in any way). Somewhere on the home page, often near the bottom, you will find a link such as "Submit a site." Just click this.

REGISTERING YOUR SITE

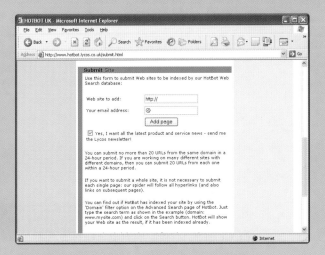

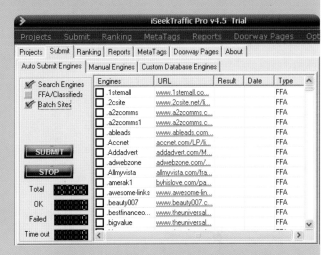

2 Other engines simply ask for a Web address, and perhaps an email address. An automated program, called a spider, then follows the link you gave and attempts to glean the information it needs directly from the webpage. It indexes the content, scans for links, and then follows these to other pages, where the process continues.

4 You can get hold of software tools for registering your site with a large number of search engines all at once, such as iSeekTraffic (*www.iseektraffic.com*). These vary in quality of service and advice—some even encourage spamming, which you should avoid at all costs, or risk being excluded from the engines' databases. You'll find hundreds of these apps if you type "free search engine registration" or similar into any search engine—but do use your common sense, and remember this is no match for doing the job yourself.

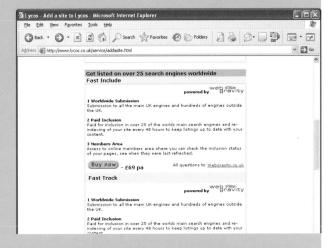

3 Some, such as Yahoo!, require you to choose a category for your site first. They then ask for a title, description, and search keywords for your site, as well as a Web address. You need to consider this information carefully if you are to attract the right people, and plenty of them, to your site—and especially if there are many other sites in your field.

5 And finally, some search engines are now offering top slots and/or speedier consideration to those who pay. The price and value of this will vary, and ultimately it will depend on the nature of your business, and who you can attract to your site in this way.

META TAGS

ADDING META TAGS WITH DREAMWEAVER

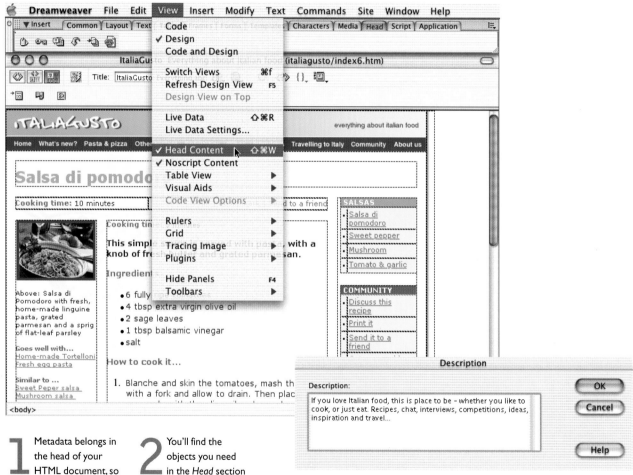

1 Metadata belongs in the head of your HTML document, so it doesn't appear on the webpage. If you can't already see it, use View>*Head Content* to see this graphically represented above your page design.

2 You'll find the objects you need in the *Head* section of your toolbox. *Keywords* and *Description* are the important elements here—you can type in the title directly below the toolbar of your document.

3 To add an element, click the object, fill in the gaps, and hit *OK*. You will see a new icon in the head section, but no change in the page itself.

META INFORMATION

IN PARTICULAR, SEARCH ENGINES LOOK FOR METADATA IN YOUR WEBPAGES TO FIND OUT WHAT YOUR SITE IS ABOUT. THIS IS SPECIAL INFORMATION CONTAINED IN <META> TAGS, WHICH BELONG IN THE HEAD OF YOUR HTML DOCUMENT AND DON'T APPEAR ON THE WEBPAGE ITSELF. THE MOST IMPORTANT ITEM OF INFORMATION HERE IS THE TITLE OF YOUR WEBPAGE. THIS IS ALMOST ALWAYS THE FIRST THING A SEARCH ENGINE CONSIDERS WHEN IT'S COMPARING WEBPAGES TO SEARCH KEYWORDS, SO YOU SHOULD MAKE GOOD USE OF IT. OTHER IMPORTANT TYPES OF INFORMATION INCLUDE A PAGE DESCRIPTION AND A LIST OF KEYWORDS, WHICH YOU SEPARATE WITH COMMAS.

CHOOSING THE RIGHT WORDS

It's likely when you're trying to attract traffic via search engines that you're going to be up against a great many other websites—maybe hundreds or even thousands. Getting near top of the list of results—even on the first page—can be hard. It's important to give a lot of thought to the words you use in your page titles, descriptions, and so on—and in your main page content too, because search engines do index this.

You should begin by trying to work out what the main search keywords are that your ideal visitor would use to find a site or product like yours. Think simple, think obvious, and think buzzwords. "Free" could be the most popular keyword in history, so you should include it in your title, description, and keywords if you have free content to offer on your site. Likewise, if you are offering MP3s, say "MP3," or your site is a portfolio of photography, be sure to say it straight. You can use services like *www.worldtracker.com* to find out what the most popular keywords are.

Because the title of your webpage is one of the main elements search engines look at, you should include a couple of top keywords or key phrases in this, as well as your company or site name. For example, "Mango World Music—Salsa, Jazz, African, and Eastern MP3s and videos" is much better than just "Mango World Music." It also helps anyone that sees your listing in their search results.

But be careful not to overstep the mark. If you have a great many keywords in your title and other meta information, the relevance of any one drops.

As an alternative, just use a couple of keywords or phrases, write different titles, descriptions, keywords, and so on for the different pages in your site. Although this can seem like a hassle, it maximizes your chances of appearing in search engines' results for different select keywords.

Finally, do use the content of your pages to push home key phrases, as well as the meta information. Many search engines index this too, particularly looking at headings marked out with traditional document structure HTML - <h1>, <h2>, and so on.

BUILDING
A COMMUNITY

ONCE YOU'VE GOT PEOPLE COMING TO YOUR WEBSITE, YOU NEED TO
KEEP THEM THERE (YOUR SUCCESS, OR FAILURE, IN THIS FIELD IS
MEASURED BY HOW MANY PEOPLE CLICK OFF AFTER THEY SEE ONE
PAGE), AND IDEALLY GET THEM TO COME BACK AGAIN. YOU NEED TO
TURN RANDOM LINK-CLICKERS INTO LOYAL CUSTOMERS.

All the usual rules of business and marketing apply here, but the web has some special tricks up it's sleeve. The most consistently successful formats for driving Web traffic are community features, such as newsletters, bulletin boards, and even the lowly guest book.

It seems odd at first, perhaps, to build a Web community around a record label site like Mango, but the bottom line is that people that share a passion want to talk and share ideas. If you provide the

medium for them to do this, they'll stick with you. This is why user-based reviews on sites like *www.amazon.com* and *www.cnet.com* have been so successful. Here, the customers provide content, they provide marketing, and they provide an incentive for people to come to the site. What could be better?

The value of a newsletter, on the other hand, is as a gentle reminder that your site is still going strong, and a quick update on what's new to see, read, or buy. But more than anything else, it gives your audience a sense of belonging to a club that shares their interests, and will help you foster a dedicated following. That's something that every successful website depends on.

These sorts of features are incredibly time-consuming and expensive to set up yourself, relying as they do on complex database and server-side technologies. But increasingly, there are companies out there that have technology and are willing to share it with you in return for some ad space or a small fee. We'll take a look at setting some of these up.

A GUEST BOOK

A guestbook is the simplest of community-oriented features on a website, but on the right site, and with the right content, it's a treasure that few can match. There are two approaches you can take: the automatic guest book, and the manual-update guest book, where you yourself add entries from a form to a static webpage. The advantage of the second option is that you can carefully edit out any abusive or unpleasant messages, which can quickly bring down the tone of a site. You can also take more control over the design and appearance of the pages.

Amazon.com—famous for user reviews. You can do this too, using a guestbook or discussion board.

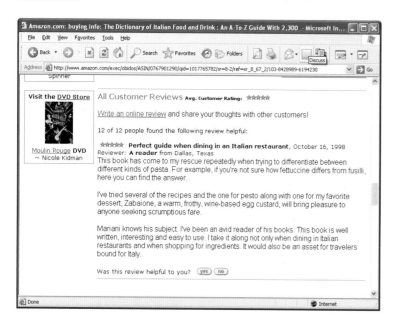

CREATING A GUESTBOOK

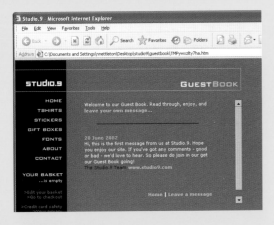

1 To create a guestbook like this, first choose what information you'd like to get from visitors—perhaps their name, email address, website, and where they are from, in addition to a message. Then coin a design to present this information, and add in a preliminary, welcoming message, asking people to join in.

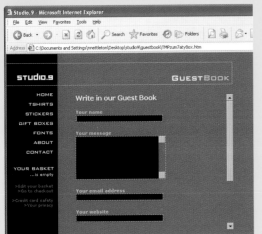

2 Now design a feedback-style form, with fields to match the information you want people to send in. Don't forget to include a statement about what you will do with people's email addresses. Then use your host's server technology to have the form entries emailed to you, link the whole lot up and upload it to your Web server. Don't forget to go to the form page and create a test entry. This should come to you by email shortly after.

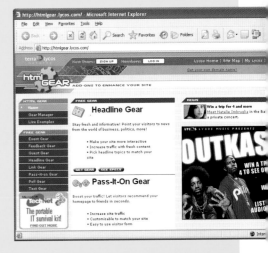

3 As real entries come in, just add them in to your guest book page, and re-upload. It'll take a while for the flow to build up, but in a couple of months you should have a guest book that makes for great reading.

4 This can get a bit laborious, however, especially if you've got a lot of other things to do. A number of sites are offering free, automated guest books that you can add to your site. They ask you to include an ad for them on your site in return. You have less control over the appearance and content, but if you're interested, try *www.htmlgear.com*, pictured, or *www.dreambook.com*. A better option may be a discussion board…

DISCUSSION BOARDS

CREATING A DISCUSSION BOARD

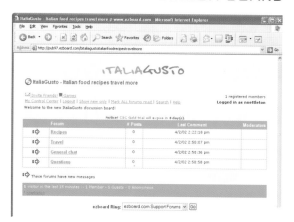

1 A discussion or bulletin board is the next step up from the simple guest book. Here, users can post replies to other people's messages, and this becomes a forum for sharing ideas, seeking advice and general banter. Web users love to hang out in communities like this, and you can easily integrate this with other parts of your site. For instance, you can set up discussion topics relating to particular products, and link to them from that product's webpage.

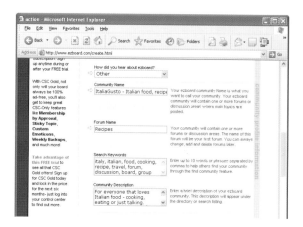

3 You need to choose a title, description, and keywords for your discussion board—you should take the same care with these as with meta information for your website, and once created submit your board to search engines.

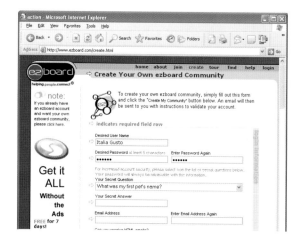

2 Manually updating a discussion board is probably not a good idea. As an alternative, ezboard (*www.ezboard.com*) is one of the most successful sites offering free discussion boards that live and work on their servers. You simply need to register on their site, set up a board, and link to it from your site.

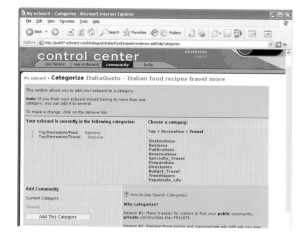

4 Once you've signed up, you need to follow instructions to activate your message board. Then you get a Web address for your message board—make a note of this, you'll need it for links on your site. First, however, add your board to a couple of categories...

5 Using the My ezboard control tab, you can customize your discussion board with colors, images, and so on. Use the colors option to adapt and match the exact colors in your website for the discussion board. You might have to experiment with this for a while to get it just the way you want it.

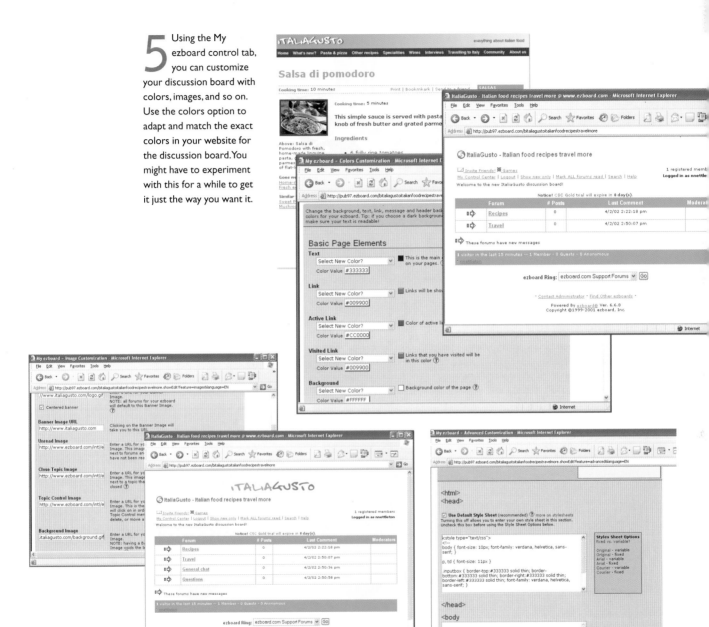

6 Now create an upload special graphics for your discussion board logo and, if you want one, a background image. Make a note of their Web addresses, and use this to customize the images that appear with your discussion board.

7 You can also use the *HTML Customization* option to add in your own stylesheets for the discussion board, as well as special HTML headers and footer content.

EMAIL NEWSLETTERS

The weekly email newsletter is a valuable marketing tool, and as you build your subscriber list, you may find this rapidly redoubles your site traffic and sales. If you want to build an effective community around your site, it is a must.

As with guest books, you could build and maintain a newsletter subscriber list by hand, adding people to your address book from email form entries. But as the list grows, this is going to become a terrible strain on your email server, and rather hard to manage. A Web-based automated newsletter service is a much better bet.

BUILDING YOUR SUBSCRIBER LIST

Microsoft's bCentral (*www.bcentral.com*) offers an excellent newsletter facility for under $50 a month, or try *www.yourmailinglistprovider.com*, pictured, for a free alternative You can set these up in much the same way as a discussion board: register, customize, and then link through from your site.

In this case, however, you'll need to include a form on your site collecting email addresses, linking through to the server-side script hosted by the mailing list service provider.

It's well worth linking to your newsletter page —or even better, including the Sign Up form itself—on every page of your site, and not just the home page. Often visitors may come from a search engine or other link to a particular webpage in your site, and never go to the home page. But if they enjoy what they see, there's a good chance they'll sign up for your newsletter—especially if you can promise no spam.

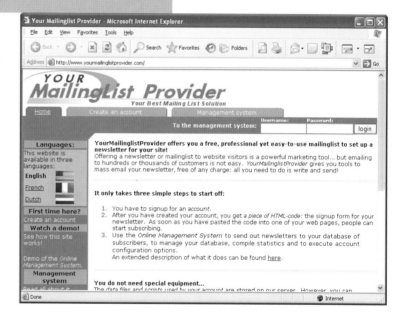

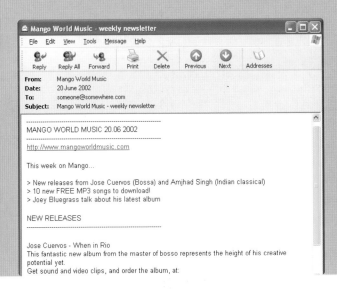

WRITING A NEWSLETTER

Creating the newsletter itself can be a difficult task, especially if you're not used to writing. But don't worry; unless your site claims otherwise, no one is expecting a literary masterpiece, just interesting information.

It's important to keep the quality of your newsletter high, otherwise people will simply delete it, and soon enough unsubscribe. (You must, incidentally, include instructions on how to unsubscribe on every newsletter you send.)

But good quality doesn't mean hard work. Some of the best newsletters simply contain a couple of links to cool new things on a website, with one or two lines explaining what each is. Others, meanwhile, discuss topics in depth directly within the newsletter, or include competitions, tips, news items, and more.

After all is said and done, how you do it depends on what you want to achieve. But keep it simple and lively, and you'll be on the right route.

Many commercial Internet ventures spent a fortune designing websites that were at the cutting edge of graphic design. Quite a few of them forgot to check their websites across all browsers and platforms. But even many of the ones that did omitted to build the most important elements of all: a viable business model, and a revenue stream. You're probably not in big business, but how can ensure that you get some money rolling in? Read on...

9

MAKING MONEY

WAYS TO MAKE MONEY

THE ULTIMATE GOAL OF MANY WEBSITES IS TO MAKE MONEY. OTHERS ARE ABOUT SAVING MONEY (BY REDUCING CUSTOMER SERVICE COSTS, FOR EXAMPLE), INCREASING PRODUCTIVITY (THROUGH SHARING INFORMATION AND ONLINE TOOLS), OR PROMOTING A CAUSE (FOR NON-PROFIT ORGANIZATIONS). MANY MORE ARE SIMPLY THERE TO PURSUE A PASSION OR A PASTIME. BUT WHATEVER YOUR OBJECTIVE, IT WOULD HARDLY BE A BAD THING IF YOUR SITE COULD MAKE MONEY SOMEHOW!

Internet business (ecommerce) has received a lot of bad publicity over the last few years. Companies with megabucks backing have plummeted from stock-market highs to bankruptcy in months, while most of the "standalone" businesses that remain have either cut back dramatically, been taken back in house, or been bought out for their technology. Free stuff is out, while advertising beckons you from every Megabyte of webspace. It's the sign of a troubled business!

But in truth, it's not that hard to make money from your website, as long as (a) you've got a saleable product to begin with; (b) you keep things simple—don't throw valuable dollars at extravagant and unnecessary gimmicks; and (c) you can get enough of the right people coming to your site. For established businesses, there should be nothing challenging in this: commerce on the Internet works in exactly the same way as commerce in the real world. But how do you go about setting up?

There are many ways to make money, but the technology you need is mostly very complex and demands high levels of security and technical precision. Unless you are running an exceedingly large and efficient operation, you will almost certainly need to bring partners on board—and that's no bad thing. Use the experts and focus on what you're good at. Here are some of the ways you can make money, and some people who can help you…

10 WAYS TO MAKE MONEY ONLINE

 wine.com

 Food & Drink — **bol.com**

① ADVERTISING

This is perhaps the simplest and most common way to get a revenue stream from your website, but you're not likely to see a lot back from it. All in all, online advertising has been an unmitigated disaster, and most sites that have relied solely on this for income are having to rethink their strategy. The trouble is that the lion's share of all online advertising spending goes to the big sites, like Yahoo and MSN, while the many thousands of others have to share a mouse's portion between them. Things may begin to change in the near future, as companies and the Web-browsing public alike get savvier, but don't expect a sudden turnaround in the market.

Who can help you? *www.doubleclick.com, http://adnetwork.bcentral.com*

Hot tip: Get appropriate advertising for your site, and allocate it a meaningful space in your design.

② NEWSLETTER SPONSORSHIP

This is really just another form of advertising, but newsletter sponsorship often turns out much better results than your standard banner-and-button ad combination, particularly where the newsletter has quality content. It should also reach a well-defined and appropriate audience that actually reads, rather than deletes, the email. At the other end of the spectrum, spam has become so prevalent that it's now a serious threat to the newsletter market.

Who can help you? Contact potential sponsors directly, or use an affiliates program.

Hot tip: Focus on quality and community: make sure yours is the newsletter people read! That means giving them information they actually need.

```
== Sponsor ========================

Get www.acoolmusicsite.com for all the latest MP3s in World Music
Jazz, Salsa, Indian and more. Free preview sound clips, online
streaming, radio and more!

www.acoolmusicsite.com today!

================================
```

10 WAYS TO MAKE MONEY ONLINE

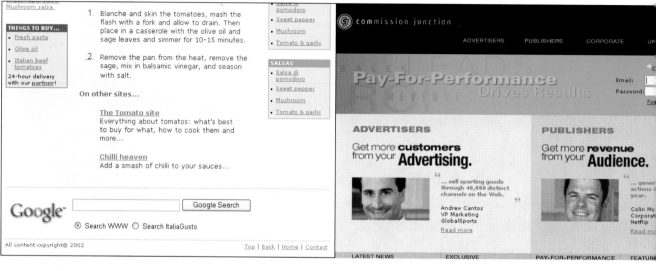

3

REFERRAL FEES

In response to hard times in Internet advertising, a new model has emerged, more open than the traditional pay-for-space, and pay-per-view models. This is pay-per-click advertising: your advertiser pays you a small fee every time you send someone to their site. In some referral programs, it doesn't actually matter how you get them there; you can choose what you want to promote, and how you want to present it. For example, you could have a list of recommended partner sites on your home page, or a handy "Things to buy" round-up next to an article. You could equally use a button ad, or automatically open another site in a new window when people hit your home page. It's likely you'll get a better response if you link people to individual product pages or product groups that relate directly to the content of your site. If you find this is working well for you, you might want to take it a step further and join some affiliates schemes…

Who can help you? *www.affiliatesdirectory. com, www.refer-it.com*

Hot tip: Here it's up to you how many people click on the ads. Just think, what would make *me* click?

4

AFFILIATES SCHEMES

Companies that sell products online have found that they can dramatically increase their revenue by offering sites with the right audience an opportunity to sell products for them, in return for a commission payment. This is a fully-fledged affiliates scheme. Joining a number of these schemes is an excellent way for the beginner to start selling without the hassle of buying and shipping products, or setting up an ecommerce system. If you put enough thought into the choice and presentation of your products, and you've got enough of the right people coming to your site, this is an excellent way to make money.

Who can help you? *www.linkshare.com, www.commissionjunction.com*

Hot tip: Choose relevant affiliate partners, and use means other than banner ads to get your visitors clicking—a text link direct to a product, for instance.

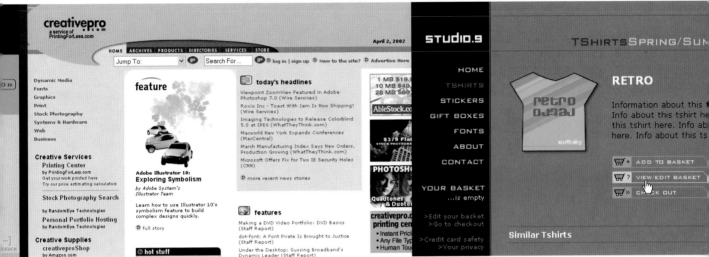

5

CO-BRANDED PARTNERSHIPS

If your site has a lot of traffic—and therefore strong marketing potential—you might be able to get a better deal than the average affiliate. See if you can work as equal partners. Well-known magazine sites and portals, for instance, often set up co-branded stores with established online retailers, in a friendly exchange of traffic and kudos for retail know-how and back-end technology. The cash aspect can be a revenue-share, profit-split, commission arrangement, or similar, along the lines of "We get this much and you get that much." The deal you come to will depend on your bargaining power.

Who can help you? Contact the companies you're interested in directly!

Hot tip: Find out which companies in your marketplace have the technology to run co-branded sites by looking at your competitors' sites.

6

ECOMMERCE

The commission rates on affiliate schemes are usually relatively low; and if you have the right systems in place for merchant business, including buying or producing—and delivering!—products, you might be better off selling it directly to customers yourself. This requires less of an investment than it did in the past, as companies are increasingly prepared to share their existing ecommerce technology with you in return for a fee, commission, or other payback. These vary from simple ecommerce sites where you have little or no control over the look and feel of the site, to sophisticated (and usually more expensive) options, where you're in the driving seat.

Who can help you? *www.store.yahoo.com, www.bcentral.com*

Hot tip: Keep it simple, present your product well, and give your users security.

10 WAYS TO MAKE MONEY ONLINE

7

SUBSCRIPTIONS

One product that you can sell online is content—perhaps via a subscription to your site. This could be a good bet if you are offering regular, high-quality, or essential content, or a Web-based service. This is becoming increasingly common, especially with traditional media brands going online, such as The Wall Street Journal (*www.wallstreetjournal.com*, pictured). But there are technical challenges: you'll need a way of stopping people looking at your content if they haven't paid up. A personal log-in is the popular way to do this, for which you'll need to run server-side scripts. To track your customers and update the content as well, a database is essential.

Who can help you? *www.payal.com*, *www.dotencrypt.com*

Hot tip: To attract subscriptions in a market where people want things for free, your content or service will have to be extremely good, accessible, and/or unique. Focus on this, and market it carefully.

8

SYNDICATING CONTENT

A new avenue of Internet business to emerge over the last year is syndication, and again this is appropriate for content-heavy sites. You'll also need a clean and effective database system, but if you fit the bill, it could be the perfect opportunity. Many commercial sites lack the staff or know-how to produce effective content for their sites, and it's cost-effective for them to buy it from a dedicated content producer. For instance, rather than hire their own news team, they might syndicate daily headlines from an established newspaper. These sites are interested in all kinds of content, not just news, depending on who their target audience is.

Who can help you? *www.yellowbrix.com*, *www.moreover.com*

Hot tip: Again, you've got to be able to create regular, high-quality, readable and marketable content to make this work for you. So check your content very carefully before issuing it to the world.

WSJ.com THE WALL STREET JOURNAL. ONLINE

THE PAGE YOU REQUESTED IS AVAILABLE ONLY TO SUBSCRIBERS.

Login Here:
User Name: [   ]
Password: [   ]
[Log In]

Forgot your User Name or Password?

☐ Save my User Name and Password
More information about saving your name and password

Not a subscriber?

(go) *Get the Online Journal*
for just **$59** for a full year!
Plus your first 2 weeks are FREE.
Print Subscribers pay only **$29** *a year!*

Tour Our Site (go) *Click Here!*

RECIPE IDEAS

- Fresh egg pasta
- 5 minute pizza
- 10 things about tomatoes
- Classic salsa

powered by ITALIAGUSTO

⑨ SELLING DATABASES

Well-defined contact databases, where you list the interests and commercial clout of the customers represented, are an immensely valuable commodity to marketing people. If you run a special-interest site, and collect email addresses or other contact details from visitors, then you may be sitting on a goldmine. However, you need to be extremely careful about privacy issues and data protection laws, which vary around the world. The bottom line is, never give out someone's personal or contact information unless they have agreed to it; and whenever you collect an email address, be clear about what you will and won't do with it. In particular, give people opt-in/opt-out check boxes for receiving promotional material from yourself and other companies. In any case, a better option may be to seek a sponsor for your site newsletter, which people are more likely to read.

Who can help you? Contact companies directly.

Hot tip: Sharing databases can be a key feature when you're negotiating a deal. The more you know about the people on it, the more it's worth.

1⃞0⃞ CREATING WEBSITES FOR OTHERS

Last but not least—and perhaps the most obvious way to make money once you've learned all this—is to create websites for other people. There are a great many Web designers and developers, but if you know how to make money, you've got a head start…

Who can help you? *www.freelance.com, www.elance.com*

Hot tip: You need a well-presented portfolio of live, successful sites. Start by creating sites for yourself, and then use these as leverage to get commercial interest from genuine customers.

GLOSSARY

aliasing The term describing the jagged appearance of bitmapped images or fonts, either when the resolution is insufficient or when they have been enlarged.

anchor A hyperlink that takes you to another part of the same webpage, rather than to a sub-page or another site elsewhere on the Web.

animated GIF A GIF file containing more than one image. Many programs, including Web browsers, will display each of the images in turn, thus producing an animation.

animation The process of creating a moving image by rapidly moving from one still image to the next. Animations are now commonly created by means of specialist software that renders sequences in a variety of formats, typically QuickTime, AVI, and animated GIF.

antialias/antialiasing A technique of optically eliminating the jagged effect of bitmapped images or text reproduced on low-resolution devices such as monitors. This is achieved by adding pixels of an in-between tone—the edges of the object's color are blended with its background by averaging out the density of the range of pixels involved.

attribute The specification applied to a character, box, or other item. Character attributes include font, size, style, color, shade, scaling, kerning, etc.

authoring tool/ application/program Software that enables you to create interactive presentations, such as those used in multimedia titles and on certain websites. Authoring programs provide text, drawing, painting, animation, and audio features and combine these with a scripting language that determines how each element of a page behaves.

bevel A chamfered edge applied to type, buttons, or selections to emphasize a three-dimensional effect.

Bézier curve A curve whose shape is defined by a pair of "direction lines" at each end. Drawing programs usually allow you to draw Bézier curves by dragging out the direction lines with a pen tool.

bitmap An array of values specifying the color of every pixel in a digital image.

bitmapped font A bitmapped font is one in which the characters are made up of dots, or pixels, as distinct from an outline font which is drawn from vectors. Bitmapped fonts generally

accompany PostScript Type 1 fonts and are used to render the fonts' shapes on screen.

bitmapped graphic An image made up of dots, or pixels, and usually generated by "paint" or "image-editing" applications, as distinct from the "vector" images of "object-oriented" drawing applications.

body One of the main structures of an HTML document, falling between the header and the footer.

brightness The strength of luminescence from light to dark.

browser/web browser Program that enables the viewing or "browsing" of World Wide Web pages across the Internet. The most common browsers are Netscape's Navigator and Microsoft's Internet Explorer. Version numbers are important, as these indicate the level of HTML that the browser supports. Another browser, "Opera", is competitive because of its compact size, efficient performance, and security. It is rapidly gaining popularity.

cell A space containing information in the rows or columns of a table.

cell padding The space between cells in a table.

cell spacing The number of pixels between cells in a table.

clip art/clip media Collections of (usually) royalty-free photographs, illustrations, design devices, and other pre-created items, such as movies, sounds, and 3D wireframes.

color depth This is the number of bits required to define the color of each pixel. Only one bit is required to display a black and white image, while an 8-bit image can display either 256 grays or 256 colors, and a 24-bit image 16.7 million colors (eight bits each for red, green, and blue, equating to 256 x 256 x 256).

color picker The term describing a color model when displayed on a computer monitor. Color pickers may be specific to an application such as Adobe Photoshop, a third-party color model such as PANTONE, or to the operating system running on your computer.

complementary colors On a color wheel, two colors directly opposite each other that, when combined, form white or black depending on the color model (subtractive or additive).

compression The technique of rearranging data so that it either occupies less space on disk or transfers faster between devices or on communication lines. Different kinds of compression techniques are employed for different kinds of data. Applications, for example, must not lose any data when compressed, while photographic images and movies can tolerate a certain amount of data loss. Compression methods that do not lose data are referred to as "lossless," while "lossy" is used to describe methods in which some data is lost. Movies and animations employ techniques called "codecs" (compression/decompression).

contrast The degree of difference between adjacent tones in an image (or on a computer monitor) from the lightest to the darkest. "High contrast" describes an image with light highlights and dark shadows, but with few shades in between, while a "low contrast" image is one with even tones and few dark areas or highlights.

copyright The right of a person who creates an original work to protect that work by controlling how and where it may be reproduced.

copyright-free A misnomer used to describe ready-made resources such as clip art. In fact, resources described as such are rarely, if ever, "copyright free". Generally it is only the license to use the material which is granted by purchase.

density The darkness of tone or color in any image. In a transparency this refers to the amount of light that can pass through it, thus determining the darkness of shadows and the saturation of color. A printed highlight cannot be any lighter in color than the color of the paper it is printed on, while the shadows cannot be any darker than the quality and volume of ink that the printing process will allow.

digitize To convert anything, for example text, images, or sound, into binary form so that it can be digitally processed, manipulated, stored, and reconstructed. In other words, transforming analog to digital.

dingbat The modern name for fonts of decorative symbols, traditionally called printer's "ornaments," or "arabesques."

dither(ing) The term describing a technique of "interpolation" that calculates the average value of adjacent pixels. This technique is used either to add extra pixels to an image—to smooth an edge, for example, as in "antialiasing"—or to reduce the number of colors or grays in an image by replacing them with average values. These conform to a predetermined palette of colors, such as when an image containing millions of colors is converted ("resampled") to a fixed palette ("index") of 256 colors—in Web use, for example. A color monitor operating in 8-bit color mode (256 colors) will automatically create a dithered pattern of pixels. Dithering is also used by some printing devices to simulate colors or tones.

domain name system/service (DNS) The description of a website's "address"—the means by which you find or identify a particular website, much like a brand name or trademark. A website address is actually a number that conforms to the numerical Internet protocol (IP) addresses that computers use for information exchange, but names are far easier for us to remember. Domain names are administered by the InterNIC organization and include at least two parts: the "subdomain," typically a company or organization; and the "high-level domain," which is the part after the first dot, such as in ".com" for commercial sites, ".org" for non-profit sites, ".gov" for governmental sites, ".edu" for educational sites, and so on.

dots per inch (dpi) A unit of measurement used to represent the resolution of devices such as printers and imagesetters and also, erroneously, monitors and images, whose resolution should more properly be expressed in pixels per inch (ppi). The closer the dots or pixels (the more there are to each inch) the better the quality. Typical resolutions are 72 ppi for a monitor, 600 dpi for a laser printer, and 2,450 dpi (or more) for an imagesetter.

download To transfer data from a remote computer, such as an Internet server, to your own. The opposite of upload.

drop shadow A shadow projected onto the back ground behind an image or character, designed to "lift" the image or character off the surface.

dynamic HTML/DHTML (Dynamic HyperText Markup Language) A development of HTML that enables users to add enhanced features such as basic animations and highlighted buttons to webpages without having to rely on browser plug-ins.

export A feature provided by many applications to allow you to save a file in a format so that it can be used by another application or on a different

GLOSSARY

operating system. For example, an illustration created in a drawing application may be exported as an EPS file so that it can be used in a page-layout application.

eyedropper tool In some applications, a tool for gauging the color of adjacent pixels.

face Traditionally the printing surface of any metal type character, but nowadays used as a series or family name for fonts with similar characteristics, such as "modern face."

file extension The term describing the abbreviated suffix at the end of a filename that describes either its type (such as .EPS or .JPG) or origin (the application that created it, such as QXP for QuarkXPress files).

file format The way a program arranges data so that it can be stored or displayed on a computer. Common file formats are TIFF and JPEG for bitmapped image files, EPS for object-oriented image files and ASCII for text files.

File Transfer Protocol (FTP) A standard system for transmitting files between computers across the Internet or a network. Although Web browsers incorporate FTP capabilities, dedicated FTP applications provide greater

flexibility. Typically, when creating a webpage, an FTP application will be used to upload this to the Web.

frame A way of breaking up a scrollable browser window on a webpage into several independent windows. Frames enable one to fix arbitrary sections of the available browser window space—e.g., a logo, a menu button bar, or an animation can be placed in one part of the browser window while another part is left available for information from a different webpage.

frame (2) A single still picture from a movie or animation sequence. Also a single complete image from a TV picture.

font Set of characters sharing the same typeface and size.

font file The file of a bitmapped or screen font, usually residing in a suitcase file on Mac OS computers.

form A special type of webpage which provides users with the means to input information directly into the website. Form pages are often used to collect information about viewers, or as a way of collecting password and username data before allowing access to secure areas.

gamma A measure of the contrast in a digital image, photographic film or paper, or processing technique. Gamma curves can be used within the software that may come with a scanner so that you can preset the amount of light and dark, and contrast on input.

GIF (Graphics Interchange Format) One of the main bitmapped image formats used on the Internet. It was devised by CompuServe, an Internet Service Provider that is now part of AOL. GIF is a 256-color format with two specifications, GIF87a and, more recently, GIF89a, the latter providing additional features such as the use of transparent backgrounds. The GIF format uses a "lossless" compression technique, or "algorithm," and thus does not squeeze files as much as the JPEG format, which is "lossy". For use in Web browsers JPEG is the format of choice for tone images, such as photographs, while GIF is more suitable for line images and other graphics.

graduation/gradation/ gradient The smooth transition from one color/tone to another. The relationship of reproduced lightness values to original lightness values in an

imaging process, usually expressed as a tone curve.

home page The main, introductory page on a website, usually with a title and tools to navigate through the rest of the site. Also known as index page or doorway.

host A networked computer that provides services to anyone who can access it, such as for email, file transfer, and access to the Web. When you connect to the Internet, and select a website, information will be transferred to you from the host's computer. Users' computers that request services from a host are often referred to as "clients."

HSL (Hue, Saturation, Lightness) A color model based upon the light transmitted either in an image or in your monitor—hue being the spectral color (the actual pigment color), saturation being the intensity of the color pigment (without black or white added), and brightness representing the strength of luminance from light to dark (the amount of black or white present). Variously called HLS (hue, lightness, saturation), HSV (hue, saturation, value), and HSB (hue, saturation, brightness).

hue A color as found in its pure state in the spectrum.

USEFUL URLS

DOWNLOAD RESOURCES
www.fontparadise.com
www.acidfonts.com
www.flashkit.com
www.fontaddict.com
www.fontalicious.com
www.fonts.com
http://htmlgear.lycos.com
www.brainjar.com
www.eyeforbeauty.com
http://infinitefish.com
www.sweetaspirations.com
www.melizabeth.com
www.thepluginsite.com
www.iconfactory.com
www.freephotoshop.com

FUN
www.the5k.org
www.surfstation.lu
www.pixelsurgeon.com
www.shockwave.com
www.linkdup.com
www.australianinfront.com.au

SOFTWARE
www.adobe.com
www.macromedia.com
www.jasc.com
www.microsoft.com
www.apple.com
www.ulead.com
www.corel.com
www.netscape.com

TUTORIALS, ARTICLES, NEWS, PICTURES...
www.webmonkey.com
www.alistapart.com
www.wired.com
www.computerarts.co.uk
www.createonline.co.uk
www.creativepro.com
www.maccentral.com
www.creativebase.com
www.webreference.com
www.planetphotoshop.com
www.zooworld.net
www.internet.com
www.wired.com
www.webmasterbase.com
www.tutorialfind.com

HTML (HyperText Markup Language) The code that websites are built from. HTML is not a programming language as such, but a set of "tags" that specify type styles and sizes, the location of graphics, and other information required to construct a webpage. To provide for increasingly complex presentations such as animation, sound, and video, the basic form of HTML is seeded with miniature computer programs, or applets.

HTML table A grid on a webpage consisting of rows and columns of cells allowing precise positioning of text, pictures, movie clips, or any other element. A table can be nested within another table. Tables offer a way of giving the appearance of multi-column layouts. They can be visible, with cells framed by borders, or invisible and used only to demarcate areas containing the elements on the page. A table is specified in terms of either a pixel count, which fixes its size irrespective of the browser or screen resolution used to view it, or as a percentage of the available screen space, allowing resizing to fit the browser window.

Hypertext Transfer Protocol (http) A text-based set of rules by which files on the World Wide Web are transferred, defining the commands that Web browsers use to communicate with Web servers. The vast majority of World Wide Web addresses, or "URLs," are prefixed with "http://".

icon A graphical representation of an object (such as a disk, file, folder, or tool) or a concept used to make identification and selection easier.

image map An image that features a set of embedded links to other documents or websites. These are activated when the mouse is clicked on the appropriate area. Often the "front page" of a website contains such a map.

image slicing The practice of dividing up a digital image into rectangular areas or slices, which can then be optimized or animated independently for efficient Web presentation. Programs that enable you to slice images automatically generate an HTML code that puts the slices back together on a webpage.

index page The first page of any website that is selected automatically by the browser if it is named "default.htm," "default.html," "index.htm," or "index.html."

interactive Any activity that involves an immediate and reciprocal action between a person and a machine (for example, driving a car), but more commonly describing dialog between a computer and its user.

interface This is a term most used to describe the screen design that links the user with the computer program or website. The quality of the user interface often determines how well users will be able to navigate their way around the pages within the site.

interlacing A technique of displaying an image on a webpage in which the image reveals increasing detail as it downloads. Interlacing is usually offered as an option in image-editing applications when saving images in GIF, PNG, and progressive JPEG formats.

Internet The world-wide network of computers linked by telephone (or other connections), providing individual and corporate users with access to information, companies, newsgroups, discussion areas, and much more.

ISP (Internet Service Provider) Any organization that provides access to the Internet. At its most basic this may be a telephone number for connection, but most ISPs also provide email addresses and webspace for new sites.

JavaScript A "scripting" language that provides a simplified method of applying dynamic effects to webpages.

JPEG, JPG The Joint Photographics Experts Group. An ISO (International Standards Organization) group that defines compression standards for bitmapped color images. The abbreviated form, pronounced "jay-peg," gives its name to a "lossy" (meaning some data may be lost) compressed file format in which the degree of compression from high compression/low quality to low compression/high quality can be defined by the user.

kerning The adjustment of spacing between two characters (normally alphanumeric) to improve the overall look of the text.

keyline A line drawing indicating the size and position of an illustration in a layout.

layout A drawing that shows the general appearance of a design, indicating, for example, the position of text and illustrations. The term is also

GLOSSARY

used when preparing a design for reproduction, and to describe the way a page is constructed in desktop publishing programs.

link A pointer, such as a highlighted piece of text in an HTML document or multimedia presentation, or an area on an image map, which takes the user to another location, page, or screen just by clicking on it.

lossless/lossy Refers to data-losing qualities of different compression methods: lossless means that no image information is lost; lossy means that some (or much) of the image data is lost in the compression process.

midtones/middletones The range of tonal values in an image anywhere between the darkest and lightest, usually referring to those approximately halfway.

multimedia Any combination of various digital media, such as sound, video, animation, graphics, and text, incorporated into a software product or presentation.

paragraph In an HTML document, a markup tag <P> used to define a new paragraph in text.

palette This term refers to a subset of colors that are

needed to display a particular image. For instance, a GIF image will have a palette containing a maximum of 256 individual and distinct colors.

pixel (Picture Element) The smallest component of any digitally generated image, including text, such as a single dot of light on a computer screen. In its simplest form, one pixel corresponds to a single bit: 0 = off, or white, and 1 = on, or black. In color or grayscale images or monitors, one pixel may correspond to up to several bits. An 8-bit pixel, for example, can be displayed in any of 256 colors (the total number of different configurations that can be achieved by eight 0s and 1s).

plug-in Subsidiary software for a browser or other package that enables it to perform additional functions, e.g., play sound, movies, or video.

raster(ization) Deriving from the Latin word "rastrum," meaning "rake," the method of displaying (and creating) images employed by video screens, and thus computer monitors, in which the screen image is made up of a pattern of several hundred parallel lines created by an electron beam "raking" the screen from top to bottom at a speed of about one–sixtieth of a

second. An image is created by varying the intensity of the beam at successive points along the raster. The speed at which a complete screen image, or frame, is created is called the "frame" or "refresh" rate.

rasterize(d) To rasterize is to electronically convert a vector graphics image into a bitmapped image. This may introduce aliasing, but is often necessary when preparing images for the Web; without a plug-in, browsers can only display GIF, JPEG, and PNG image files.

resolution The degree of quality, definition, or clarity with which an image is reproduced or displayed, for example in a photograph, or via a scanner, monitor screen, printer, or other output device.

resolution (2): monitor resolution, screen resolution The number of pixels across by pixels down. The three most common resolutions are 640 x 480, 800 x 600, and 1,024 x 768. The current standard Web page size is 800 x 600.

RGB (Red, Green, Blue) The primary colors of the "additive" color model, used in video technology, computer monitors, and for graphics such as for the Web and multimedia that will not

ultimately be printed by the four-color (CMYK) process. CMYK stands for "Cyan, Magenta, Yellow, BlacK".

rollover The rapid substitution of one or more images when the mouse pointer is rolled over the original image. Used extensively for navigation buttons on webpages and multimedia presentations.

rollover button A graphic button type that changes in appearance when the mouse pointer moves over it.

saturation A variation in color of the same total brightness from none (gray) through pastel shades (low saturation) to pure (fully saturated) color with no gray.

scan(ning) An electronic process that converts a hard copy of an image into digital form by sequential exposure to a moving light beam such as a laser. The scanned image can then be manipulated by a computer or output to separated film.

shareware Software available through user groups, magazine cover disks, etc. Although shareware is not "copy protected," it is protected by copyright and a fee is normally payable for using it, unlike "freeware."

A WORD ABOUT FLASH

Flash offers high-impact, fast-loading graphics of a kind that just aren't achievable with GIFs and JPEGs. One of the best uses of this application on your site is in the navigation. After all, this is going to be on practically every page you create, so why not give that little bit of extra oomph. Creating buttons and rollover effects is a breeze in Flash, and combined with a bit of animation, you can come up with something really impressive. The possibilities are limited only by your imagination and understanding of the software. Part of this is due the fact that you can easily embed buttons within animation, animation within buttons, and animation within animation in Flash—an ability that opens many doors for the creative thinker...

spacer A blank, transparent GIF, one pixel wide, used to space elements on a webpage.

tag The formal name for a markup language formatting command. A tag is switched on by placing a command inside angle brackets, i.e., < and >, and switched off again by repeating the same command but inserting a forward slash before the command. For example, <bold> makes text that follows appear in bold, while </bold> switches bold text off again.

text path An invisible line, either straight, curved, or irregular, along which text can be forced to flow.

thumbnail A small representation of an image used mainly for identification purposes in an image directory listing or, within Photoshop, for illustrating channels and layers. Thumbnails are also produced to accompany PictureCDs, PhotoCDs and most APS and 35-mm films submitted for processing.

TIFF, TIF (Tagged Image File Format) A standard and popular graphics file format originally developed by Aldus (now merged with Adobe) and Microsoft, used for scanned, high-resolution, bitmapped images and for color

separations. The TIFF format can be used for black-and-white, grayscale, and color images, which have been generated on different computer platforms.

tile, tiling Repeating a graphic item and placing the repetitions side-by-side in all directions so that they form a pattern.

transparency Allows a GIF image to be blended into the background by ridding it of unwanted background color.

tween(ing) A contraction of "in-between." An animator's term for the process of creating transitional frames to fill in-between key frames in an animation.

typeface The term (based on "face"—the printing surface of a metal type character) describing a type design of any size, including weight variations on that design such as light and bold, but excluding all other related designs such as italic and condensed. As distinct from "type family," which includes all related designs, and "font," which is one design of a single size, weight, and style. Thus "Baskerville" is a type family, while "Baskerville Bold" is a typeface and "9 pt Baskerville Bold Italic" is a font.

Uniform Resource Locator (URL) The unique address of every webpage on the WWW. Every resource on the Internet has a unique URL which begins with letters that identify the resource type, such as "http" or "ftp" (determining the communication protocol to be used), followed by a colon and two forward slashes.

vector A mathematical description of a line that is defined in terms of physical dimensions and direction. Vectors are used in drawing packages (and Photoshop 6 upwards) to define shapes (vector graphics) that are position- and size-independent.

vector graphics Images made up of mathematically defined shapes, such as circles and rectangles, or complex paths built out of mathematically defined curves. Vector graphics images can be displayed at any size or resolution without loss of quality, and are easy to edit because the shapes retain their identity, but they lack the tonal subtlety of bitmapped images. Because vector graphics files are typically small, they are well suited to Web animation.

webpage A published HTML document on the World Wide

Web, which forms part of a website.

Web server A computer ("host") that is dedicated to Web services.

website The address, location (on a server), and collection of documents and resources for any particular interlinked set of webpages.

World Wide Web (WWW) The term used to describe the entire collection of Web servers all over the world that are connected to the Internet. The term also describes the particular type of Internet access architecture that uses a combination of HTML and various graphic formats, such as GIF and JPEG, to publish formatted text that can be read by Web browsers. Colloquially termed simply "the Web" or, rarely, by the shorthand "W3."

World Wide Web Consortium (W3C) The global organization that is largely responsible or maintaining and managing standards across the Web. It is chaired by the UK's Tim Berners Lee, progenitor of the Web.

INDEX